Organizing for
Women

Organizing for Women

Issues, Strategies, and Services

Dale A. Masi
Department of
Health and Human Services

LexingtonBooks
D.C. Heath and Company
Lexington, Massachusetts
Toronto

Library of Congress Cataloging in Publication Data

Masi, Dale A
    Organizing for women.

    Includes bibliographical references and index.
    1. Women in community organization—Study and teaching—United
States. 2. Feminism—United States—Societies, etc. I. Title.
HV41.M29   362.8'3'0973   78-19577
ISBN 0-669-02577-1

Copyright © 1981 by D.C. Heath and Company

Published simultaneously in Canada

Printed in the United States of America

International Standard Book Number: 0-669-02577-1

Library of Congress Catalog Card Number: 78-19577

*To all the women in my life who made a difference,
especially my daughters Renée and Robin*

Contents

List of Figures

List of Tables

Preface
and Acknowledgments

In 1975 six female students staged a sit-in at my office at Boston College. I was the only tenured woman professor in the Master's in Social Planning Program in the School of Social Work. They were students in the department and wanted to know what it was like to be a woman in a man's profession [community organization (CO), administration and planning]. They poured out all their concerns: how had I managed raising children; did they have to be supermoms; would it affect their careers; how did the men treat me?

From that moment my professional and personal role took on a new dimension. I am embarrassed to say I had not thought of myself in this perspective. I was shaken by these earnest young women who became my friends as well as students. I was intrigued. Together we agreed to start meeting.

What soon evolved was a support group of women in CO, including a part-time female faculty member and myself, meeting every other week. As we struggled with a plan, because we were planners, we quickly saw what we needed was process: an opportunity to share our concerns within the context of the CO group. Each of us would talk about where we were professionally and personally. For me, it was the catalyst to humanize relations with my students. I would never again just lecture; nor would I be concerned with sharing myself. I developed much closer relationships with my students, both men and women, because of this new awareness.

What also evolved was the need to conceptualize the principle we were addressing, that is, CO from a woman's perspective. Together, these students and I designed an outline and advocated a course in the school: Community Organization for Women. It was touch and go convincing the faculty and executive committee, but it was finally approved, and in the spring of 1976 the first class started. I taught the course for three years, and it proved to be one of the most exciting learning experiences I have engaged in.

My CO background started in the early fifties when my philosophy professor at college told me I was making a mistake going into law, it was CO that I wanted. I did not know what he was talking about but looked into the schools he suggested. The Boston College Admissions Office asked why, as a woman, I wanted this field. They told me later that I was the first woman accepted into the CO program. I enrolled in the Catholic University master's program and knew from the first day of classes that I was in the right field. I continued working in it through the years, but the awareness of my uniqueness as a woman in CO never really penetrated until the day the students came to my office.

I have gone through several stages as a feminist. The first was that of becoming aware. It was like suddenly putting on another pair of glasses. The next stage was anger as I realized what I had done and how much I had not seen. I realized how fully acculturated I had been by society. It reminded me of the story the beloved Whitney Young, national executive director of the Urban League, told of himself. As an example of how institutionalized racism is, he said, the first time he had a black pilot on an airplane, he (Whitney) was frightened. I had accepted so many inequities without even being aware. The anger came out in a variety of ways: heated discussions, impatience with people who did not understand, and fury with society that let this continue. In the next stage I channeled the awareness and anger into some plan. I found the way to do this through the women's group and the course, and by developing a mentor system by sponsoring certain female students and acting as a role model for them. As I became more skilled at this, my own career was rising in a separate field, employee counseling programs, bringing human programs of alcohol, drug, and mental health into the workplace.

I began to see that as we controlled our emotions we needed, as feminists, to develop strategies, to learn the importance of power for women, to respect and appreciate the value of money, and to develop organizing and planning skills.

As my course developed, I saw that my own field, human services, had not addressed women's concerns from a woman's perspective. It needed reorganization. I also realized that its failure to apply CO principles was one reason the women's movement itself was having problems.

My next stage was commitment. Awareness of and anger toward societal inequities was not enough; I had to do something. So an opportunity arose to do a book on the subject, I knew I had found a way to satisfy part of that commitment to women. I also realized I had been very fortunate to be one of the few women professors in this area, to have worked in it for so many years, and now to share its principles with my sisters to help them move ahead in some small way.

This book addresses two matters relating to the women's movement. First, it enumerates the organizational techniques exhibited thus far by women activists. An analysis of the movement from a community organizer's perspective interweaves this description. Second, this book describes the responsiveness of human services to the women's movement. Because these services are vital to the lives of women, it is important that they be analyzed from an organizational standpoint. Analyzing case studies set forth in this book achieves the goal of relating women's issues to human services. This book assumes that the analysis resulting from the case studies applies to all human service areas.

Since this book is about organizational strategies, it is important that we begin with individual strategies. I offer the following ten as mine.

1. Learn to fight back psychologically. It is important to realize how much we have been socialized into the place we find ourselves.

2. Develop support groups.

3. Learn to trust and help women and not compete with them. On the other hand, do not automatically distrust men. Find those who are our allies and use their skills and influence.

4. Find a mentor and be a mentor.

5. Understand power and see most issues from this perspective. Learn to use power and be comfortable in using it. Do not assume you lack power. Look again. You have more than you think.

6. Take assertiveness-training classes. Consider feminist therapy if you need any at all.

7. Strategize with other women.

8. Call on women in high positions and expect them to support you.

9. Learn to use such resources as the National Women's Political Caucus, the Women's Agenda, and other women's groups.

10. Do not get discouraged. Learn the strategies of organizing and planning.

Acknowledgments

I want to thank all those people, men and women, who contributed advice, time, criticism, and efforts toward the realization of this book. Though too numerous to name, I am grateful to my students, relatives, friends, and associates. My special thanks go to Nancy Kaufman.

Part I
Organizing for Women:
General Perspectives

1

Community Organization: A Theoretical Perspective

Community Organization

Definition

Community organization (CO) has many meanings and each definition conjures a variety of associations. The word *community* triggers a wide range of sociological and anthropological references. The word *organization* relates to the bureaucratic process as well as the grass-roots unionizing process. However, each definition of CO falls into one of two basic categories: residual or institutional. Until the 1960s, a residual model regarded social services in a rehabilitative context: "Community organization is a process by which a community defines its needs or objectives, develops the confidence and will to work at them, finds the resources to deal with them, takes action with respect to them and in so doing extends and develops cooperative and collaborative attitudes and practices in the community."[1]

The institutional category, popular through the 1960s, envisioned societal institutions as responsible agents for allaying social inequities. Charles Grosser's definition of institutional CO therefore espoused advocacy efforts, exerted on behalf of clients and social workers, as the critical tool for successful community organization. "Sufficient power to overcome a condition willfully created by society . . . as opposed to education or persuasion to overcome a condition created unintentionally by the victim."[2]

Kramer and Specht emphasize the *purposive* change directed by a professional person.

> Community organization refers to various methods of intervention whereby a professional change agent helps a community action system composed of individuals, groups or organizations to engage in planned collective action in order to deal with social problems within a democratic system of values. It is concerned with programs aimed at social change, with primary reference to environmental conditions and social institutions. It involves two major and interrelated concerns: (a) the processes of working with an action system, which include planning and organizing, identifying problem areas, diagnosing causes, and formulating solutions; and (b) developing the strategies and mobilizing the resources necessary to effect change.[3]

CO has therefore evolved into a professional practice employed by social workers to alter society's institutional behavior.

Community organizers work with all classes of people. The method sets no limits on the population groups to be served, and is practical in a variety of settings. Organizers are in schools, communities, welfare agencies, and a range of social-service agencies. Practice areas for organizers also continue to evolve. For example, the business community has recently been developed. This area of development by community organizers was virtually inconceivable several years ago.

Since the emergence of the political state such institutional forces as government, religion, and law placed women in a second-class position. As this is not an individual matter for each woman to overcome, CO can be directly applied to women. Using Grosser's approach, altering society's institutional perceptions of women should be a primary goal for supporters of women's rights.

History

In 1912, CO was first referred to by Roger Baldwin in his paper titled "Community Organizing for Children." By 1939, CO was so popular that Robert Lane in his report argues that CO should be integrated in the social work profession. The first two schools of social work to integrate CO into their curricula were Boston College and Ohio State University. These schools were the training ground for United Way executives.

It is two historical roots of CO (collaboration and reform) that account for the definitional differences in the residual and institutional models. Ross's residual definition is tied into the collaborative, cooperative approach of the United Way whereas Grosser's institutional model identifies with the social reform approach. Eventually the reformers became professionalized in social work and began doing group work, with a group therapy orientation rather than a client advocacy model. The latter reform approach became associated with CO and is still carried on today in CO practice.

The professionalization of CO occurred in 1962 when the National Association of Social Workers adopted its *Working Definition of Community Organization*.[4] This formally established it as a professional method alongside casework and group work in social work. It delineated the various dimensions of the practice and put CO in its appropriate theoretical context and subsequently paved the way for future developments in education and practice.

Perlman and Gurin pointed out that the *Working Definition* incorrectly applied CO as a tool for addressing citizens or agencies.[5] The application of CO to both citizens and agencies, however, is its true definition.

CO is necessary for working with women as well as working with services for women. To exclude either services or women would preclude a successful women's movement. For example, many efforts have been made to raise women's consciousness; this helps develop their awareness of their oppressed position. What follows, however, is the need by women to implement the goals resulting from these awareness efforts. Thus, one of the keys to successfully applying CO to the women's movement is the treatment of both women and the service-delivery system alike.

With the explosion of social consciousness of the 1960s, social welfare, like many other parts of society, was forced to reexamine itself. Social work providers, especially caseworkers, were accused of several things: (1) over-concern with professionalism, with an interest in social work rather than social action; (2) overemphasis on Freudian psychology which placed the problem of the client on the individual rather than society; (3) perpetuating the middle-class value system by excluding the client in community planning; and (4) ignoring the paradox of poverty in the midst of plenty.

Through the Office of Economic Opportunity, the Johnson Administration poured millions of dollars into CO efforts as an attempt to advance the war on poverty. CO methods had somehow escaped the criticism previously attributed to the social work profession and was therefore thrust center stage as the panacea for all mistakes previously caused by the allied helping profession. Respected community organizers now included Richard Cloward, Francis Piven, John Ehrlich, and Whitney Young.

In attempting to resolve the war on poverty, community organizers adopted concepts that are now basic to the community organizational approach:

1. Participation by members of the client group in addition to the community at large is essential for ensuring successful planning.
2. Perception by community organizers of the federal government as an ally of social change is essential for ensuring successful social reforms.
3. Treatment by the community organizers of advocacy as an appropriate tool for their work is essential for ensuring successful social change.
4. Treatment by community organizers of communities of interest, or functional communities such as minorities, is becoming increasingly important in ensuring social change. The civil rights movement, for example, showed that blacks succeeded in their reformation efforts because they specialized their strategy and organizational forays.

To fully understand the history of CO, it should be seen as a continuum from process to task. The 1960s emphasized the process approach; the 1970s, the task orientation. In the case of the war on poverty, CO efforts failed because either the process or task approach was emphasized separately. For CO to succeed as a strategy, an equal emphasis must be placed simultaneously upon both the process and the task approach. Gilbert and Specht summarize these approaches in the following manner:[6]

	Process Orientation	*Task Orientation*
Goals of practice	Facilitating social relationships and enhancing capabilities	Achievement of more delimited concrete outcome
Role of practitioner	Nondirective	Directive
Primary skills to be used by practitioner	Interactional, social, and political	Analytic and technical

Theoretical Framework

The working definition of the social work profession proposes that it is in essence a grouping of several discrete but interdependent categories. These are values, knowledge, methods, roles, and sanctions. I added principles and concepts and put the entire grouping under the section "Professions in Relation to Science." This explains the analytical reasoning for the basic assumption of the framework; that is, social work is a profession and CO a specialty within that profession (figure 1-1). Figure 1-2 pictures CO as the center of a wheel with the categories of a profession as the essential spokes.

Science

Science is either formal or empirical. A formal science is based on a set of established and proven techniques applied in a methodological manner. An empirical science is based on experience or observation and does not rely on a specified theory or methodology. The formal disciplines provide the empirical sciences with the concepts which allow for systematic observation and manipulation. The formal sciences are for the most part based on logic.

The empirical sciences are primarily observational; examples are physics, economics, psychology, and zoology. Empirical sciences are classified into three groups: physical, biological, and social. The five principal social sciences are anthropology, economics, political science, psychology, and sociology.

The social sciences provide conclusions as to knowledge, concepts, and methods. The practical sciences (overt professions) imply postulates which allow them to answer the question how. Social work postulates, taken from the social sciences which in turn drew them from the formal sciences, are the code of ethics and values of social work.

The profession uses both the concepts of the formal sciences and the acquired knowledge of the empirical sciences. A profession is neither a science nor an art but combines the sciences with skills. Science without practicing professions is an intellectual exercise. A profession provides the opportunity

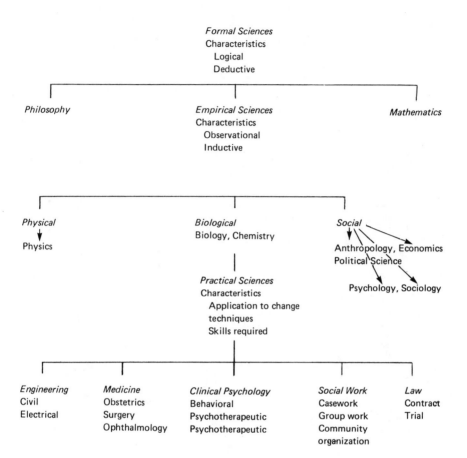

Figure 1-1. Theoretical Framework: Professions in Relation to Science

to apply scientific principles to achieve results that will improve the social condition.

Each practical science or profession has its own specialty with its particular postulates. CO is a specialty of social work. Its professional framework and assumed values distinguish it from other social work approaches. It represents a disciplined choice of acts which are guided by the application of CO practice theory.

Values. Values are learned from four sources: role models, peer groups, membership in large reference groups (conferences, professional associations, and journals), and the external environment. Values are gained intellectually,

Figure 1-2. Profession of Community Organization

emotionally, and ritualistically. Practitioners also have their own set of values which they bring to their work environment.

The following values in CO form the basis of guidelines for practice. The dignity and worth of an individual is the most important value. For women, this is critical. Human integrity has not been traditionally honored in our society. The right of self-determination by the individual is essential. The dignity and self-worth of groups such as minorities, ethnics, and women should now be recognized. A belief in the democratic process is essential for the practice of CO. The rights of individuals, groups, and communities to have differing perspectives is crucial to the development of an identity. In addition, by becoming involved in the decision-making process these oppressed groups, such as women, will begin to make their presence felt. Women must opt for total involvement and active participation in the decision-making process that affects them if they are to realize any significant change in their status.

Perlman and Gurin describe the process of making values dynamic. Translation of values into a dynamic process means the progressive identification of specific objects and their relation to each other in a continuous end-means chain. Choices must be made every step of the way, since the situation is such that not all values can be maximized simultaneously. But value positions are not static. They emerge, develop, and are modified in the course of social interaction, including that between the practitioner and the people served.[7] Perlman and Gurin further state that one reason planned change has been unsuccessful is because we have used broad values as our goals, such as the elimination of poverty and the development of community. They suggest that value premises and choices must be separated from the technical action available so that selective action can be taken.[8] The women's movement should consider this. In addition to the goal of the equal rights amendment (ERA), women need realistic subgoals or little victories to help them see that gain is indeed possible. Achieving subgoals is necessary to support the larger issues as well as to provide the needed psychological impetus.

Richard Means identifies another problem associated with value development. He claims that the values necessary for solving social problems lack clarity. Understanding our value traditions helps us to understand the social problems of our communities. There is no doubt that this holds true for the history of women. To appreciate how deeply embedded are the values in society is to appreciate the magnitude of the task ahead.

Social problems derive from the gap between ethical standards and the consequences of value positions that produce behavior deemed unethical by traditional ethical concepts. We analyze social problems from other than moral grounds. We need to say openly that certain things, such as racism, are unethical.[9] The same obviously holds true for sexism, yet too often feminists hesitate to put it in a moral context. If women could face the unethical, immoral position into which they have been put as women, they might become aware of the rightness of their position. It would save unnecessary ambivalence by some women on women's issues.

People often assume their values are right and they become inflexible. For example, we must understand that the opponents of the women's movement come from a different value orientation. It is why the conflict is so controversial. It does not mean one should change values, but an appreciation of how the lines are drawn is critical before designing a strategy. The lines of battle for the advancement of women in our society are clearly value issues that run very deeply in our culture.

Value conflicts are realities that we often experience but do not consciously recognize. For example, American society places high value on the concept of free will and self-determinism. The opposite value sees social problems caused through societal conditions as poverty and disease. Thus we have the individual versus society value discrepancy. In the United States as we adopt more social welfare legislation, we are saying it is the responsibility of the society to provide certain things to its people. Opponents claim it is each person's responsibility to take care of oneself and the pull between the two approaches continues.

Another value conflict which has emerged since the civil rights movement is the monolithic versus pluralistic society. For years perpetuating the melting pot was the goal of American society. As generation after generation of immigrants arrived, a gradual melting of cultures was accepted. In the fifties, liberals were classified by the extent of the melting they would support. Racial intermarriage was seen as the true liberal position and goal. Since recognizing the concept of black power we now have racial as well as ethnic groups wanting to maintain individual identities. Clearly this is a different value than was formerly espoused.

There are value conflicts in the women's movement which will have to be addressed. Examples are the sensitive issues of abortion and lesbianism. All do not have to agree on these questions, but there needs to be an understanding of the value differences. There must be movement together for the advancement of the role of women: the common value.

In CO, one of the clearest value conflicts regards violence. The author defines this as a deliberate intent to harm, such as guerrilla warfare, kidnapping, and hijacking. The threat of violence must be used very carefully, if at all. One may find oneself in an unanticipated situation where violence is the only means of escape. This differs from planned violence. Under most circumstances, the use of violence should not be encouraged. However, if one considers, for example, the recent oppression of women in Iran and the threat to women the new government poses, violence may be used as a last resort. It is a difficult and a serious dilemma.

The value of belief in the democratic process is rarely challenged. Unfortunately, this has stifled the women's movement in many respects. The concept of democracy translates into consensus causing many women's programs to fail because a consensus in decision making could not be reached. Understandably, the point of consensus is to ensure that each member participates. Often accomplishing the goal is sacrificed to accomplishing the process.

The concepts of group dignity and worth catalyze intergroup hostility. For example, women often compete with minorities for program funding. Typically, minority women choose their minority identification over their feminism. Ideally they should not have to make that choice. Both minorities and women need jobs and programs. Strategically, it would be better to join forces than to compete.

Each of these values could be examined from many dimensions. It is important to realize they are dynamic and sometimes subjective. Understanding that the feminist value system may be in conflict with itself but can be fluid, would be beneficial as strategies are set for the movement.

Principles. Principles are fundamental assumptions associated with rules for behavior. They are seen as a step away from values as the beginning application to a code of conduct. They are the path to implementing the values. The following are the critical CO principles.

In CO, the client should be identified or defined. The relationship between the community worker and the client is a key in CO. Recent studies of welfare mothers show that the manner in which the welfare worker treated the client had a direct relationship upon the client's ego and self-image. The more positive the relationship and the more ego-reinforcing, the higher the client's self-image.

In CO practice, study of the community is necessary to ascertain its strengths and weaknesses and to discover its needs and problems. CO should use factual data as the basis for subsequent action. In the formulation of a plan of action, representation and participation of appropriate and significant groups in the community must be encouraged from the outset. To execute the plan of action the community organizational structure must be simple and flexible. Identification, involvement, and development of appropriate and qualified leaders is essential. Coordination and communication among the people within the community and cooperation among the communities must be facilitated and encouraged by CO practice. Coordination and mobilization of resources in the community is essential for CO practice. Continuous evaluation forms part of the CO practice.

It is obviously essential to know the particular community. The skill of the CO worker lies in understanding the community so as to identify and nurture its leadership. Communities are used to having men serve on boards and in legislatures while women do volunteer work and rarely ask questions. There is a wealth of untapped leadership ability among women that should be channeled to ensure its development.

The principle of evaluation has frequently failed. Too often evaluation will be done, if at all, at the completion of a project rather than while the project is in progress. Continuous feedback is important in operating programs. For this reason, more women should be trained as evaluators and researchers. Women should develop this expertise so they can evaluate women's programs and not rely upon men.

Concepts. Concepts are defined as abstract ideas generalized from particular instances and conceived as thoughts. They can be essential in the development of CO theory. They can, however, also have a sterile effect as Lane points out. Rarely can they be applied directly. A concept at best is partial and tentative and must be seen in relation to all the complex elements in a situation.[10]

Goal, power, change, process, participation, readiness, need, conflict, confrontation, task, and interaction are all concepts. Each sustains a crucial role in defining CO. As mentioned previously, interaction of process and goal has been described in the Gilbert and Specht model. Without a doubt power is the single most important concept for women to understand and acquire. Power is force, energy, and potency. Power is acting with effect. Phyllis Chesler claims:

> There are twelve major forms of power. Seven are almost totally con-trolled by men and are fluid and interchangeable with each other (phys-ical, technological, scientific, military, and consumer power; the power of organized religions and secular institutions). Two powers may be controlled equally by women and men interchangeably (social position and influence). Three forms of power are almost exclusively female and are noninterchangeable or nonfluid spheres (beauty, sexuality, and motherhood). Money, the thirteenth power, can buy and control the twelve powers. It is a power sacred to most men and foreign to most women.[11]

Community organizers must recognize and utilize the necessary techniques for obtaining power. In doing so it is important to first assess one's power base which can often be overestimated. For example, at the crucial moment supposed allies may desert. For groups without power the sheer numbers of persons organized can become potent. Alinsky consistently claimed, however, that numbers without organization can accomplish nothing. Elite power is shared by the few at the top, whereas pluralistic power is composed of various power bases with differing decision-making influence.

In planning strategy, a power base must be identified that can make the decision for the organization's goal. For the women's movement this targeting is crucial. Then the target is zoned in on and strategies developed for influ-encing it. Power in itself is neutral. Too often women have seen it as a negative. What one does with power is another thing. Power does not have to be corrupt. Women need to become more comfortable with gaining power as well as using it.

Participation by community members as well as client groups is a valuable concept in CO. How one chooses participants is most important. Too often we say we have representatives from a group duly authorized to delegate repre-sentatives when in effect we do not. For example, it is better to have an elected representative from the group rather than one appointed or picked only because he/she is a member of that group. The latter cannot speak with as much authority as the former. Whenever possible it is better to get representatives from several groups who can thus participate with more authority. There are inherent problems with the concept of participation of which we need to be aware. Today, especially, participation is seen as a sacred idea and not ques-tioned. Frequently the concept is exploited by mere lip service. Misleading pictures are presented of existing real participation which in fact does not. Too often participation becomes an end in itself. There is an overemphasis on the members participating for their own needs rather than the needs of the group.

For example, a consciousness-raising group seeks to enhance each individual member's development as a primary goal. This is actually closer to group therapy. If we take a group designed to accomplish a task, the same emphasis on individual development should not be stressed. Sometimes in women's groups this change in focus from the individual to the group becomes difficult to accomplish. The difference between group therapy and CO needs to be clearly kept in mind.

Alinsky said that if 5 percent of a group were effectively organized, they could accomplish their task.[12] But is success a statistical measure? It is not necessary that all members of a group or even a majority be present. For the women's movement there may obviously be times when a tight organization, not a percentage, is the effective strategy.

Confrontation is a concept often hard for women to practice. Because women have been raised as passive acceptors and the expression of assertion seen as unwomanly, confrontation tactics are not practiced by women. This is why assertiveness training is so important to women. It is a basic necessity for women to be comfortable at confronting in order to accomplish one's goals.

Readiness and need are both concepts that are tied into timing. When the group is ready and the need so great that mobilization can take place, is a sensitive perception that the worker must develop. This must be emphasized because if the sense of timing is off, a major battle can be lost. It also means one must help a group become more aware of a need through various means and that the readiness stage may be accelerated. It often means that groups cannot be moved until the time is right. One must be able to perceive when that time is and then act.

Knowledge Base. The factual foundation of CO comes through many knowledge areas. Knowledge of the following areas are needed for effective CO. Although it is impossible to be versed in all these, an awareness of their importance and an ability to take the resource that may have specific access to what is needed is essential. The areas are community, power structures, community dysfunction, human service institutions, social systems structure, decision making, determination of priorities, roles which a practitioner uses at various times, knowledge of change, organizational behavior, leadership, political systems, economic systems, planning methodology, and planning theory.

Information about community theory is essential for the CO worker. The community is the client, not the target population. Traditionally communities were seen from a geographic perspective. Recently, the importance of functional communities or those that share a common interest have been recognized. Women are obviously such a functional community. As one looks at specific groups of women, be they drug abusers, offenders, and so on, one speaks of even more functional communities. Roland Warren is one of the leading theorists in the study of communities. He characterized communities as having horizontal (local) influences or vertical (nonlocal, usually state and federal) influences. He also describes communities as moving at a pace very much in line with the previously discussed topic of timing. He contends that communities have capacity for growth and that they can be studied and diagnosed.[13] Generally the latter is done by describing the group from many perspectives. Interviews are usually conducted to accomplish this. Most community studies have been on geographical limits. Akenfield in England[14] and Middletown in the United States[15] are two examples. The importance of studying the community before designing a strategy is equally applicable for the functional community. Whatever group of women with which one is working, one needs to know specifics such as age, socioeconomic status, work experience, educational background, and health.

One important distinction between minorities and women is that the latter are put in functional communities whereas the former can be in both. Minorities can be placed geographically, sometimes by neighborhoods. Therefore the same strategies may not be applicable to both, though often the two groups tend to be viewed together.

Knowledge of community dysfunction and what brings this about is important information for the CO worker. Dysfunction is essentially the problem. How it is viewed and how it is diagnosed can obviously determine the plan of action. For example, when women's issues are seen from the concept of lack of power the solution is very different than if viewed as an incapacity for women to adjust. *Corporate Wives: Corporate Casualties* by psychiatrist Robert Seidenberg presents an excellent explanation of why suicide and alcoholism are so high among corporate wives.[16] In essence, he attributes it to their way of life, from constant moving and culture shock. Instead of blaming each wife for not adjusting to the situation, he suggests that companies recognize their responsibility and possibly hire women. He also points out that in the future wives may not be expected to undergo such trauma for the sake of a husband's job. Women in particular have been seen as a dysfunctional group for many reasons. This has invariably been a diagnosis by males looking at the problems through male lenses. When one approaches what appears to be a problem from the perspective of the women, things can often look very different.

For example, male alcoholism counselors may refer women to rehabilitation treatment centers for thirty days without planning for child care. When the woman resists going, it is interpreted as resistance to treatment rather than the real problem of caring for her children. This is not necessarily intentional on the part of males. It is because there are two different perspectives, one male and one female, to many situations. The health and mental-health system as well as many social welfare programs frequently operate from the male perspective. Chapters 7 through 10 of this book describe in detail how programs designed by women for women can look quite different than those designed by men.

Understanding human service institutions as a knowledge area is related to the understanding of systems. Unless one knows the organizational and bureaucratic structure of the system, there is no way of working within it to bring about change. In any one of the human service areas there is a network of federal, state, and local agencies as well as national, state, and local private agencies involved in the particular problem area. In addition there are many crossovers. For example, health-service agencies which do all our planning for health facilities crossover into mental health as well as substance abuse. Not only is it important to know the structure, it is also necessary to see the power structure as well as identify the leadership in each. Again how to find out about the power structure as well as identifying the leaders requires the requisite information channels. What can often look like the overt power structure may well not be. In the classic study of Atlanta community power structure, Floyd Hunter found that the five key decision makers in the community operated behind the scenes, not visibly.

A leader is identified as one who has power and can make decisions to effect change. Knowledge of leadership concepts is essential. Leadership is frequently charismatic, political, or tactical. Susan B. Anthony symbolizes the charismatic leader for women, as do Betty Friedan and Gloria Steinem. Political leaders are Bella Abzug, Mildred Jeffries, president of the National Women's Political Caucus, and Eleanor Smeal, president of NOW.

During the civil rights movement an example of tactical leadership in the sixties was explained by Whitney Young to a group of my students. The Urban League, National Association for the Advancement of Colored People (NAACP), Core, Southern Christian Leadership Conference (SCLC), and SNICC were the five main national organizations representing the blacks. The Urban League and NAACP were seen as the conservative groups, SCLC in the middle, and the other two as more radical. Often people would not want to identify with one or the other because they did not share its philosophy. As Young explained to the students, the organizing strategy was deliberate. Once a month the five leaders met and planned a united strategy and one of them, in this case Young, chaired the group. Radical groups are needed for the more conservative to be able to negotiate. Urban League money supported SCLC as well as some CORE activities. The activities of the five were often orchestrated together.

I fear there is no overall tactical plan in the women's movement, but feel that the development of a planned strategy is essential. It may in some ways have happened inadvertently. For example, without the radical bra burners who are willing to get out on the front line, we might never be able to get any legislation that even looks moderate passed. Bella Abzug being fired from the President's Committee on Women created a furor. Hopefully concessions would be developed before the new leadership took over.

Two other knowledge areas that should be addressed are planning theory and methodology. I come from a philosophy of CO that sees planning as an intrinsic part of the process. A strategy of planned social change for the women's movement as well as for the women's human-service delivery system is essential. Too often planning is done on an annual basis, especially in human-service planning. Unfortunately, annual budgets are confused with plans. Planning requires projecting into the future and designing ideal models as for human services. In relation to women as a whole one must ask what women need and want by the year 2000. Then what do we specifically need for each of the human-service areas as well as other areas. A major women's movement plan with subdivisions projected over twenty years at least is needed. The following chart depicts this theoretically.

Strategies	Year	Goal
Legislative	2000	What laws do we want passed?
Education	2000	How many university presidents and other senior officials should be women?
Economic	2000	What percentage of the gross national product should be owned by women?
Political	2000	How many women senators, representatives, and governors should there be? What about a vice-president and president as a woman?
Industrial	2000	How many women should be on boards of directors of of Fortune 500 companies, company presidents?

Each of these divisions would be subdivided by many subgoals with time goal estimates placed alongside each. Allocation of resources for the accomplishment of these goals would also be assigned. Program evaluation review technique (PERT), a planning technique which utilizes time, money, and woman power ingredients, would be one approach that could be used to develop such an over-all plan.

Such plans must also be in each of the human-service areas. For example, in the case of women with alcohol problems, what would be our goals for the year 2000?

Strategies	Year	Goal
Prevention	2000	How do we reach all ages?
Training	2000	How many female professionals do we want in the field?
Research	2000	What are the major questions that should be studied that concern women and alcohol?
Treatment	2000	What are our goals for residences, outpatients, and other forms of services?

Remembering that social planning is a process as well as a thinking methodology we need to involve women in developing such plans. These plans cannot be done in a vacuum; they must be developed now and clear deadlines established.

Method. The method in CO spells out the rational operational steps necessary to get from the identification of a problem to the evaluation after the change process has been implemented. Of course the worker has to be aware of these steps, remembering that some can occur simultaneously or in a different order. The community organizational method (dynamic process, not necessarily incremental) is as follows: identification of client system, doing a community assessment, problem identification, diagnosis, planning and building communication by mobilization of energy and resources following evaluation and maintenance of change process, leadership development, use of conflict, and management of power must be balanced. A plan of action is designed and implemented. Lastly, follow-through and evaluation are needed. Without these steps there can be problems. It is the methodological approach that the worker must know. Often people try to act through instinct or to go with particular situations without analyzing the procedure. Skill at implementing the method is the real test of the worker. One might be excellent at knowledge areas and conceptualizing but it is implementation that is crucial. If all this cannot be put to use so change can occur, the whole community organizational effort serves no purpose.

Certain personality types are obviously more skilled than others. An ease with oneself as well as with others is essential. Community-workers must be able to express themselves well on their feet and in writing. Speaking before groups, regardless of size, is another important ingredient. Other skills include appropriate use of parliamentary procedure and ability to write grants and chair meetings. Some of these characteristics can be learned, some cannot. Usually women need more confidence in their potential ability in these areas. Training women in these skill areas can effectively accomplish this goal. If a woman can chair a meeting, she can go a long way toward influencing its outcome. If she knows parliamentary procedures, she can often get legislation and motions passed. All women in the movement should learn these basics. They are the organizational tools needed in order to rebuild the social system.

Roles. Roles are defined as the actual behavior of an individual as the occupant of a position. A variety of roles can be utilized in CO. The practitioner must be skilled in applying the appropriate role to the problem or task to be accomplished. An ability to move in and out of roles is important. The following defines the most common roles which are utilized.

The enabler or catalyst awakens and focuses discontent, facilitates its expression and translates it into aspirations and needs, and sustains morale during the long process of organizing. The expert provides information and advice and knows community analysis and research. The expert is aware of the experience of other communities and is a technical resource. The expert speaks with authority but does not necessarily make concrete recommendations. The advocate is a leader and directs resources toward eliciting information, arguing the correctness of a position and challenging the stance of an institution. The advocate can become a partisan in a social conflict. The broker puts people in touch with community resources they need but are unable to locate. The activist rejects a neutral or passive stance and encourages the community to move and take such action as boycott, strike, or picket. The planner helps the community set a goal and methods of achieving the goal, and advocates a rational approach to problem solving. The administrator is the executor of social policy.

Sanctions. Sanctions for CO give all the others the authority to practice. Any profession gets its legitimization from the society to practice. This is the acknowledgment by the society that the group has arrived at the level of a profession. By so doing, the society accepts the particular professional group and hires them to accomplish a certain function. The following are the sanctions for the profession of CO: educational institutions (through schools of social work), organized profession (as National Association of Social Workers), government agencies, voluntary agencies, community development programs, private practice (as individual planning associations), industrial auspices, state licensing, the community, and religious groups.

It is obvious why various groups fight so hard for various forms of sanction. Battles are waged in state legislatures over licensing and today one hears much about credentials and recognition. Various groups are striving toward the same end, that is, community acceptance as the group to practice this particular method.

The framework thus goes from finding the way for CO as a form of social work professional practice to being sanctioned by the community to practice. This has taken eighty years and still CO is in its infancy compared to other professions such as law and medicine. The status of a profession is related to its age in society. Although young, CO has now accumulated experience in these various aspects of the framework. It seems a loss for the women's movement not to take advantage of this experience and use it for their efforts. There certainly have been a variety of organizational efforts and strategies by women as we will see in the next chapter. A more serious combination of the theories prescribed and applied to the women's movement is still needed to accomplish the major social change that is needed. Basically it is a social change process and that is what CO is all about.

Theory in Practice. Using a systems approach the theoretical framework is then applied to social needs (figure 1-3). The input of the values and principles are then combined with the concepts and knowledge and specific methodologies, and roles are utilized. What results is the application to program and policy change under the respective sanctions. This is fed back again to the concept and knowledge base after the first go around, and thus the living application is continued. The cycle then goes on. For our purposes we would apply social needs to particular social needs of women. Applying our values and principles as well as the concepts and knowledge we have acquired in this area, we decide on what method and roles we want to utilize. We apply this to various social policies and programs under the various sanctions we have with the appropriate change. We then repeat the cycle putting in new input and developing further social growth.

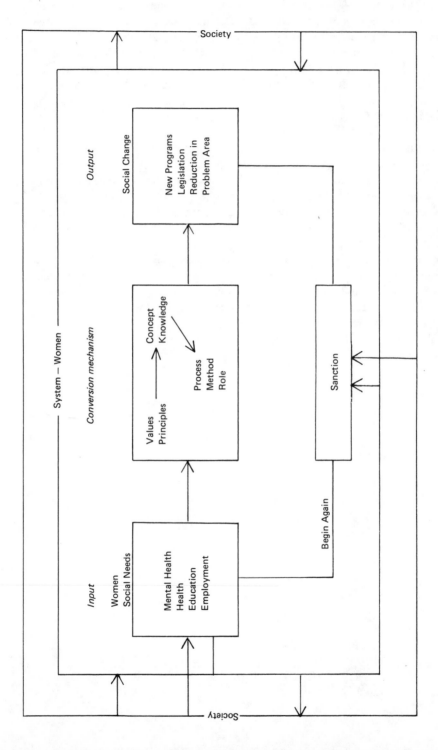

Figure 1-3. Community Theory in Practice: A Systems Approach

2 Historical and Organizational Perspectives of the Women's Movement

Introduction

An examination of past political and social movements organized by American women can be helpful in planning effective movements to influence the status and rights of women today. We can thus learn from past strategies how to avoid their mistakes and absorb their strengths. An analysis of past efforts, following the model detailed in chapter 1, raises pertinent issues that the women's effort cannot afford to ignore. The suffrage movement, for example, strikingly resembles the struggle for passage of the equal rights amendment (ERA). Although suffragists gained women the vote, they also diffused the movement for years to come.

An understanding of the historical efforts of women to organize themselves for social and political change is essential to an analysis of present trends and services for women. The fact that organizing was not a concept invented in the sixties is clear from the written history of women since presuffrage days. It is true, however, that women have traditionally structured their organizing on the basis of strategies learned from men. It is when these strategies have been combined with the creativity and energy of particular women that they have achieved successful outcomes for women. It is no surprise that change in woman's condition has been so difficult to achieve when one realizes that the efforts to force change worked within a system structured and controlled by men. Success has come only at a high cost from the intensive efforts of women who dedicated their lives to the cause of women's rights.

Echoing their mistakes must be eschewed while carrying on the struggle for women's rights. If today's movement combines a historical perspective and a people-oriented approach with a well-planned task and goal strategy, it could succeed through planned social change and continue to grow in power and impact as goals are met.

The Movement

Seeds of Movement: Pre-Seneca Talk, 1790-1850

At the turn of the nineteenth century, women shared few of the freedoms for which men settled in the new continent. In the colonies, religious orders adhered

21

to English common law until the advent of the Quakers. As Eleanor Flexner points out in *Century of Struggle*, women, especially at marriage, succumbed to "civil death." They had no legal existence: they could not sign contracts or own property, including their personal earnings. The wife's place was definitely tending children and hearth.[1]

While some dissatisfaction spread among women across the land, the few who spoke up relied on their own writings. These earliest feminist thinkers tended to be members of the urban intelligentsia. During the late 1700s, societal ideology was influenced by enlightened philosophers who believed that reason guided action and that free inquiry was the simplest path to truth. The earliest feminist writers felt that education would change women's inferior status. These writers included Mary Wollstonecraft, on the rights of women; Fanny Wright, on education and free inquiry; Harriet Martineau, the first female sociologist, on society in America; and Judith Sargent Murray, on sex and equality. John Stuart Mill was one of the few male intellectual and political writers of the time to advocate women's rights.[2]

These writers directed their appeal to the democratic political system where male power was viewed as analogous to political tyranny. They earnestly believed that reason, when properly cultivated through education, could set people free.[3] These early feminists fueled what would emerge as a full-fledged movement for women's rights in the mid-1800s. Despite its quiet, intellectualized beginnings, the movement would later erupt into action, marches, petitions, conventions; even violence would emerge as a tool for reform.

How did women emerge from their subordinate positions to organize a struggle for their basic rights? In the late 1700s, the society began to grow and change rapidly. The rise of Protestantism and industrialism, among other forces, altered traditional attitudes. And as the country expanded, pure survival dictated that women must work at a variety of tasks, often alongside men. In addition, some women were spurred on by social issues such as slavery and intolerable working conditions. Others responded to pressures unique to their particular part of the country; social conditions varied across the country.

In the North, the Church and its Puritan theology dominated life. With the onset of industrialization, women's energies were exploited for profit. Even though women entered the work force, the attitude remained that their real place was in the home.[4]

In contrast, the southern stereotype was that women led lives of leisure even while serving as dutiful wives to plantation owners. Any luxury white southern women enjoyed, of course, depended on hardworking black women slaves. While there were actually few southern belles, the myth elevated the white male to a kingly status. He ruled the house and protected his white women from the imagined lust of the black male. The black women, however, was fair game for the lust of the white man. The emphasis in the South was on race as well as sex and class. Thus, the women's movement in the South emerges most noticeably from the abolitionist struggles of the 1800s.

Western women lived still another life-style. During the first half of the nineteenth century, thousands of families headed westward to settle. Women had no choice but to work hand-in-hand with the men. While in the North and South, families formed according to class and social status, western families had diverse backgrounds. The puritanical values of the East never existed in the West. Women gained new freedoms from the frontier's challenges, with the exception of Mormon women who lived in a strictly male-dominated culture. Despite their new freedom, however, even the non-Mormon woman lived under a moral code created and enforced by men, the controllers of important business.

However different their personal lives, women throughout the United States were affected by the growing antislavery movement in the early part of the century. Some women saw similiarities in the struggles for black rights and women's rights. And when women found themselves excluded from abolition-ist societies in the North, they formed their own. Sarah and Angelina Grimke were among the earliest feminist abolitionists. Unable to live alongside slavery, the Grimke sisters left their South Carolina slaveholding family to settle in Philadelphia. They found an oasis among the Quakers and other abolitionists and began appealing to Christian women of the South. But slavery was not the only social ill they protested. They fought inequality of the sexes as well.

The Grimkes advocated social change; their strategy used basic Christian tenets as moral arguments for the inherent injustice of slavery and sexual in-equality. Initially, they spoke to small parlor gatherings of women. But their meetings quickly outgrew the parlor. The Grimkes spoke at churches and public forums, often addressing large, mixed audiences throughout Net York and New England. False translations and perverse interpretations of the Scripture, they said, had obscured God's true intent.

In "Letters on the Equality of the Sexes," Sarah Grimke wrote, "How monstrous, how anti-Christian, is the doctrine that woman is to be dependent on man! Where, in all the sacred Scriptures, is this taught?" She compares the condition of woman to that of the slave who "has too well learned the lesson, which man has labored to teach her. She has surrendered her dearest RIGHTS, and has been satisfied with the privileges which man has assumed to grant her . . . The doctrine of dependence upon man is utterly at variance with the doctrine of the Bible."[5]

The church responded to the Grimkes' outspokeness with a storm of con-troversy. Such attacks took a toll on these and other women who, driven by their moral consciences, came into conflict with the conduct expected of them. The resulting inner turmoil they suffered was particularly severe for Angelina who was overcome with the strain in 1838 and did not speak again for many years.[6]

Despite their deep suffering, the Grimkes and other feminist abolitionists learned from the opposition. At times, they turned opposing arguments to their favor in arguing for equality of the sexes. They continually linked women's rights to antislavery. Their dual struggle received mixed reactions from other abolitionists. Some felt struggling for women's rights diluted antislave arguments. But most women felt their true role in society was analogous to that of the slaves. They continued to argue for their own rights, justifying them with scriptures and pointing out inferior educational and work opportunities for women.

While these middle- and upper-class female abolitionists, led by the Grimkes, linked slavery to the condition of women, working women began to speak out about the wretched conditions of the factories. Women working in slum dwellings and sweatshops contacted each other for support and action. At first, these short-lived networks failed to make a significant impact. The women had no experience in organizing; and they lacked support from their male colleagues, many of whom feared competition for wages.[7] Then women became involved in strikes. In 1824 women factory workers joined a strike—for the first time—in Pawtucket, Rhode Island. Men had organized the strike against a wage cut and longer hours. Four years later, the first all-woman strike took place in Dover, New Hampshire. Throughout the 1830s, women held strikes in the Northeast. They would leave the factories, attend demonstrations and meetings, and then slowly return to work in a matter of days or hours. Sometimes their demonstrations turned militant, with rock-throwing and storming. Violent or not, the leaders were often fired and blacklisted. Factory workers were doubly plagued by poor working conditions and lack of support.

At first, the women made no gains from such actions; they lacked systematic organization. They also lacked the leisure of middle-class abolitionist women who could afford to devote more time to the movement. Then in 1845 came the Lowell Female Labor Association, an auxiliary of the New England Workingmen's Association. Under Sarah Bagley, the first notable woman trade unionist, the association developed a well-planned strategy to replace the hitherto fruitless strike efforts. Armed with witnesses and facts for support, the members initiated petition campaigns directed at the Massachusetts state legislature. Their motto was "try again," and indeed they persisted. Even without the vote they brought about the defeat of a state legislator with sexist views. That legislator later discredited the association and its leaders.

Similar associations sprouted under Bagley's leadership in other Northeast towns. Again the fact that they were well-organized led to their success and impact. Their strategies ranged from public speaking to pamphlets and a weekly newspaper (which lasted more than a year). The members of all these organizations worked in the mills. Due to their hard work and commitment to their cause, these women gained respect from working men. But the Lowell Female Labor Association, for all its strengths, had a fatal weakness: it was too dependent on one person. When Sarah Bagley later suffered a breakdown, the group could not survive the loss of its leader.

By the mid-1800s, women had reached some landmarks. The Grimkes' feminist/abolitionist movement and organization of working women were giant steps foward. While the immediate goals of each group differed, in each case women stepped forward for the rights they deserved. But the fate of Angelina Grimke and Sarah Bagley (which caused their respective groups to disintegrate) graphically shows the handicap of organizing a movement without financial or moral support from society. It also highlights the vulnerability of women leaders. The personal loss of Grimke and Bagley was monumental. In effect, they were martyrs for the cause of women. Women leaders today, still pioneers, need to heed this experience. The movement must incorporate supports which will maintain its leaders and not let them be destroyed in their fight for justice.

The efforts of the abolitionist and mill workers were notable but lacked cohesion. Although women's growing discontent was visible, only a thoughtfully planned program could have allowed this discontent to have an impact on the whole society. It was not until 1848 at the first women's rights meeting, at Seneca Falls, New York, that the movement found the leadership it needed for action.

Seneca Falls: Birth of a Movement, 1848-1860

The first women's rights meeting in American history took place in a Methodist Church in Seneca Falls, New York, in July 1848. Until this momentus convention, the fight for women's rights lacked unity and leadership. The discontent among women was visible and growing, but a concrete strategy was needed in order for it to have an impact on the nation. The Seneca Falls Convention, led by Lucretia Mott and Elizabeth Cady Stanton, provided the agenda necessary for action.

In London in 1840, the World Anti-Slavery Convention planted the seeds for the Seneca Falls meeting. For the entire ten days of the convention, no women were allowed to be seated. Lucretia Mott, a delegate to the convention, and Elizabeth Cady Stanton met as they sat passively in the gallery. The convention's discrimination against them spurred the two women to fight sexual inequality as well as racial inequality. They pledged to organize a women's rights convention upon their return to America. But the convention did not materialize until eight years later. For several years, Stanton led a life of relative leisure as a wife and mother with house servants. She was surrounded by friends, many of whom were reformers. Not until she moved to Seneca Falls in 1846 did her quiet life change. There, she lacked the support system she had found in Boston, and she faced growing family responsibilities.

In 1848, Stanton and Mott reunited at the home of a mutual friend in Waterloo. Stanton was extremely discontented with her life as housewife and mother of three boys under age 6. Though Mott's youngest child was 20, she sympathized with Stanton. As Rossi points out in *Feminist Papers*, these were not enlightened feminists who would channel their anger into books and lectures. They were women set on social action, moral crusaders who saw organized participation as the way to begin.[8]

Eight years after their vow to hold a convention, planning began. Seated at Jane Hunt's dining room table, Stanton, Mott, Martha Wright (Mott's sister), and Mary Ann McClintock wrote an announcement for the local paper to advertise the convention which was to be held a week later. The women adapted the Declaration of Independence into a Declaration of Principles, a strategy learned from abolitionists who often used it at their gatherings.

The declaration is in Rossi's book as it appeared in the *History of Women's Suffrage*, written by Elizabeth C. Stanton and Susan B. Anthony. It not only asserts "that all men and women are created equal," but also gives a history of the "repeated injuries and usurpations on the part of man toward woman":

> He has never permitted her to exercise her inalienable right to elective franchise.
> He has compelled her to submit to laws, in the formation of which she had no voice. . . .
> He has made her, if married, in the eye of the law, civilly dead.[9]

The declaration describes still more injustices and inequities perpetrated upon women by men. The authors concluded with a call for action: "In entering upon the great work before us, we anticipate no small amount of misconception, misrepresentation, and ridicule; but we shall use every instrumentality within our power to effect our object. We shall employ agents, circulate tracts, petition the state and national legislatures, and endeavor to enlist the pulpit and the press on our behalf."[10]

Following the declaration was a series of twelve resolutions on the changes needed to redress these injustices. Most of the resolutions dealt with a control of property and earnings and with the rights of married women to divorce and to win guardianship of their children. Only one resolution concerned the vote. It was the most hotly debated resolution, and the only one not accepted unanimously by the women. Those who spoke against it feared that the demand for the vote would defeat other resolutions they deemed more rational. Ironically, the vote would become the rallying point for the entire movement and overshadow the resolutions which dealt with the economic status of women.

Both men and women signed the declaration. But the proceedings of the convention at Seneca Falls received wide publicity and ridicule by the media and the clergy. Many who signed the declaration later withdrew their signatures due to pressure and humiliation.

Early Suffrage Years, 1860-1890

The Seneca Falls Convention along with the smaller conventions it spawned launched the women's rights movement. The conventions supported the legitimacy of women's discontent with their plight. They were a rallying point for women throughout the country. In Ohio, Rhode Island, and Kansas, similar conventions followed. New leaders emerged to spur women toward action. In Ohio, Sojourner Truth, a black slave from New York, gave a fiery speech linking the plight of women to that of slaves. And she wished that fate for no person, regardless of color or sex. She said: "If the first woman God ever made was strong enough to turn the world upside down all alone, these women together ought to be able to turn it back and get it right side up again."[11]

From 1850 to 1860, national women's rights conventions met each year except 1857. Some people charged that the women did nothing but talk. But in fact, the women were challenged to develop a common ideology based on their verbalized dissatisfaction, to use that ideology as a basis for a permanent organization. But they did not form such an organization because they feared that to do so would restrict individual initiative. Only during the Civil War did they learn that these fears were misguided.

While the conventions raised women's consciousness and served as the necessary first step in a full-fledged movement, women still lacked power. Without the vote as a tool for access to those in power, their only means of communication were public speaking, coverage by the press, and petitions. The church proved relatively useless as a means of support, as it remained hostile to the cause. For a while, women tried to make a point of adopting a daring costume, a loosely belted tunic and shirt. While this was a creative, attention-drawing strategy (as bra-burning would be a century later), it did not gain much concrete change.

One of the most important effects of Seneca Falls was that it stirred the interest of Susan B. Anthony. After hearing of Stanton and Mott's efforts at Seneca Falls, Anthony met Stanton in 1851 and subsequently joined the movement. Anthony brought to the movement a strong sense of politics and organizing. She came from a long line of Quakers where equality for women was a traditional value. Her father was a colleague of Garrison and Douglas and she "cut her teeth" in organizing for antislavery. She was a paid canvasser for the New York State antislavery society.[12]

She initiated well-organized petition drives in every county in New York. Her first petition campaign asked the New York Legislature for the following reforms: women's control of their own earnings; guardianship of children in case of divorce; and the vote. In her time, Anthony's strategies were innovative. Starting with sixty women, one for each county in New York, she had each serve as a captain to collect signatures; in ten weeks, they collected

6,000. And using her political savvy, Anthony planned a statewide women's rights convention in Albany at the same time the legislature was in session.

Naturally, the reforms were not passed at the time. But a new energy entered the movement. The women who were involved persevered, resolving to continue to enlist support throughout the state. Four years later, in 1860, the bill did pass the New York Legislature. This victory led to an important and powerful partnership between Anthony and Stanton. Other notable women joined in their work, among them Lucy Stone, Ernestine Rose, Abby Kelley Foster, Frances Gage, Lucretia Mott, and Sojourner Truth. As women supported each other to improve their lives, they developed what is crucial for any movement: leadership.

The Civil War: The National Women's Loyal League, 1865-1870

In 1861, the Albany Women's Rights Convention met. It was the last one held before the outbreak of the Civil War. Thereafter, all activity on behalf of equal rights for women ground to a halt. Many women accepted the reality of war and the changes it brought; they were busy in the workplace filling in for men at war. Farms and factories continued functioning because of the labor of women. Some women participated in war-relief work assisting their husbands and sons and concern for women's rights was not a high priority.

Elizabeth Cady Stanton and Susan B. Anthony, however, had grown too accustomed to active intellectual and political work to accept roles as helpers. And they were critical of the administration's policy toward slavery. They distrusted Lincoln and feared he might make compromises with the slave states. They and other ardent abolitionists demanded unconditional emancipation. In the winter of 1863, Stanton challenged Anthony in a letter: "The country was never so badly off as at this moment . . . . We must not lay the flattering unction to our souls that the proclamation will be of any use if we are beaten, and have a dissolution of the Union. Here then is work for you. Susan, put on your armor and go forth."[13]

Anthony and Stanton set out to enjoin women all over the country to New York for a meeting of the loyal women of the nation. The gathering drew hundreds of women. Lucy Stone, Ernestine Rose, and Angelina Grimke joined Anthony and Stanton as leaders. They adopted resolutions pledging women's support to the government as long as it continued to fight for freedom. They also pledged to collect 1 million signatures to petition Congress to pass the Thirteenth Amendment. Before the gathering adjourned, it organized the National Women's Loyal League, with Stanton as president and Anthony as secretary.

The league taught women the value of organization as a means to accomplish their ends. It acted as a powerful force in changing women's views that formal organization was a negative force because of its bureaucratic and often restrictive nature. As Flexner explains, the National Women's Loyal League is not often mentioned in historical accounts of the Civil War. It was, however, unique at a time when women were known mostly for their concern with doing good, not for their activism in national politics. Flexner points out that no similar organization existed among women of the Confederacy. The more common forums for women were hospital-relief societies or sewing circles.[14]

Despite these efforts, the Thirteenth Amendment granted freedom to slaves, but little for women. However, women did begin to recognize their own capabilities and to enjoy the freedoms afforded them by having to work outside the home. Yet they had performed essential services during the war, and for the most part their efforts went unnoticed. Women realized that the passage of the Thirteenth Amendment, while a victory for female abolitionists, did not hasten the suffragists' goals. In fact, most men and some women reformers felt that the Civil War was the black's hour and that feminists should wait to press their claims until black male suffrage was secured.

Considering the status of blacks at the time, feminists must have been quite humiliated that white men would support the vote for black men yet oppose suffrage for women of any race. Perhaps naively, they thought when peace came, a grateful country would reward women with the vote. Their inexperience with politics created a simplistic analysis of the forces at work against them. While they were used to the argument of conservatives who believed suffrage for women would mean the downfall of home, church, and state, they were totally unprepared for the opposition of Republican politicians. Nor did the women expect abolitionists to desert the feminist cause once the slaves were freed.

The Fourteenth Amendment to the Constitution, proposed to Congress in 1866, introduced for the first time in the U.S. Constitution the word *male*. It gave all men equal rights under the law, including the right to vote. It benefited black men and ignored, once again, the issue of enfranchisement for women. Women had been duped: they had put aside their own campaign during the war to join in the campaign for freedom of slaves and, as a result, had fostered a setback in their own movement. Now women saw clearly that, to white men, freedom for "slaves" meant freedom for black slaves, and that white men would sooner support equality for black men than for women of any color. A profound lesson exists here for the present women's movement. By allying itself with civil rights issues, women may be repeating this mistake; that is, today's women's movement may find itself in reality helping minority men but not women of any color. This potential misalliance also has particular relevance for minority women who often feel they must choose between two causes: race and sex. Often they choose race. They may be hurt by such a strategy should history repeat itself. If white men continue to choose men over women, then women (white and minority) will have to counterattack against all men regardless of color.

The Movement Splits: Suffrage Early Years, 1860-1890

From the beginning of the movement, women had disagreed on the relative weight to give the vote. As mentioned earlier, it was the only resolution which did not receive a unanimous vote at Seneca Falls. Women could not agree on whether it was the only issue or one of many in the fight for women's rights. The Stanton/Anthony forces felt women should fight the Fourteenth Amendment and its discrimination against women. Others, led by Lucy Stone, felt it was indeed "the black's hour" and women should support the amendment.

Soon after ratification of the Fourteenth Amendment in 1868, the fifteenth was introduced. It read: "The right of citizens of the United States to vote shall not be denied or abridged by the United States or any state, on account of race, color, or previous condition of servitude." Stanton and Anthony argued that the word *sex* could easily have been inserted. They failed to recognize, however, the deep-rooted emotional basis among men for not wanting to grant women the vote. When slaves won their freedom, black males reached the legal status of men, and received all the rights intended for American men, at least on paper. But women, white or black, did not attain that status. They were not and still are not legally the equals of men.

The passage of the Fourteenth and Fifteenth Amendments deepened the rift in the women's movement. The rift was not ideological; both conservatives and radicals desired the vote. The split was a strategic one. The two factions did not agree on how the vote should be won. The radicals, led by Stanton and Anthony, regarded women's rights as a broad cause in which the vote was primary, but in which other matters of importance for women also figured. They recognized that some women were exploited in the workplace and some were social outcasts, and they wanted to speak out for those women.

But the more conservative group, led by Lucy Stone and Julia Ward Howe, did not want to address any issues which might risk the support of influential members of society. They had no interest in working women, in criticizing the church, or in the question of divorce. While giving lip service to the idea of a federal woman suffrage amendment, they concentrated on the state level.

Unable to reach agreement, the two factions finally split. In 1869, Anthony and Stanton organized the National Woman Suffrage Association (NWSA), for women only. They believed that the large number of men in the movement had betrayed women's interests. Here again is a lesson from history which should not go unnoticed. If today's struggle is to gain power from and equity with men, it well may not be possible to utilize men in the organizational structure of the top level leadership. This lesson seems to have been heeded today in the movement. This is not to say appropriate coalitions may not be utilized with men, but in the actual decision-making levels Anthony and Stanton were clearly correct in ruling them out. They opened membership in the new association to any woman who believed in suffrage and who agreed with the broad-based strategies and demands of NWSA. In 1870, they founded a newspaper called *The Revolution* which survived for about two and half years.

The conservatives, led by Lucy Stone and her husband Henry Blackwell, founded a second organization, the American Woman Suffrage Association (AWSA). This group, led by both men and women, maintained a narrow focus on the vote and refused to recognize the church and family as sexist institutions. They also used a newspaper to communicate with the membership, the *Woman's Journal*. It spoke for club women, professionals, and writers, many of whom were not yet ready to espouse the cause of women's suffrage.

The division in the movement hurt the struggle for women's rights. But there is a lesson to be learned from the split. The radicals were ahead of the times in their strategies. The movement was not ready for their approach. Their drive and impatience to gain the vote may have been necessary for change in the movement. While the immediate result of their action was a division in the movement, in the long run their actions were significant in moving the fight forward. Conflict can be definitive in creating social change.

By 1890, the two factions reunited to become the National American Woman Suffrage Association (NAWSA), with Elizabeth Cady Stanton as its first president. But the movement as a whole had become fairly conservative and conventional by then. While society no longer considered suffragists strange, the gap had widened between privileged women suffragists and working women in the factories and trade unions. Also the immigrant movement further stymied liberal beliefs as to what the role of women should be. In many instances, the votes of immigrant men blocked suffrage for women at the state level.

In the 1880s, the movement suffered from lack of an ideological framework. Many previously active women were drawn away from suffrage to temperance or other social-reform movements. Even Stanton became increasingly interested in the divorce question and in criticizing the sexism of the Old Testament. She focused much of her energy on writing a Woman's Bible, which set out to redress the sexism of the Old Testament.

Susan B. Anthony replaced Stanton as president of the suffrage association in 1892. She became distressed when the association decided to hold Washington conventions in alternate years rather than every year. She was skeptical of any attempt to divert attention away from a national movement in favor of state-by-state constitutional strategy. Anthony's fears were proved correct when, between 1893 and 1913, the move for a federal amendment vanished as a political issue. Clearly Anthony was a giant. Her understanding of strategies as well as issues was unparalleled. History consistently showed her to be correct. The more radical of our women leaders today may be the Anthonys of tomorrow in the history of the movement.

Social-Reform Years: The Late 1800s

During the 1800s, while the suffrage movement languished, other social reform movements flourished. In the late 1800s, more women than every before became educated and entered the labor force. Industrial advances freed middle-class women from some of the drudgeries of daily household chores. Increasing immigration provided unskilled females to work as their cooks and housemaids. Middle-class women had more leisure than ever before. Many focused their energy on social reform but withdrew from the suffrage movement. They worked for the temperance movement, the settlement house movement, the consumer movement, and the trade union movement.

Instead of political power, many women sought a token place in the world of men. They were willing to work alongside men even if it meant placating the white male power structure. They joined the society-at-large in viewing women's issues as sectarian and men's as universal. Nevertheless, these reform movements had a profound effect on the power, unity, and skills of women.

The Temperance Movement: Liquor Industry versus Suffragists

Women reformers had been concerned with the temperance issue since the 1840s. For many, temperance was their hope for gaining relief from the abuse and abandonment of drunken husbands. In November 1874, the Women's Christian Temperance Union was organized in Cleveland. It strongly supported the suffrage movement's goals and, as a result, provoked the liquor industry's campaign against women's suffrage.

Frances Willard led the national temperance organization. She viewed the fight for temperance as another way to gain support for the vote. Gradually, she taught women that they could not protect their homes and families from liquor and other vices without a voice in public affairs. She used her organizational skills and spoke publicly to impress upon people the critical relationship between temperance and the vote.

Although Willard had a potentially potent strategy, she underestimated the power of the liquor interests. The more the Women's Christian Temperance Union linked its cause to the vote, the more money the liquor industry poured into antisuffrage activities. The conflict remained until the liquor companies, threatened by a prohibition amendment, shifted their energies away from suffrage to their own survival problems. Whatever problems it may have raised for the suffrage movement, the Women's Christian Temperance Union succeeded in reaching and influencing more women than any other organization of its time.[15] Alcohol continues to be a major problem today for men and for women. The liquor lobby is still very powerful. Perhaps a negative strategy of ensuring that the liquor industry is aware that temperance is not a strategy of the women's movement today may head off a repeat of alienating the same powerful group again.

Settlement House Movement: The Classes Unite

The settlement house movement, albeit another diversion from the struggle for suffrage, had profound effects on uniting middle- and lower-class women. Furthermore, it taught women some important lessons in strategy. The movement began when Jane Addams established Hull House in 1889 as a vehicle for social action in the slums. Not all the settlement houses which began at that time had the same activist mission. Many were created by altruistic middle-class women to improve the lives of the poor. Still, most women in the settlement house movement agreed that to improve slum life would require a change in the societal conditions that breed poverty. Inevitably the leaders of the movement found themselves involved in struggles to improve working conditions. The houses became focal points for change in all aspects of a woman's life.

While designed for the poor of both sexes, women organized the settlement houses, and women and children predominantly occupied them. The movement was a new organizing strategy for women. It brought to the fore the importance of local organizing as part of any national movement for change. It introduced the importance of fellowship and support for women. Finally, it provided role models for emancipated women. In Jane Addams, the movement produced a vital leader. Many other great women lived in the settlements. As O'Neil explains:

> No other aspect of the women's movement, except for suffragism itself, received so much attention from the national press. Best of all, the settlements reassured conservatives that liberated women would interest themselves in traditional womanly concerns, ... Settlement workers played a key role in the women's movement.[16]

Interestingly the settlement house movement played a vital part in the early history of community organization (CO) and social work. It was here that occurred the birth of social reform and what was later to become social activism. The split that followed in social work had the social activists turning to CO while the conservatives from the group settlement house orientation went into group therapy and casework. The interface of the women's movement and CO occurred here.

Consumer Movement: Rise of Activism

The National Consumers' League (NCL) grew out of the social-reform interests of middle-class women. Organized by a small elite group of well-educated New York women in 1890, it became a powerful activist organization. The women were outraged by reports of the deplorable working conditions of retail-shop workers as well as their low pay and long hours.

The prominent organizers of the league used their positions in New York society to advance the interests of working women. Their wealth and influence advanced the league considerably. One of their tactics was to promote a "white list." It carried the names of retail establishments meeting their standards for working conditions. The women encouraged buyers to patronize white-listed stores rather than stores which exploited retail salespersons.

New York's was the first league, but by 1899 consumers' leagues had spread to large cities throughout the country, coordinating various local groups. Florence Kelley, chief factory inspector of Illinois and one of the league's strongest leaders, used her organizing skills and energy to expand the scope of the NCL. Within several years, she had facilitated ninety local leagues, twenty state leagues, thirty-five auxiliary leagues, and numerous college branches.

The NCL adapted their white-list strategy into a white-label campaign. They authorized clothing manufacturers with good labor policies to put an NCL white label in their garments. By 1914, some seventy manufacturers were using the label. In addition, league members lobbied for protective legislation and publicized poor working conditions in various industries. After 1907, the league successfully concentrated its efforts on maximum hour and minimum wage laws for working women.[17]

The NCL was a successful and powerful organization of women, for women. The leaders turned the league's small size to an advantage: they mobilized quickly when action was needed. They believed, as most progressive era thinkers, that to change society, they needed cooperation, reason, and morality. Women such as Kelley, Josephine Shaw Lowell, Maud Nathan, and Frances Perkins used their leadership and organizing skills to put together a successful campaign for action.

Women's Trade Union League of 1903: Working Women Grow Stronger

The NCL and the settlement house movement, while organized by middle- and upper-class women, recognized the need for joint efforts of working- and middle-class women. The National Women's Trade Union, founded in 1903, went a step further in uniting the classes.

The time was ripe for such a league. Many socialists and workers, unhappy with the American Federation of Labor's (AFL) lack of effort to organize women, gathered in Boston for the annual convention of the AFL. The settlement house women had seen the deplorable conditions of women working in factories. Several wealthy Bostonians had been trying since 1892 to organize women in trade unions. William English came up with the initial idea for a National Women's Trade Union League (NWTUL). A wealthy socialist intellectual, English had seen such an organization work in England.

The settlement leaders involved in the NWTUL knew that facts were crucial in making a case. Thus, they worked to get Congress to pass a bill appropriating funds for an authorized, comprehensive inquiry into the conditions of women workers. The report took four years to complete. It produced a nineteen-volume document on the condition of children and women wage earners.

Because of the overriding importance of the AFL's mission to its own cause, the NWTUL chose to work within AFL's system. It organized women for existing unions rather than founding its own unions. But within these boundaries, the NWTUL made some important accomplishments. It brought many wealthy women into direct contact with the labor movement; and it developed a body of working women who eventually led the NWTUL, thus making it the only feminist organization primarily composed of working women. Futhermore, the liberal stance of the NWTUL reminded the AFL of its own moral shortcomings. For instance, while the AFL excluded Orientals, the NWTUL refused to do so. But while the socialist and immigrant Jewish members influenced the NWTUL, the leaders quieted their revolutionary fervor by immersing the more radical members in practical work. Although the NWTUL ultimately became a rather middle-class reform movement, it thrived on the coalition of socialists, workers, and wealthy members. Most important, it showed that if the vote was ever to be won for women, a similar coalition was exceedingly necessary.[18]

The movement just described today remains a source of potential strength or dilution of strength for the women's movement. The alcohol issue, social reform for the poor, consumer concerns, and the labor movement are major examples of social issues. Many women are involved in these causes. The critical issue is that women in these movements must not opt for them over the women's movement per se. They must see them as part of the same cause. By seeing the women's issues involved in these social concerns from a woman's perspective, they will also be able to move their cause ahead as well as that of women. History again shows that women separated these things from the women's movement and that to do so is a mistake. This is the main theme in part II as it makes the transition from the movement to issues.

Suffrage: The Later Years, 1906-1920

While the social-reform organizations did not always directly address the issue of women's rights, they did give women opportunities to work for change in the social fabric. Some of the clubs and organizations which grew out of the social-reform era were token attempts to given women a role in issues of concern to a male-dominated society. But others gave women much needed experience in organizing to fight the longest battle of them all: the struggle to gain the vote.

The suffrage movement received a much-needed shot in the arm in 1907, with the return of Harriet Stanton Blatch from a twenty-year stay in England. Blatch, daughter of Elizabeth Cady Stanton, had participated in the militant woman's Social and Political Union in England. She believed that to achieve the radical goals of her mother, women needed militant tactics. She recommended renewing the push for an amendment to the federal constitution, the strategy favored by the Anthony/Stanton faction of the suffrage movement. But the movement was due for change. It was not long before the American militants, led by Blatch and Alice Paul, split off from the conservative NAWSA to form the Congressional Union (which later called itself the Woman's Party).

Under the leadership of Carrie Chapman Catt, NAWSA continued to pursue a strategy of individual state referenda. They felt that Blatch's Congressional Union's goal of a federal amendment was premature and unattainable. The rift between the two groups widened until it split the energies of women working to gain the vote. Still, NWTUL continued its hard-driving campaign. During the 1914 election, it sent organizers into states which had won full suffrage to swing women's votes against Democratic candidates, regardless of their stands on suffrage. The women felt that the party in power had to be held accountable for the lack of a national amendment. Alice Paul explained the practice in *The Suffragist* in 1914: "If the party leaders see that some votes have been turned they will know that we have at least realized this power that we possess, and they will know that by 1916 we will have it organized. The mere announcement of the fact that the Suffragists of the East have gone out to the West with this appeal will be enough to make every man in Congress sit up and take notice."[19]

The Congressional Union used new strategies which are often incorrectly attributed to the whole suffragist movement. These included open-air meetings, card files of members by political districts, and speeches at factory gates for the workers. The members campaigned actively against politicians opposed to suffrage and fought for the right of women to serve as poll watchers on election day. The group also initiated parades and "trolley tours" to bring their message to small towns and larger cities. The Congressional Union had become well-organized and truly political.

These events brought a new drama to the suffrage movement. Mobbings, beatings, and hunger strikes were not uncommon as the increased publicity brought new blood into the movement. Unlike the conservative feminists who were willing to stop at gaining the vote, the militants saw the vote as only one of many goals for women. They wanted to win it and then move ahead to other important issues.

The Congressional Union, then calling itself the Woman's Party, turned to militancy only in the last three years of the campaign, 1917 to 1920. Meanwhile, the conservative NAWSA began to work for a federal amendment, but dissociated itself from the militant strategies of the Woman's Party. Instead, the NAWSA worked within the establishment to gain the vote, ignoring the beatings and punishments of their more militant sisters.

It is hard to say what or who was responsible for the final victory. Certainly, it was a combination of factors built up from years of planned activity by the various women's organizations. The Nineteenth Amendment had been introduced to every session of Congress since 1878. It was finally ratified on 26 August 1920. Just to achieve the vote took:

> Fifty-two years of pauseless campaign . . . fifty-six campaigns of referenda to male votes; 480 campaigns to get state constitutional conventions to write women suffrage into state constitutions; 277 campaigns to get state party conventions to include woman suffrage planks; thirty campaigns to get presidential party conventions to adopt woman suffrage planks in party platforms, and nineteen campaigns, with nineteen successive congresses.[20]

The battle had been won but the war was certainly not over, and is not over today. Unfortunately, the energy it took to win that one battle crushed the women's rights movement for years to come. Because women emphasized the vote alone, they did not develop a broader consciousness. When they won the vote, they became lulled into the belief that other victories would easily follow. Much is to be learned here for the ERA. As critical as ERA is to the women's movement, it cannot be the only issue. Much energy again may be put into its passage which could in turn bring about a period of dormancy similar to that which followed the suffrage war. Equally important is the violence that was necessary in order to obtain the vote. This may well occur again before ERA is passed. This time women have history to teach them. They need not be unprepared and caught by surprise.

The Movement Sleeps: 1920-1960

The decline of social feminism after World War I disappointed many, but it was a sign of the times. There was a nationwide, postwar swing to the right. Suffragists quickly realized that the fight to win the vote was more rewarding than actually having the vote. Carrie Chapman Catt attempted to keep women together in their new roles as voters by founding the League of Women Voters (LWV) in 1920. But the LWV's neutrality and broad issues did not replace the NAWSA, which appealed to many with its single focus. Strategically, the neutrality of the LWV may well be incorrect. By remaining objective and neutral, women's powers in voting were neither mobilized nor utilized for the attainment of concrete goals. This in effect may well have been one of the major mistakes of the movement. Even a third party may have been more effective. Often, by controlling some of the votes, bargaining can transpire if the two major parties are in a close fight. This still may be a viable strategy for today.

Once won, suffrage for women was no longer an issue for organizing. Women were swallowed up by established political parties; they no longer had the distinct voice which characterized them during the progressive years. Suffrage did not alter the power balance between men and women. Women were still economically dependent and no closer to self-determination.

In the 1920s people turned inward, seeking self-fulfillment. Freedom became a more personal issue. In the roaring twenties, people searched for glamour; they valued romance and eroticism. Conformity was in; conservatives were absorbed and radicals ridiculed. As most women searched for personal fulfillment, politics were far from their minds.

The 1930s brought a startling halt to the pleasures of the twenties. But the devastating effects of the depression further stymied any organizing around women's issues. Firestone explained:

> With the myth of emancipation going full blast, women dared not complain. If they had gotten what they wanted, and were still dissatisfied, then something must be wrong with them. Secretly they suspected that maybe they really were inferior after all. Or maybe it was just the social order. They joined the Communist party, where once again they empathized mightily with the underdog, unable to acknowledge that the strong identification they felt with the exploited working class came directly from their own experience of oppression.[21]

By the end of the thirties, women had gained little as a result of the vote. They excelled in lobbying, but they had lobbied without the vote. In presuffrage years, women were strongest when speaking with almost a single voice. As O'Neil points out, this has never again been the case. Women were joined together in presuffrage years by a variety of forces which could not be preserved in the postwar, postsuffrage, and postprogressive world.[22]

What organizing did go on in the twenties and thirties was largely around the issue of equal rights. In 1921, the old Woman's Party was disbanded and a new one created. For a while, women thought of the new Woman's Party as an alternative to the major political parties, but eventually this Women's Party devoted itself entirely to lobbying for the ERA. It was hoped that the struggle for a federal amendment would recapture the enthusiasm of the presuffrage days. O'Neil explains that in making these calculations, the Woman's Party committed two important errors: it overestimated its political strength, and underestimated the strength of the opposition to an amendment granting such blanket equality between the sexes.[23]

As women's movements before and after suffrage can attest, the lack of coalition building and joint problem solving hurt the already declining activism of women in the twenties. In fact, by 1924 every important social feminist organization had attacked the ERA as a threat to protective legislation for working women. While the Women's Party members did not oppose legislation, they firmly believed that it should be based on industrial lines, not sex. The two factions were not really so far apart in their ideals, but emotionalism and lack of good organizing skills made it seem that they were fighting each other. The Woman's Party believed in social welfare, but strongly felt sexual equality must come first. They often took a haughty, uncooperative attitude, however. They were labeled extreme feminists, agitators, and antidemocratic.

Evidently, their strategies did not suit the times. At first, they attempted to hold the party in power responsible for all of society's ills. Later, they believed that with a sufficient number of congresswomen in office, the ERA would pass. They supported all women candidates, even those not supporting the ERA. Eventually, they supported only women who endorsed the amendment, but all of them were beaten. In the meantime, the Woman's Party received much hostile publicity.[24]

The differences between social reformers and social feminists of the presuffrage years continued into the twenties and thirties. It appears that women felt the need to choose between joining a cause or seeing themselves as a cause. They did not seize the opportunity to build coalitions based on points of agreement. Rather, they fought one another when what they needed was unity. The problem was not one of ends; it was one of means. Extreme feminists, while astutely analyzing the situation, underminded their own goals by giving society the opportunity to label them as weird and abnormal.

In the thirties and forties, Freud's writings gave credence to the "abnormalties" of the Women's Party feminists. Freud viewed women as passive, childlike creatures suffering from penis envy, the crucial aspect of their emotional existence. He based his central thesis of women's inferiority on lack of a penis. According to his theory, men develop social virtues and strong superegos when they overcome the Oedipal complex. The fear of castration enables them to do so. Since women have no such fear, they never free themselves from the Oedipal complex. Thus, they have a weaker capacity for sublimation than men. In Freud's view, women are inferior to men; their only chance for equality is to embrace their procreative function.[25] It was the theories of Freud and his followers that set the stage for the rebellion against "the feminine mystique."

The Feminine Mystique, 1960-

In 1963, Betty Friedan described the feminine mystique as follows:

> The suburban housewife—she was the dream image of the young
> American woman and the envy, it was said, of women all over the
> world. . . . She was healthy, beautiful, educated, concerned only about
> her husband, her children, her home. . . . As a housewife and mother,
> she was respected as a full and equal partner to man in his world. She
> was free to choose automobiles, clothes, appliances, supermarkets: she
> had everything that women ever dreamed of.[26]

Friedan explains that the mystique, after World War II, became the self-
perpetuating core of contemporary American culture. Nobody discussed
whether women were superior or inferior to men. Nobody used words like
emancipation and career. These were strange concepts which had been buried
for years. If a woman had a problem during the fifties and sixties, she blamed
herself. Women were so ashamed to admit dissatisfaction that they did not
know how many others shared it. Marilyn French vividly portrays the feelings
of women in these decades in *The Women's Room.*

During the fifties, women closeted their dissatisfactions. They accepted
their homemaker role, tending duties as wives and mothers. If problems emerged
in their marriages, it was their problem. If they did not have a career, they had
only themselves to blame. The country's introspective mood discouraged women
from looking outside themselves for the causes of their discontent. They were
seen as sexual beings, fulfilled once their maternal needs were met. Male psycho-
analysts molded them to fit into a world dominated by male values. Quite
simply, women were enmeshed in an identity crisis. To deviate was a risk few
women would take: they had no support from men or women.

It was as if women spent half a century fighting for their rights and the
next half wondering whether they wanted those rights after all. Friedan raises
the possibility of the history of early feminism repeating itself today. Women
had worked hard to dispel prejudices against them. But while their efforts at
first appeared successful, those stereotypes had only gone underground for a
while. They reemerged in the forties disguised as psychological theory, under
the shroud of education and social science, supposedly the chief enemies of
prejudice. As Friedan asks, "how can a woman presume to tread the sacred
ground where only analysts are allowed?"[27]

No one was willing to answer her question until women again stood up
for their rights in the late sixties. This reawakening of the movement, according
to Friedan, is analogous to the earliest struggles for women's rights; she pointed
out that women had to fight a similar battle: "They had to prove that woman
was not a passive, empty mirror, not a frilly, useless decoration, not a mindless

animal, not a thing to be disposed of by others, incapable of a voice in her own existence, before they could even begin to fight for the rights women needed to become the human equals of men.[28]

Women's Liberation Movement Reemerges: The Sixties

During the fifties and early sixties, the seeds of discontent were sown. Women began to question whether psychotherapy, diapers, and the PTA were the only vehicles to personal fulfillment. Spurred on by Friedan's timely book, women began talking to each other about their condition. The knowledge of their ancestors' struggles lay dormant, but not dead. The dissatisfaction of the suburban housewife combined with the idealism of college youth began to feed the fire. Racism emerged as a social issue as had slavery 100 years earlier. Responses to racism and the escalating war in Vietnam created a social movement unlike any seen for years. Somewhere in the search for solutions, the Women's Liberation movement was born, with far-reaching effects.

In 1961, President Kennedy created the National Commission on the Status of Women. In 1965, a year after the Civil Rights Act banned sex and racial discrimination in employment, the commission published a report documenting that such discrimination against women still existed: women's wages were half those of men, and the percentage of women in professional and executive jobs was declining. The commission recommended that women be counseled on using their abilities in society. It further suggested that child-care centers and other services be provided to allow women to combine motherhood and work.

To Friedan, the report was nothing but empty talk. The social structure had not been changed, only peoples' consciousness. She felt that the time was ripe for a political and social movement like that of the blacks. In the mid-sixties, she went to Washington, armed with the supposed power behind title 7 of the Civil Rights Act banning sex discrimination in employment. There, she found an underground network of women in government, press, and labor unions who felt powerless to stop the sabotage of that law. They asked Friedan to start an "NAACP for Women."

In 1966, the National Organization for Women (NOW) was born around a luncheon table in Washington, D.C. Friedan and the original twenty-eight members committed themselves to "take action to bring women into full participation in the mainstream of American society now, exercising all the privileges and responsibilities thereof, in truly equal partnership with men." Friedan wrote these words on a napkin, marking the beginning of the Women's Liberation movement.[29]

NOW was the first women's organization to be founded in fifty years. That same year, the New Left and the civil rights movement embraced women's issues. In those two movements, however, women worked for the greater good of society instead of focusing on their own plight.

In the late sixties, New Left women began defining themselves either as politicos, who wanted the feminist movement to remain part of the New Left, or as feminists, who favored an independent women's movement. By the end of 1969, consciousness raising C-R groups had been formed in at least forty American cities. Membership continued growing with regular monthly meetings of 30 to 300 women held in most major cities.[30]

While not every woman interested in women's liberation participated in a C-R group, hundreds of women did use them as the first step in a long process of liberation. As the movement increased in size, what began as an informal network within the New Left movement branched out into its own identity.

Conclusion

Today, women have still not won the battle for an ERA, an amendment first proposed in the 1920s. Perhaps women activists are fighting the same issues with the same strategies. In the past, women worked for temperance, settlement houses, freedom for slaves, and suffrage. Now, women work for an end to wife abuse, shelters for abused women, equality for blacks, passage of the ERA, and abortion. In 1914, the NAWSA opposed the party in office because suffrage had not been granted women. Today, there is talk of voting out the present pro-ERA administration for not working hard enough to pass the amendment. Arguments used against the suffragists are now used against pro-ERA women; the amendment will mean the downfall of home, church, and state, say conservatives.

Worst of all, feminists once again are split on the issues. There is disagreement over whether to make ERA the central issue for the movement or to see it as just one of many steps toward equality. This disagreement recalls the split between earlier feminists over the issue of suffrage: a split that was ultimately damaging. Where to stand on abortion and lesbianism causes further arguments among contemporary feminists. And women still struggle with the question of whether to fight for their own rights or for the rights of minorities. The issue is even more complex today, as black and Hispanic women decide whether to fight for racial equality or sexual equality.

In deciding what emphasis to place on the push for ERA, women should keep in mind what their sisters learned in the past. While there is enough opposition to ERA alone to occupy all women's energy and power, will total concentration on one issue destroy the movement? Once ERA is passed, will the movement die out for lack of a single organizing point? Perhaps, ERA, like the supposed power gained from suffrage and the Civil Rights Act, will provide paper rights only; and perhaps inequality for women in her church, in her workplace, in her home, and even in control of her own body will continue. Feminist leaders must be powerful and alert enough to avoid these disasters. They must choose effective strategies for change while recognizing and rejecting mistakes which repeat the past.

Women's organizations today carry a heavy responsibility for reaching the goals of the women's movement. They must be organized to accomplish these goals. NOW, the National Women's Political Caucus, and hundreds of other organizations that have been born in the last several decades should strategize together. The Office of Women at the White House has a plan for implementing issues in relation to the federal bureaucracy. The Women's Action Alliance is an organization of women's groups who form an annual national strategy for priorities in their effort. The more organizations work together like this, the better off the movement will be. History has clearly shown that the capacity to have a lasting structure is one of the most critical elements the women's movement needs. The structure should be comprehensive as well as having the capacity to act. This requires numbers of women in support, money, and power. It requires an organization of organizations with leadership and a strategy plan.

**Part II
Organizing for Women:
A Particular Perspective**

3 Woman as Worker

Think for a moment of a nuclear family . . . husband working, wife not working outside the house and at least one child under college age living with parents. What percentage of American families do you think this comprises? . . . Only 17 percent.

Sarah Weddington
Special Assistant to the President
Radcliffe College Lecture Seminar, 1979

Women and work are major aspects of women's issues which must be viewed separately from the history of the women's movement. This chapter shows the economic importance of work to women and points out the occupational segregation that exists for women. It also points out issues in the workplace which are especially relevant to women and descriptions of particular forms of institutional discrimination against women which exist in current employment practices. Lastly, the strategies for combating these conditions are suggested.

In recent years, public media and popular literature have been filled with stories of working women. Articles concerned with the new women managers, the female executives, and the feminine professionals have surfaced at nearly every newstand. At face value, America's women seem to be making tremendous progress and seem to be quickly advancing in the business world. However, deeper investigation into the statistics and facts reveal that this progress may not be as tremendous as it seems. In reality, there has been and will continue to be a steady influx of women into the labor market; but the economic conditions of women are not improving despite their increased participation in the labor force. For example, in 1976 the average fully employed, white woman earned $8,285; her male counterpart earned $14,071. A woman of a minority race earned $7,825; her male counterpart earned $10,496.[1]

The only change which has really occurred is that more women are now experiencing the same kinds of discrimination that have kept women dependent and subservient for generations. The new heroine of the magazine articles—the strong, independent female executive—represents only the tiniest proportion of working women. Worse yet, she is often a token representative of her sex, employed to satisfy the requirements of the government. Because she has a position, her employer is eligible for government contracts and grants. In effect, her employer profits from her work and from her presence.

The workplace has been and continues to be male-dominated and almost completely lacking in responsiveness and equality for female workers. American women began to move out of the home and into the labor force at the end of the Civil War. There has been a steady but gradual increase in the numbers of women in the workplace since then.

America's young, single women entered the workplace first; they crowded the small mills and factories of New England, working for a few years before marriage or sending the money home to help struggling families on the farms. Not long after the mill girls entered the labor force, older, married women began to trickle into the mills. These women were often poor, immigrant women, and soon the female labor force became associated with the economically needy.

Almost all categories of women were represented in the female labor force during World War II. With men fighting overseas, women were substitutes in the fields and factories. Women's labor became critical to the survival of the nation's economy. No one complained about the negative effects working mothers had on the development of their children. No one wondered if women were physically strong enough to handle industrial machinery. No one said women were losing their feminine identity. No one even hinted that women were only secondary to the nation's working economy. Women were seen as and accepted as vital participants in the country's struggle for more resources and toward a new upsurge in productivity. As the nature and scope of women's participation in industry grew, a new generation emerged of economically solvent women. These women began to have dreams and aspirations of upward mobility and economic and social independence. But this promise of upward mobility was an illusion. When the wave of victorious veterans returned, they reclaimed their slots in the labor force and displaced the "vital" women workers. Thus dispensed with, women resumed the struggle for economic survival in "pink-collar" professions.

Over the past decade, more women have worked outside the home than at any time in our nation's history. Forty percent of the country's labor force is female between the ages of 18 and 64. Twenty-three percent of all working women are over 55. About 43 percent of the female labor force is married, and 37 percent of these women are mothers of children under age 6.[2]

There are many reasons for the steady increase in female labor force participation over the last nine years: delayed marriage, beginning families later in life, increasing numbers of divorced or separated women facing the issues of self-support, inflation, recession, the women's rights movement, and a growing belief in the opportunities for women in the marketplace. Whatever the reasons, women are entering the labor force in ever-increasing numbers, they are staying in that labor force over their life spans, and they are taking their career and economic pursuits seriously. Most women enter the labor force before they begin their families, they tend to stay in their jobs during pregnancy, and they tend to remain in the labor force after their children are born.[3]

During the last ten years, the fastest-growing demographic category has been the female-headed household. These households, which usually have at least one dependent child present, have grown at ten times the rate of two-parent households; from all indications, this group of single mothers will continue to grow in the future. One explanation for the increase is that the remarriage rates are not keeping up with divorce rates. By 1978, the Bureau of Labor Statistics (BLS) reported that in every socioeconomic group one out of every six children under age 18 lived in a family headed by a woman.

Certainly the fact that women are now major bread-earners for families deflates the argument that women do not take their jobs seriously or that women are merely supplemental wage earners. In the book, *The Subtle Revolution*, editor Ralph Smith points out that two out of every three American mothers will be in the labor force by the year 1990. A total of 11 million women will enter the labor market during the next decade, and a large percentage of these women will be single heads of households. "The stereotype of a wife as someone who stays home to look after the children will only fit one-quarter of American mothers."[4] Within the next twenty years, women will constitute the majority of the labor force in the United States.[5]

The fact that women are working is nothing new. The fact that wives and mothers of small children are working is also not new. What is new is their numbers, the extent of their participation, and the mounting pressures and responsibilities they face. To face these pressures and responsibilities, in this century and the century ahead, working women need to develop new strategies in the workplace to allow for their full and equal participation.

Occupational Segregation: Economic Implications

Although more and more women are working, their general well-being, both economic and social, has not really improved much. Chapman states the issues involved in women and work particularly well: "Since the postwar period, women's overall economic condition is still characterized by dependency, poverty, low wages, tax and social security disincentives, and credit discrimination."[6]

In 1956, the median earnings of a full-time working woman were only 63 percent of that of a full-time working man. At the beginning of the 1970s, the same woman earned 59 percent of her fully employed male counterpart. With the reemergence of the women's movement, women began to demand equal work, and the press and public media broadcast the great developments in equal rights for women through affirmative action and social awareness. But by 1974, eleven years after the passage of the Equal Pay Act and two years after the establishment of the Equal Employment Opportunity Commission, women were earning 57 percent of men's wages.[7] Although more women have been working, their economic condition has been losing ground.

Even when women function as the heads of their households, the wage discrepancy gap persits. In 1956, female heads of households brought home 56 percent of what male heads of households earned when each was the sole provider. By 1974, these women brought home only 47 percent of what their male counterparts did.[8]

The greatest myth in this discrepancy of income is that women earn less than men because they are less educated. Recent statistics indicate that a female college graduate can expect to earn 60 percent less than a male college graduate of the same age. Annual earnings for a woman who completes high school is $7,103, whereas a male high-school graduate can expect to earn an average income of $12,260. The median income for a woman who has completed four years of college is $10,519, whereas her male college counterpart is earning $17,129. One reason for this discrepancy could be that one out of every five females that graduated from college works in a clerical position, and these positions are notoriously underpaid and economically devalued.[9] In fact, the median annual income for a female college graduate is less than the median annual income for a male who has graduated only from high school.

The great gap in income which exists between the sexes is largely a part of the occupational segregation which has become particularly prevalent within the last eighty years. There are in fact two labor forces in the United States. One labor market is marked by low status, low pay, and stagnation. This labor market employs women. The other market is characterized by diversity, broad-pay scales, and a wide range of opportunity for advancement. This labor market employs men. The Equal Pay Act, as well-intentioned as it was, could do little to change the duality in the labor force. In this society, the kinds of jobs women customarily do are not considered equal to the kinds of jobs men do. And pay scales reflect this imbalance of values.

Division of labor by gender is becoming more polarized. In 1900, one-third of all working women were in domestic-service jobs. Valerie Kincade Oppenheimer found that between 1900 and 1960 fully one-half of all working women were employed in occupations in which at least two-thirds of the labor market were women.[10] Today, this is still true. In 1978, Louise Kapp Howe wrote: "the more detailed your analysis of a particular occupation becomes—by specific type of work, by industry, by firm, by department within the firm, by level of advancement achieved—the higher the rate of occupational segregation becomes."[11]

In the 1970s, two-thirds of working women were in white-collar sales or clerical positions. So vivid is occupational segregation that traditionally female professions have come to be known as "pink-collar" professions.

Whenever a particular occupation has a female population of 80 percent or more, that occupation qualifies as a pink-collar profession. Nursing is a pink-collar profession; 97 percent of nurses are women. Ninety-five percent of sewers and stitchers are women. And 99 percent of secretaries are women.[12] Only 20 percent of the male labor force works in 10 percent of the occupational categories. The fifty-seven occupations employing the most male workers employ fewer than 52 percent of the entire male labor force. In contrast, 15 percent of all professional women in the labor force work in only four job categories. Clearly, as Stellman wrote, "occupational opportunity and achievements of men are much more diversified than those of women."[13] Even in social work and teaching, female-dominated professions, males hold most top-management positions.[14] Within their own professions, women are not able to penetrate the higher levels of management, positions that have higher-pay scales. In 1972, for example, women accounted for 30.7 percent of all full-time federal employees. Yet only 5.8 percent of the highest-level GS-13 to GS-18 positions were held by women. Most women employed by the federal government possessed the lowest-grade ratings of GS 1 through 6: 73.6 percent.

Oppenheimer also discovered why women are making strides in labor force participation, at least in terms of their numbers. Women have not been demanding and gaining entry into the labor market across the board. Women are entering the labor force mostly in pink-collar professions.[15] The reason for this is, with the rise of corporate power and industrialization, the greatest labor demands have been in traditionally female labor markets: clerical and service positions. Women have simply responded to increased demand for semiskilled labor. Contrary to the public notion that the rise in the numbers of working women means economic progress for women, women are doing what they have traditionally done: they are not infiltrating the myriad levels of the corporate structures; they are merely filling new openings in old professions and filling them in greater numbers than ever before. The large strides are largely illusion.

Howe discussed the illusory strides of women in their work with news reporter, Ellie Grassman. Grassman wrote: "All we've heard about these last six months is Barbara Walters and her million-dollar contract," says Louise Lapp Howe, author of *Pink Collar Workers*. "We don't hear that the gap between working men and women is higher than ever," she says. In 1956, the average earnings of full-time working women were 63 percent of men's; in 1974, they had shrunk to 57 percent. "Women comprise 40 percent of the country's workers, but only 15 percent of them are 'professionals,' mostly teachers and nurses, traditionally female categories." The rest are pink-collar workers, Mrs. Howe's term for the underpaid, undervalued yet socially useful beauticians, sales workers, waitresses, office personnel, and homemakers whose stories she relates in her book.

Grassman highlights the distinctions between male and female beauticians. The male is addressed as Mr. and earns plaudits, sycophancy, and a very handsome salary. The female is addressed by first name, earns less, and lacks job security. Yet males and females perform the same functions. Grassman makes equally pertinent observations about waiters and waitresses. He secures better-paying jobs in prestigious establishments: fine restaurants, hotels, and private clubs. She works in fast-turnover, counter-service eateries, coffee shops, and cocktail lounges, which offer less money and no fringe benefits or job security.[16]

The forces that govern occupational segregation are subtle and elusive and have to do with social, psychological, and economical factors. Many pink-collar professions are characterized by some form of help or support given to others in the line of duty. The secretary takes care of her boss, often functioning as an extension of his or her spouse or parent. The homemaker takes care of the sick in the home; the nurse, in a clinic or hospital. The social worker cares for the weak and the poor. The mother cares for dependent, young children and often for an old and struggling parent or a disappointed husband. Many female professions are simply extensions of the traditional female role within the family structure. Women gravitate to these professions because they are consistent with the socialization into female roles imposed on them during their education. These roles and therefore these particular occupations are reinforced. Teachers subtly reward young girls for excellence in art, English, and home economics the same way they reward young boys for excellence in math, science, and athletics. The American educational system encourages boys to compete, girls to cooperate. In an economic system that functions almost entirely by competition, the training of young girls does little to prepare them for much besides helping, nurturing, cooperative occupations. It is critical that women head into the proud sciences of physics and mathematics. Women need to become engineers and nuclear experts. Because of the disproportionate numbers of men in these fields the National Science Foundation (NSF) was instrumental in influencing Senator Edward Kennedy to recommend the following legislation.[17] "We have to establish benchmarks to measure performance", Senator Kennedy said.[18]

1. A requirement that every federal agency involved in research and development establish the advancement of women in science as a priority
2. A research, development, and demonstration program to encourage women's participation in science
3. Science-education programs specifically designed to encourage young women to continue in science through their precollege years
4. A recruitment and fellowship program involving the NSF, the nation's scientific societies, and the Civil Service Commission
5. Requirements for adequate representation of women on all federal advisory panels and peer-review groups
6. Employment goals for both the federal and private sectors, and a reporting system to keep track of their progress

There may be significant change in women's occupational status in the near future. There have been strides made by females in school over the last five years, but there is still a long way to go. In 1979, Harvard Law School claimed 25 to 30 percent of its current class was female. Johns Hopkins Medical School's student body is only 12 percent female. In 1973 in the University of Virginia's prestigious Colgate-Darden School of Business, student population was only 9 percent female; however, by 1979, 30 percent of its students were women. So women are making progress; but the population of professional schools does not reflect the population of women in the country (more than 50 percent). Therefore, it will doubtless be a long time before equality in higher education becomes actual, especially in professional schools that promise higher status and incomes for their graduates.

Hiring practices are also involved in the split and shift of men and women into specific occupations. First, women seek out female-specific jobs; and personnel departments within companies and employment agencies, upon which many women rely for finding jobs, send women to interview for lower-paying, traditionally female jobs. Women apply for "people" jobs; men apply for management or physical work. These jobs connected with people seldom result in rapid advancement; the jobs are associated with female roles and functions; they are devalued. Second, once in these traditionally female positions, women usually find themselves excluded from training programs which could lead to advancement or promotion. The young male salesman is more likely to be placed into a management-training program than his female secretary.

The prevalence of occupational segregation prevents women from making professional progress to accompany their increased participation in the American work force. Testifying before the Senate Committee on Human Resources in 1978, the National Commission on Working Women representative pointed out that 43 percent of professional-level women and 59 percent of women in blue- and pink-collar jobs expressed dissatisfaction with the lack of opportunity for job advancement.

Women hold 2 percent or less of middle-management positions. In over three-fourths of 163 American companies with more than 1,000 employees, one survey showed no women in top-management positions. On the other hand, women hold 98.6 percent of stenographic, typist, and secretarial positions. And only 4 percent of those who earn over $30,000 per year are women. Furthermore, because of the presence of systematic occupational segregation, women are subject to economic disadvantage. The ultimate form of occupational segregation is unemployment. A discussion of women in the work force would not be complete without considering women who are looking for work, who want to work, but who cannot find even pink-collar jobs.

Despite the steady increase in female labor force participation, there has also been a dramatic increase in the numbers of women who are unemployed. In 1947, women constituted 28 percent of the labor force and 27 percent of the unemployed. In 1979, women constituted 42.2 percent of the labor force and 49.9 percent of the unemployed. The segregation is by race as well as by gender. Black women have twice the unemployment rate of white women. Black teenagers and older black women have the highest rate of unemployment. In fact, black female teenagers have a higher rate of unemployment than any other demographic group.[19] Getting a job, any job, is more difficult for women than it is for men. The number of women who were sole supporters of their families increased by over 30 percent over the last decade, but at the same time the number of women who were unemployed rose by 24 percent.[20]

Special Populations

Blue-Collar Workers

Women started thinking about breaking the occupational segregation gap in recent years. This is especially true in blue-collar professions in which 5.1 million working women earn their living. One out of every seven working women has a blue-collar job. As a group, blue-collar women have begun to make important strides into traditionally male areas, but they have run into traps no one could have anticipated.

Female blue-collar workers themselves come from various cultural backgrounds with their own cultural biases toward women. One expectation is that women, not men, cook, clean, and care for the children whether they want or not. In addition, according to Nancy Seifer, the blue-collar woman is usually the wife of a manual laborer; she generally earns less than $5,000 a year.[21] Most frequently, she lives with her family in an ethnic-oriented community in an urban center. The blue-collar woman is seldom actively involved in the women's movement and while she is frequently aware that her wage is substantially less than the blue-collar male's, she can justify this because of the differences in the nature of the jobs men and women hold in the factory. This unique form of occupational segregation can be seen by a simple walk through a factory. Men operate the heavier machinery while women line up on the assembly lines doing the more intricate and detailed wiring work. The problem is that heavy-machinery jobs pay more than the detailed assembly-line work even though there is some question as to which kind of job requires more skill. In addition, if the blue-collar wife were to push for increased wages and benefits, she would more likely do so for her husband rather than for herself. One reason for this is that, although these women might be unhappy about their positions and paychecks, to push for women's rights might fuel an already inflammatory home situation. Blue-collar women have indicated that their husbands become more restless as wives' wages increase, resulting in more domestic quarrels. Such husbands tend to regard the growing social and economic independence of their wives as a threat. Myra MacPherson summarized in 1977: "Breaking into jobs traditionally held by men is not all it's cracked up to be. Women in telephone companies and auto industries talk not only of sexism but of sex on the assembly line, jealous husbands, who don't wnat their wives to work with men, of male coworkers hostile about a woman taking over a male job, of male against female battles over seniority, of the strong blue-collar male attitude that women should stay at home."[22] Women who challenge the status quo by entering the blue-collar workplace may do so at considerable cost.

Women's Unions

Women have been members of labor unions for nearly a century. The early unionization efforts of the mill workers of New England were almost all spearheaded by women working in the textile mills and living in company quarters. But several problems have persisted between women and organized labor groups. First, women have not participated in organizing efforts in numbers great enough to influence their own working conditions and wages. Second, women who have participated in these efforts over the years have not learned much from their more successful organizing brothers who have become skilled and effective in winning benefits for male workers.

As members of unions, women are theoretically entitled to equal pay for equal work; but according to the BLS even organized women are concentrated in the female-dominated occupational categories in much the same way as their nonorganized sisters. These sex-specific job categories are further characterized by low wages and unequal benefit packages. In addition, not many blue-collar women are members of unions. Most of these women workers are concentrated in industries which are not organized and which have not been known for aggressive organizing efforts. Whereas 27 percent of the male labor force is unionized, only 10.5 percent of the female labor force belong to organized labor groups. This trend toward minimal participation by women workers in organized labor has been true since the efforts of the mill workers in the late 1800s.

As a result of this trend, women have achieved little through unions in the way of benefits and wage increases. During the nineteenth century, 98 percent of all working women were not represented by any union. At the turn of the century, 1.5 percent of full-time working women belonged to unions.[23] Today, union membership by females has increased only to 10.5 percent. To put it another way, six out of seven women who work are not represented by organized labor.

Occupational segregation is partly responsible for this trend. Several unions which serve female-dominated professions have low percentages of women leaders. For example, the International Ladies' Garment Workers Union (ILGWU) has a membership of 430,000; 80 percent of the members are women. Yet this union has only one female on its board of directors.[24] And the AFL-CIO, of which the ILGWU is a member, has just appointed its first woman to its executive council.

It was not until the birth of the Coalition of Labor Union Women (CLUW) in 1974 that women began to unite to address their particular economic issues or the unique needs and problems of blue-collar women in the marketplace.[25] Fifty-six percent of the female apparel workers, who dominate their union, are the sole supporters of their families. Yet the male workers in comparable blue-collar positions in the clothing industry consistently earn more than their female counterparts.[26] The failure of the apparel industry and the union representatives to resolve such an inequity is symptomatic of the slow progress of unionized women. The changes that Burleigh Gardner calls for cannot develop too quickly. He wrote: "What we are witnessing today . . . is a basic change in the attitudes and aspirations of the female working class segment of our society . . . a change that will require new ways of accommodation and communication."[27]

Organizational efforts, such as the formation of the CLUW, symbolize the direction women in unions must take in order to obtain inclusion at the collective-bargaining tables and in all phases of labor-management negotiations. Because women meet overt and often subversive resistance in their family, personal, and work lives, the process of organizing may remain painful and slow.

Divorced women and single mothers are fully discussed in chapter 4. However, since both groups are also working women, they warrant consideration here under special populations.

Divorced Women

There are more than 5 million divorced women in the United States. These women form a new group of economically disadvantaged in this country. Contrary to public opinion, divorced women are not "on easy street" because of the steady flow of alimony checks from their ex-husbands. Only one woman in seven is ever awarded alimony, and fewer than 50 percent receive any form of child support. Yet most divorced women are responsible for the care of their children.[28] So divorced women work.

However, if a woman has been out of the work force during marriage or has only worked part-time, she is at a disadvantage following a divorce. Her husband was already earning more than she was. Her earning power would be less even if she had been a full-time wage earner. But if a woman was less than a full-time wage earner during her marriage, after divorce she necessarily starts at a lower level. Her standard of living is lower at a time when her resources may be lowest. Any children she has will compound her depressed economic status. In most cases, a man has few increases in his expenses as a result of divorce and no change in his employment capacity. The divorce courts tend *not* to take this state of affairs into account, so divorced women in America often suffer financially and professionally for reasons which actually have nothing to do with their capacity to work.

Single Mothers

Divorced or unmarried mothers of young children constitute 20 percent of the American female population. The economic necessity for them to work is self-evident. But because they must simultaneously be full-time mothers and full-time workers, single women with children are almost forced to take personal risks which nonparents or pairs of parents need not take. Single mothers encounter the psychological stresses of economic difficulty, social isolation, solitary child rearing, and lack of complete freedom to develop their careers because of child-related constraints.

The economic strain under which an individual finds himself or herself may be measured by the person's level of access to material goods and resources. Unmarried or divorced mothers must provide food, shelter, and medical care for themselves and their children on a single income that is usually lower than that of the children's father. This group of women suffers more psychological pressure caused by economic strain than any other group in the country.

The single working mother along with single people in general experience more social isolation than paired parents. In addition, Pearlin and Jackson, studying "Marital Status, Life-Strains, and Depression" in 1977, found that the formerly married have difficulty in establishing a single life again. The working mother does her job at the workplace during the day and her home responsibilites in the evening, leaving little time to become active in the social scene. Unfortunately, this group is then especially vulnerable to depression.[29]

All parents of young children are susceptible to depression caused by the increased responsibility of parenting. The implication of this fact for working mothers is obvious. Most courts award custody of children to the mother. In two-parent households, depression in parents is highly correlated with the age of the children in the family. The younger the children, the greater level of parental responsibility and the greater the probability of depression. A female parent alone risks depression even more.

Reports on recent trends in child psychology in popular and academic literature have alerted women to the effect their working may have on the development and well-being of their children. Many women have been caught in the guilt-producing situation of making some decision about work which might advance their career but which might not be ideal for their children. Some women have actually let promotions pass by because of the potential effect on their children. Furthermore, single working mothers are not free to relocate as companies may demand, or take a position that entails extensive traveling when they have responsibilities for young children and little or no assistance.

Single mothers of young children are almost a special population within a special population. They may experience higher stress then other working women because of the necessity to work, and they are most prone to mental-health problems. It is ironic that in 1980 the movie *Kramer vs. Kramer* became such a smash hit. Millions of Americans sympathize with the father who sacrificed some of his employment opportunities to be able to adequately care for his child. Yet thousands of women have been doing this for decades. He is a hero to society; she is expected by society to do it.

Part-Time Workers

Many women work part-time because in full-time work they cannot meet the demands placed upon them by home, family, and society. Although some federal agencies provide benefit programs for part-time workers, most private employers do not. So women who can work only part-time seldom receive such fringe benefits as paid vacation, medical insurance, or sick leave; and they often sacrifice promotions, seniority benefits, and pay raises. Yet part-time workers have low-turnover rates, fewer absences, and usually bring more energy and more ideas to their work.

Job sharing, in which two part-time workers share the same job, has gained popularity recently. It is a trend which could facilitate part-time careers for women. Industries which have experimented with job sharing found that job sharers exhibit the same positive characteristics as part-time workers.[30] The success of job sharing may contribute to improving working conditions for all part-time workers.

Volunteers

Segregation of the sexes also exists in the world of volunteerism. Historically, volunteerism has been inaccurately regarded as the domain of women. Men serve as volunteers too, but the kinds of organizations in which they participate and the positions they hold in them differ from those of women. Usually, men are administrative volunteers, and women are service volunteers. An administrative volunteer holds a decision-making role, that is, board of directors. A service volunteer works hours or days without compensation in an agency, hospital, and so on. No authority resides in the service-volunteer role. Women volunteer in hospitals as pink ladies (compare pink collar) and in garden clubs. Women stuff Christmas baskets for the Salvation Army and go door to door for the Heart and Cancer Funds and for innumerable other organizations. But even women who are active and demonstrate leadership ability in these local-service groups rarely use their influence and leadership to their own advantage. Women tend to define volunteerism in terms of selflessness. My 76-year-old mother continues to volunteer two days per week in a thrift shop in Yonkers, New York. She has donated this time for the past forty years. For twenty-five years she also donated one day per week in the hospital running their library. Incidentally, her mother had done the same for years. For women this is expected. If a man did such volunteer work he would be proclaimed a hero like Kramer.

The definition which men most often use differs strikingly. Some men contribute to their communities through volunteerism in the same ways women do. But for others, selflessness is coupled with self-interest. Men volunteer with other businessmen through such organizations as the JCs, Rotary Clubs, Shriners, Retired Citizens Consultants groups, and Junior Achievement. It is within these "charitable" and civic organizations that men meet other business-men and develop friendships that will further their own professional interests. The strength of a Rotary Club is in the economic viability of its membership; when the successful and influential join, others equally successful and influential follow. This does not mean that these organizations do not contribute substantially to the communities within which they operate; but their members help themselves while helping their communities.

Male volunteers have different rules and goals than their female counterparts. And as in the pink-collar professions, top-administrative positions in our voluntary agencies are held by men. For example, the United Way and the American Red Cross (the latter was founded by Clara Barton) have never had women executive directors even though most of their volunteers are women. Men seem to use volunteerism to further themselves and their careers; women seldom gain as much as they give.

Volunteerism has advantages if used correctly. It can be especially useful to women who have been out of the labor market for a long time and find reentry into the paid labor force difficult. Volunteerism can provide the experience for a woman that an employer says she lacks. Women should regard volunteerism as fulfilling two different goals. It allows her to assist in a worthy cause, and it enables her to work at something which may subsequently lead to remunerative activities. When selecting an organization to volunteer for, women must determine the status other female volunteers have in the organization. Women must also determine what that organization can contribute to their own development and well-being. The key to beneficial volunteering is having a goal. Women should regard volunteering as a tool to implement obtaining a gain of some sort, a gain more substantial than simple helpfulness."

Issues and Strategies in the Workplace

Sexual Harassment

Supervisors, managers, and employers have a tremendous amount of influence and power over employees. They have the power to upgrade positions and to recommend personnel for training and promotions, to regulate work loads and to influence the mood of the working environment, and to hire and fire. Many persons in supervisory roles use their powers constructively, but some abuse it. Sexual harassment is a form of abuse male supervisors, managers, and employers sometimes exercise against their female employees. Sexual harassment covers a wide range of behaviors. A woman may be as sexually harassed with a gesture or whisper as she is with an overt offer or threat. Any time a male with power or influence over a female employee's job or financial security uses that power or influence to bargain for sexual favors, that male is guilty of sexual harassment. Not only is sexual harassment a form of discrimination, it is illegal. "Sexual harassment is deliberate or repeated unsolicited verbal comments, gestures, or physical contact of a sexual nature which are unwelcome. Within the Federal Government a supervisor who uses implicit or explicit sexual behavior to control, influence or affect the career, salary or job of an employee is engaging in sexual harassment."[31]

Representative James Hanley of New York conducted congressional hearings on sexual harassment in late 1979 which revealed that this illegal activity is quite widespread. A majority of the women surveyed in a number of government departments said they had experienced some form of behavior from male bosses or supervisors that they would classify as sexual harassment. The nature of the problem women face in instances of sexual harassment is that when an employer makes sexual demands, women lose a form of freedom. Women who refuse or ignore the demands risk provoking retaliatory actions that can have professional cost. A spurned supervisor may damage the status of a female employee's job, pay, or future opportunities. It is no wonder that women often allow themselves to become intimidated or coerced. In addition, women report that fighting sexual harassment head-on is a dangerous proposition. Many people still blame the victim. A woman who has been harassed may be said to have "asked for it" because of the way she dresses, flirts, and teases. Being a victim of sexual harassment threatens a woman's self-image when the attitudes of others make a woman question herself and how her behavior may have been interpreted. The fear or ignorance of coworkers and friends may isolate a woman fighting sexual harassment, leaving her to handle a difficult situation alone.

In most instances of sexual harassment, the offending male denies the accusation made by the offended female. The word of a respected male manager with many years of service is often taken more seriously than the word of a female subordinate. Frequently, the manager receives little more than an empty reprimand from his superiors. The woman who protested his actions may again be harassed, this time in revenge for her protest.

For all these reasons, women who are sexually harassed in the workplace often feel that they have no recourse. Frequently, women remain silent, handle the situation as best they can without making waves, and endure the outcome alone. Because women's work is so important to their economic well-being, quitting is seldom an option. However, in a 1979 study Arthur Fleming, the U.S. Civil Rights Commissioner, found that a statistically significant number of women who are sexually harassed at work resign their positions, thus forfeiting their benefits. But an ethical response to sexual harassment is not the negative posture of leaving a job, remaining silent, and fighting a one-sided conflict alone.

There have been some successful fights against sexual harassment in recent years, and these successes have been characterized by two important elements: detailed and accurate documentation of the instances of harassment and support from other female employees who have experienced the same treatment. Documentation entails accounts of the times and dates and exact descriptions of conversations and actions and events along with assistance from anyone who may have been present and witnessed or overheard what occurred. Documentation also entails compiling data regarding those promotions, training opportunities, and pay raises that may have been denied as a consequence of resistance to harassment. Women who have successfully protested sexual harassment have become familiar with personnel regulations and with their own personnel files in particular. They have also become familiar with the memos and reevaluations that have been done by the offender. Some women have received support from staff members of personnel departments.

The Office of Personnel Management of the federal government recently developed a procedure to help individual agencies deal equitably with instances of sexual harassment.[32] The Merit System Protection Board is currently undertaking a survey of federal women on sexual harassment. These two developments are constructive and helpful, though somewhat conservative.

Sexual harassment is one of the largest and most widespread problems working women face. It can be subtle or blatant. It is also an issue riddled with moral judgments, values, and emotional unrest. It is a problem requiring women to provide support and assistance for other women. A supportive group of coworkers can be extremely helpful to the woman who has experienced sexual harassment. On a larger scale, such groups can become instrumental in encouraging companies and businesses to specifically address incidences of sexual harassment and to adopt policies to protect employees from such occurrences.

As with many of the issues and problems working women face, women must control the problem and its solution by uniting for common goals and safety and must not rely on outside sources for protection or redress. Because the government has recently taken the lead in combating sexual harassment, private industry will follow. Since sexual harassment is illegal, it is important for women to familiarize themselves with their agency or company policy on this. Women should know the company designee who receives complaints of harassment. Often the Employee Asssistance program (EAP) can be utilized to help a woman clarify what is happening and to support her through legal channels if necessary. The EAP is based on problems affecting job performance and is an appropriate resource. Women should be cooperative and supportive in a harassment case; besides, class-action grievance is always more effective. The government is taking the lead in trying to help sexually harassed women; it is up to women to utilize this assistance.

Work Environment and Women's Health

In 1977, the Department of Health and Human Services (then Health, Education and Welfare) estimated that 1 million women of childbearing age work in environments that were potentially hazardous to their and their offspring's health. These women were constantly exposed to chemicals and solutions that are known to cause birth defects or miscarriages.[33] Instead of improving the dangerous working conditions, the companies responded to pressure from the Occupational Health and Safety Administration (OHSA) by offering their female employees the following options. A woman could (1) obtain a sterilization operation at her own expense and then show written proof from her physician that she could not become pregnant; (2) transfer to another department and possibly lose seniority or suffer a reduction in pay; or (3) be dismissed.[34]

Male workers were also tested, and their sperm was abnormally affected by the same working conditions which posed a hazard to female workers. But the men were not forced to choose among any of the above options. The OHSA policies were structured so that women between the ages of 18 and 40 who worked in certain unsafe surroundings were required to damage themselves, if not physically then professionally. In addition to being fundamentally immoral, this state of affairs constitutes a conflict between the 1970 Occupational Health and Safety Act which guarantees the right to safe working conditions and the 1964 Civil Rights Act that protects the right to equal employment opportunity. Because of this conflict and the options presented by their employers, some women find themselves in an untenable situation. As Stellman says, "if women cannot have economic backups when they wish to work because they may be exposed to something injurious to their fetuses while they are pregnant and also are not allowed the option to continue work, what then are their real choices?"[35] These women still need incomes; they still need to work. Yet they should have a right to do so without risking their health and that of their future children.

The American female worker has not had a health advocate for more than a quarter of a century. At the same time, a disproportionate number of women have been entering job categories with high-health risks in the twenty largest occupations.[36] Considering that 1.5 million women have children every year and that 40 percent of the female labor force is married and of childbearing age, the lack of a health advocate to address the special concerns of working women is intolerable and dangerous.

In addition to the effect of the work environment on pregnant and future pregnant women in the workplace, there has been little research into the differential reactions to various toxic substances between the sexes. Little is known about women's physiologically different reactions to industrial wastes or chemicals. Women workers have not been subjects of much research in the field of occupational health. However, one recent study revealed that certain female clerical workers do have a higher rate of cardiovascular disease. In 1979, a ten-year study by the National Heart, Lung and Blood Institute indicated that clerical workers who are mothers and who are wives of blue-collar workers endure stress-related heart disease at a higher rate (12 percent) than other working women (8.5 percent).[37] More such studies should be undertaken so that sex-related occupational hazards can be eliminated from the workplace.

Some health hazards associated with traditionally female occupations are already widely known. Clothing workers are exposed to thick amounts of aerosols, spray adhesives, and other chemicals used to treat the fabric they handle. Oils and oil mists are used to treat thread in the mills and factories; yet companies do not protect their employees from the harmful effects of these substances.

Nurses and hospital workers are necessarily exposed to infectious illnesses. To a certain extent, this risk is unavoidable. However, fewer hospitals and nursing homes make safety adjustments for pregnant workers. Back strain, exposure to radiation, and new drugs often pose hazards to personnel in the health-care professions, most of whom are women.[38]

Byssinosis (brown lung disease) is a chronic respiratory ailment that results from inhaling large amounts of cotton dust in cotton mills. Women constitute the majority of workers in textile industries. Women work on the spinning and weaving machines, and they usually remain on these jobs because they are not promoted to other positions. The exposure of women to cotton dust is greater than that of men, thus increasing the risk of byssinosis among women.[39]

Attempts to legislate labor laws for women over the last 100 years have been protective and well-intentioned. But the laws have consistently reflected social assumptions about women's "natural" function, and in reality have been used to prevent women from getting into better jobs with better pay. Judith Fair points out: "Special labor laws for women have never been a simple issue of owner-employer vs. workers, or government guarantees of good working conditions. They have always been inevitably mixed with basic issues of women's rights and society's general perceptions of the role and limitations of women."[40]

Policymakers in this country first addressed the issue of protective labor laws for women in the last part of the nineteenth century when only the very poorest of immigrant women were forced into the dark, unhealthy, and hazardous factories. These women worked long hours under the most unhealthy conditions, so the first female-specific labor regulations were passed to address this particular population. The protective labor laws for women came about the same time the protective labor laws for children were also being debated and instituted. Women often received protection along with child workers which worked against women's advancement. In addition, women were not part of the organized labor movement that was gaining tremendous strides for its workers, so women did not share this progress. Male labor unions almost at once managed to have the workweek cut from sixty to fifty hours. Most women still worked sixty hours.

Legislators slowly responded, but many of the protective laws which did come into being addressed the nature of women, their roles and physiology, rather than identifying the harmful conditions and health hazards in the workplace. Instead of protecting women from the physical effects of their work, industries used these new regulations to exclude women from employment. The laws restricted women without changing the dangerous conditions.

Obviously, women have the right to be both protected from dangerous working environments and unrestricted in their choice of work. Fortunately, agencies such as OHSA are required to implement policies which enable this. But the conflict between the Occupational Health and Safety Act and the Civil Rights Act must be resolved to ensure maximum protection of women in their work environments. In addition to working toward appropriate action cited above, a coalition with men should be considered in some of the health areas. Men should be informed of potential threats to their fertility so that they too will want to fight for a healthy work environment. The fetus and how it is affected should be the concern of men as well as women. Men do not want their children aborted or born with handicaps.

Institutional Discrimination

Overt sexual discrimination in the workplace is both socially unacceptable and illegal. Yet the practice of subtle discrimination persists in some systems and policies of the federal government. The federal job classification system, veterans' preference legislation, the Internal Revenue Service, and the federal retirement benefits system, all contribute to continuing de facto sex discrimination. Working women should be informed of these discriminatory practices. Private employers often mirror federal practices. So any conclusion about sex discrimination existing in the government may also imply that the same discrimination is being practiced by private businesses and industries.

In 1975, Mary Witt and Patricia Maherny studied the way in which the federal job-classification system affected women working in the Department of Transportation (DOT). (This classification system is used by every federal agency, so this study may be said to constitute a random sample.) Both men and women received a classification by skill. DOT usually classed women into positions which had traditionally been held by women, were people-oriented, and did not require a degree. Men most often received classifications which allowed them to enter apprenticeships and take staff training, and these steps led in turn to promotions. By misapplying the federal job-classification system, DOT was systematically excluding women from career opportunities and economic mobility.[41] Working women should not infer that all federal employers misuse the classification system. But women should be aware that the possibility for misuse exists, and monitoring classification procedures should be encouraged.

Veterans' preference is another federal policy which is not designed to discriminate against women but does. Veterans' preference applies to all veterans who have received an honorable discharge. Any veteran automatically receives a five- to ten-point increase on the score of a civil service exam when he produces a letter from the Veteran's Administration declaring his eligibility for the preference rule. Since civil service exams are ranked and openings are filled with applicants who score highest, this is a definite advantage for men since most veterans are male. Veterans' preference is currently being challenged by women's advocacy groups. The Civil Service Reform Act provided a breakthrough recently. Senior government executives are now excluded from veterans' preference. Agencies are instead obliged to implement affirmative action policies for senior executives; this step will help women. But the majority of the female working population is not affected by this ruling. Women's advocacy groups need further support as they challenge agencies to permit women to compete for government jobs equally with veterans. The state of Massachusetts should be commended for moving ahead and striking out veterans' preference in their state system. Unfortunately this has been challenged by the state attorney general, and the decision is now before the Supreme Court. Veterans' preference needs to be challenged in every state as well as the federal government by women's groups.

The Internal Revenue Service has a reactionary conception of working wives. Wives' salaries are considered supplemental, a bonus or option to the salary of a male head of a household. There is an extra cost in taxes, almost a tax for being married, to any couple earning between $8,000 and $40,000 per year. As noted earlier, women work because of economic need. A woman works for the economic survival of the family and yet if she earns 25 percent of their joint income, the couple pays far more heavily in taxes than they would if they were single and filed separate returns. The White House Conference on Families has this issue on their agenda. Following meetings in 1980, recommendations may be forthcoming from the conference that will press for changes in the law.

As Chestler and Goodman noted in 1976, "Mothers and married women are victims of special economic inequities including tax disincentives which keep them from working outside the home (except at the lowest-paying jobs), overcharge them when they do, and give them no relief or reward for working inside the home."[42]

In addition, Chestler and Goodman also pointed out that helpful deductions, such as cost of doing business, are not possible for many women to take advantage of because so few women own businesses. Even the deductions women can take are severely limited. Working wives may deduct child-care costs only if both parents are working full-time and if the deduction is taken as a personal expense after gross income. The Internal Revenue Service, in other words, does not consider child care a cost of doing business.[43] This policy also reflects the social attitude that women's real function is to care for children and not to become economically capable individuals. Work is treated as if it were optional. Child care at home is regarded as a norm. Chestler and Goodman summarized, "A mother can't get adequate child care, can't get adequate income, can't get tax deductions; if she does a job, she will be paid less, will get no business deductions for the cost of child care."[44] And they also stated that a woman who volunteers her skills and services outside the home "in addition to the free work she does inside the home, is an Internal Revenue Service nonentity."[45] Women cannot pay taxes on or take deductions for work they are not paid to do.

In a survey of social security beneficiaries who retired from private business in 1969 and 1970, only 21 percent of the females as opposed to 46 percent of the males had been covered by any form of pension plan. One of the major issues facing working women is that occupational segregation also contributes to the failure to ensure financial security in the retirement years. Women are still concentrated in occupations that do not have pension or retirement plans and benefits.[46]

Even women who work in companies and industries that have pension and retirement plans receive benefits far below their male counterparts. This is also true of women working in the federal government. Female government employees may retire after the same amount of time as male employees. But they may not expect benefits that are equally high. The median annual pension in this country, according to Chestler and Goodman, is $2,080. The average pension received by women is $970. Part of the problem is that retirement benefits are almost always calculated by earnings, and since women continue to earn substantially less because they hold lower-paying positions in business and industry, this earning discrepancy translates into a drastic reduction in living standards upon retirement.

Many women assume they will receive benefits from their husband's retirement plan. But Congresswoman Pat Schroeder, long an advocate of equal retirement benefits for women, told me that in 1979, 50 percent of married federally employed men elected not to pay the insurance premium which would guarantee their wives 55 percent of their retirement should they die. (This is true not only of men employed in domestic federal agencies but also in the military and the State Department.)

Worse yet, a divorced woman who resides in a noncommunity property state is not entitled to any portion of the federal or military retirement regardless of how long she has been married. It is wise for women to learn the various state laws before filing for divorce. Military wives and State Department wives may have moved frequently enough to be able to establish and claim residencies in several states. Other women should consider moving for the divorce period to establish residency because the financial difference can be great when dealing with retirement. Schroeder has introduced bills in Congress for the past several years trying to get this into law. Unfortunately, an all-male committee will not schedule hearings. She needs the support of women's groups.

Day Care

This is one of working women's greatest needs. When both parents of young children work, they must find child-care services. These services are often difficult to find and expensive. The necessity for providing day care for her children can be even more problematic for a single working mother. A brief study of day care in America describes the status quo and some of the problems faced by working parents.

Theories of early childhood development which became popular in the 1950s and 1960s seemed to imply that a mother who let her young child be partly reared outside her home was harming the child in some way. This implication, which has since been refined into a less negative concept, created much unnecessary guilt among working mothers; the implication also negatively influenced some of the early legislation on child-care issues. For example, in the 1960s the Children's Bureau declared that "day care was not something to be preferred but a service prescribed by a social worker as a remedy for parental failure or inadequacy."[47] Because of these prevailing attitudes and their influence on policies, day care was often associated with poverty and maternal neglect. Several current policies prevent the strong legislative and political activity required to develop adequate, well-run, and greatly needed day-care facilities for children of the ever-increasing numbers of working mothers.

The child and Family Service Act of 1975 states the following: "the family is the primary and most fundamental influence on children; child and family service programs must build on and strengthen the role of the family, must be provided on a voluntary basis to children whose parents or legal guardians request such services with a view toward offering families the options they believe to be the most appropriate for their particular needs."[48]

The act clearly indicates that family service programs should be available on request to those who need them. Yet the gap between the demand for day-care services and the supply is great. There are 4.4 million working mothers with children under the age of 6, and 5.6 million children under 6 with working mothers. There are 905,000 day-care slots in the entire nation.[49] So despite the provisions of the Child and Family Service Act, more than four out of five children who should have day care provided for them do not have it. Rather than being an end, day care is actually a means, a strategy for working people. But day-care programs do not presently operate maximally for the people who need them. The insufficient number of day-care slots is only one aspect of day care which warrants improvement.

About 60 percent of all mothers with children under age 6 are in the labor force; 44 percent of working mothers have children under 6. These children have varying day-care needs depending on their ages. Children who are in school during the day may only require after-school care. Infants and young children require more specialized facilities, and they also need more attention from day-care personnel. Different requirements notwithstanding, day-care facilities in any form are few. Almost all of them as restricted in one way or another, even though the federal government spends $2.2 million in direct and indirect costs of day-care facilities. Use of most government facilities and programs is usually restricted by income level. The following breakdown of current available day-care programs indicates how much the government is presently spending on day care and who may receive it.

Program	Cost in 1000s	Restrictions
Title 20 social security	$ 808,600	Low, moderate income
Head start	477,600	Low income
Title 1, ESEA	136,000	None
Child-care food service	120,000	Low, moderate income
AFDC	84,000	Low income
Work incentive program	57,000	Low income[50]
	$1,683,200	

One of the problems involved in ensuring good day care for working mothers is that the existing programs are essentially limited to the poor, who often lack the political skills to improve a situation. Working middle-class mothers are virtually excluded from obtaining most federally supported day care. They must find costly or inconvenient care for their children. In 1976, only 1.6 percent of the children of working mothers went to day-care centers. Some 26 percent were cared for by relatives or friends, and 50 percent of all day care took place at the child's home.[51] The average annual cost of child care in a day-care center is $1,630, but most working mothers (69 percent) found less formal care was not as expensive, averaging less than $520 per year.[52]

The status quo of day care is marked by the lack of availability of day care, the cost of providing it often by a woman on a single income, and the ineligibility for federal day-care programs of many working parents who need the services. Yet the number of working mothers who need day-care services is increasing among both low- and middle-income mothers. This growing group of women will have to have support from public and private institutions if they are to continue to work full time.

When support has been available, the value of day care has been clear. Women's Bureau statistics show that studies of mothers and children benefiting from industry-based day-care centers reveal higher efficiency, lower costs, greater productivity, lower absenteeism, and easier school adjustment for the child.[53] And the positive impact of child-care programs is not limited to businesses. It clearly has value for women involved in any other important activities. In academic settings that provide child care, more women both entered school and completed their courses than ever before. Grace Hermandez Cargill found in 1977 that 40 percent of all colleges and universities provided some form of child care for their staff, faculty, and students.[54] More assistance of this kind is what is needed in the future.

Day care may be structured in a variety of ways. One popular model involves the use of public-school facilities and resources; this accomplishes three things. First, this model puts to use school facilities that are in financial trouble due to the drop in birthrates and consequent reduction of student registration. Second, using public-school facilities provides jobs for teachers that may have been laid off because of drops in student enrollment. Third, such a model provides the community with high-quality and necessary care by trained personnel. Different models may work effectively too. Each community and each population of women needing day care is different. Day care can be provided by companies, schools, and the state with assistance from the federal government. (The latter may provide grants or stipends to families that desire less formal day care for children.) Much can be learned by studying the more advanced day-care programs which exist in many European countries. For example, in many Mediterranean countries, employers often furnish day-care services as an employee benefit.[55] Social workers in the United States have heard about these day-care services but little has been done about investigating them. In 1968-1969, I studied the day-care nursery system in Italy under the sponsorship of the National Institutes of Mental Health. The following describes some of the forward-looking thinking which existed then in Italy and ten years later is still not evident in the United States:

> The asilos as a national system were started by Mussolini, originally under the Department of Child and Maternal Health. Because of the fascist emphasis on health among the young, they were originally geared toward ensuring that children were at least well-cared for during the day and provided with one good meal. Children were examined and, ideally, any physical problems detected. Up to 1967, many asilos were subsidized by the national government but there was no uniform system. Remembering the special relationship of church and state, it is not surprising that many orders of nuns receive government money to run asilos. This accounted for the low fees charged. In 1967, an Italian government fell on the question of the asilos. The winning group argued that the asilo was also necessary for the education of all children. Nursery school education was seen as a vital part of the educational process. The asilos were then transferred to the Department of Education. This schooling was to be provided at no cost to the children. Serious thought is now going on as to whether it should be mandatory for children to attend asilos.

> To have the government consider this from an educational viewpoint for all children rather than a program for deprived children or a project for working mothers seems to me far ahead of the American approach. I cannot help but wonder why day-care nurseries are provided in our country only for children whose mothers are very poor and who must work. Where is our education system in exploring the value of teaching at this important age of two to five? The following describes a visit to an asilo.

> Asilo, Rome: Large industrial city in southern Italy. Agazzi and Montessori methods used.

> The asilo itself is totally housed in a large palace 100 years old. Again the director, Signorina Silvana, was warm, knowledgeable, and most expressive in her comments and awareness of children. The interview was conducted wholly in Italian, but there was little difficulty in understanding. Signorina Silvana was also most expressive about her feelings about Montessori and Agazzi. This asilo is specifically for children whose mothers work at the AAI (similar to our HHS). There are seventy-five children and they are grouped in sections. Since women are granted eight weeks' maternity leave after the birth of a baby, the youngest there are 2-month-old babies. In the group from 2 months to 1 year old, they had 12 children at that time. A ratio of one staff member to six babies is maintained. For the group from 1 to 2 years old, the staff ratio is one to eight. From 2 to 3 years, the staff ratio is one to 12. Certainly, with the infants this is child care. However, a look at the ratio of adults to children shows their emotional growth is a prime concern. Maternal type love is all important.

The remainder of the children were over 3 years old. The asilo is open year round except on Sundays and Mondays. It is located back of the AAI building. The children arrived at 8 A.M., were fed breakfast at 8:30 A.M., and were then washed or bathed. They were free to play or nap until they had lunch. This asilo was closed at 2 P.M., when the children went home. Government offices frequently close at 2 P.M. in Italy after a six-hour work day. Only senior officials will return for the 4 P.M. to 7:30 P.M. afternoon hours.

The nursery housed the infants. This was an isolated section and the rest of the children and staff were not allowed to enter. The kitchen facilities were separate and there were obvious rigid sanitary restrictions. There was a play room for the babies; of course, each had its own crib. A pediatrician checked all children weekly and was on call if needed. A small, but well stocked, infirmary was maintained.

Another section of the asilo was for the children from 2 to 3 years of age, and this was strictly Montessori. Signorina Silvana brought us into the three rooms and the outdoor section reserved for Montessori learning. Her opinion, which I quote because I'll never forget it, was "for the intelligence Montessori is good, for the emotions and discipline it's a disaster." She explained something I thought very crucial. She said that after her children had been under the Montessori method for a school year they broke all the equipment at the end of the time. She saw it as the children's way of wanting to be free, breaking out of the bounds of the method. She showed me the Montessori equipment that the children had broken.

Only a few children were present but it was obvious from the things around that this was a very creative asilo. There was a puppet theater with puppets made by the children. I saw large life-size playing blocks which were for free play; the children could use them in any way they desired. Again there was the use of the outdoors, and the outdoor Roman theater was used as a swimming pool when the weather permitted. Each child had his own garden. There were numerous paintings, papier-mache items and creative crafts made by the children.[56]

An appropriate strategy is to consider day care on two levels: that for women and that for children. Then it may gain the support it so badly needs and will help both women and children. The working women of America must solve the problem of day care for themselves and their children. To do so, women require cooperation from their employers and from the country-at-large which, after all, should invest in its future population. This is an area where a coalition with a group of men could also be an effective strategy. In this case, working fathers would be a valuable ally. Day-care is a working *parent* issue and the more it is seen this way, the quicker the problem of lack of facilities will be solved.

Women as Owners of Businesses

Women have been severely underrepresented in business ownership. Recently the Small Business Association granted low-interest loans to women going into business. In addition, once the women's business becomes so designated, women may specially qualify under affirmative action policy for government contracts and grants. This development is critical for women to be aware of. American Woman's Economic Development (AWED) Corporation is a federally funded organization to assist businesswomen trying to succeed on their own. Strategically the women must learn to control and have a voice in owning and administering companies.

Legal Issues and Resources

Several laws and executive orders already exist which protect women from discrimination by sex. An understanding of this legislation and these presidential orders is basic to formulating strategy for future action. The following discussion of the Equal Pay Act, the Civil Rights Act of 1964, and affirmative action programs serves to introduce the working woman to her current legal resources.

The Equal Pay Act of 1963 guarantees all workers the same pay for whatever work they do regardless of their race, age, ethnic background, or sex. However, women who have sought to use this act to deter discriminatory practices in their workplaces have encountered difficulty because the act specifically excludes workers in certain positions. These positions—office workers, retail sales workers, workers in the service occupations—are predominantly held by women. In addition, the act permits workers with senior status to earn more than those who do the same work but do not have the same level of seniority. At face value, this practice seems justified. If people work longer, theoretically they do their jobs more efficiently. They therefore can be said to be more valuable to the companies they work for, so they should be paid more. However, women have the least access to seniority because they take time from work to have children or they work in professions which tend not to have seniority systems. So the contingency of the Equal Pay Act permitting higher pay to workers with senior status to exclude women from receiving equal pay.

In addition, the Equal Pay Act does little to affect the occupational segregation problem. As long as women stay in low-status, low-paying occupations, the Equal Pay Act cannot serve them. Individuals must be doing equal work to qualify for the guarantees of this act. Fortunately, documented cases already exist in which women have been hired or promoted into jobs at salary rates substantially less than men in the same jobs. Also documented have been instances of a woman doing the same work as a man under a title matched with a lower-paying job description. In both these situations, the Equal Pay Act is applicable, and women who know that they are getting less money than men doing similar work should realize that this federal law stands behind them.

The legal resources of the future may be involved to a lesser degree in matters of equality and discrimination. New concerns will influence new legislation. For example, as previously discussed, the NSF recently influenced Senator Kennedy to propose legislation advancing the position of women in the scientific professions. Kennedy's legislation includes federal support for programs which recruit women into scientific professions and which recruit women to pursue their education in scientific fields of study.[57] But such legal assistance in all fields will doubtless require time to initiate.

The Civil Rights Act of 1964 prohibits any industry employing fifteen persons or more from discriminating by sex in its hiring. The act requires that entry levels, pay, promotion, training, education, and retirement (virtually all benefits) be distributed equally among the sexes.

National practices of affirmative action began in 1965 when President Johnson signed Executive Order 11246 and followed it in 1967 with Executive Order 11375. Since then, some states have initiated their own affirmative action regulations as well. According to these orders, any company entering into contracts with the federal government in excess of $10,000 must certify that it does not discriminate against certain classes of people; women are included in those classes. In addition, companies must show that they are actively developing policies that will assist these economically underserved populations to attain better positions, pay, and status. Companies fulfill the affirmative action requirements through a number of identifiable programs involving active recruitment of women, access to training, and promotion of women into management positions. Often companies have an affirmative action specialist. This specialist, usually in the personnel department, should be of particular use to women seeking career advancement and higher pay.

An important strategy for female employees is to determine what the company's affirmative action program offers and to examine the plan. This plan lists hiring goals and potential promotional and salary levels, and must be shown on demand as required by federal law.

Women can use the power afforded by affirmative action regulations after employment with a company for various periods of time. To effectively use any of these acts or executive orders, women must take care to document in detail the dates and individuals involved along with complete descriptions of the circumstances surrounding their complaints of discrimination. Women who undertake to prove that they have been discriminated against should consult other women who have successfully done so; they should also seek legal assistance from attornies with experience in discrimination cases. Fighting discrimination is often a lonely, anxiety-producing battle. Support from knowledgeable professionals in this area can lessen the stress and can indicate to the employer that the woman seeking redress should be taken seriously.

Combating Attitudes and Role Expectations of Women

Women have traditionally been taught that they are less valuable than men, that they should gauge their lives to support others' creative goals and efforts, and that competition is unfeminine. Recent challenges to these traditional teachings proved them false notions. And now, women of every race and age have begun to move away from tradition-bound images of women. Urban women, rural women, and blue-, pink-, and white-collar women have begun to struggle for access to the worlds of influence, status, and money.

As already seen, increasing numbers of young women are entering law schools, medical schools, and graduate schools of business. Ten years ago, these women were minorities. Although still in the minority, this expanding group of aspiring women have different goals and different ideas about themselves than previous generations of young women had. Today's women can begin to form core-support groups within institutions. The concept of the support group is an essential strategy for several reasons. Although males have been brought up in this culture to understand and respect competition, they have also been raised to understand the concepts of team play: concepts which lend assistance and support to an otherwise lonely corporate game. More often than not, one of the issues confronting young women seeking career opportunities is that they enter the work force or begin professional education as individuals without support from anywhere and subject to challenges and criticism aimed exclusively at their gender. Team play provides a natural peer setting with the accompanying empathy from those who have experienced similar situations and challenges. Wisdom and experience pooled by peers can lead to collective action and united, creative strategies. A woman who operates with the support of a group need not fight a battle alone. The power and effectiveness of a group are far greater than the power and effectiveness of a single individual no matter how much law is on the books in her support, no matter how right she is in her fight.

Academic settings are not the only places where support groups can be effective. Friendships form on assembly lines and in employee lounges as well as in schools, libraries, and classrooms. Studies indicate that working women have an average of four close friendships through their jobs and that these friendships are important sources of emotional and social support. Women should use these friendships to form strategy groups to combat discrimination on the job. Professional males have been doing just this for years. Rotary clubs and monthly business luncheons provide inside information, contacts, and professional support for men. Many of these organizations refuse to admit women professionals to their tables. The careers and professions of working women have been subtly damaged by such exclusion both in the long and in the short terms. Women must develop their own networks around the concepts of career advancement.

Such groups can provide women with inside information about resources, job openings, training, and financial opportunity. Along with emotional and social support, groups of working women, creating their own inside track, can do a lot to ensure that their members are privy to information necessary for financial and professional growth. In addition, women's groups can work toward common goals and toward solving common problems. Groups can organize to ensure pregnancy benefits, to restructure workdays to accommodate demanding roles of work and family, to ensure promotion of women into management and better-paying jobs, and to equalize pay discrepancies within a profession. Support groups can work to change company policy that affects and harms group members individually and collectively; and groups can provide the necessary support for members who are waging individual wars on sexual harassment or on alienation by gender within their work roles.

Women Organized for Women

All around the country, women are organizing to combat specific types of discrimination. Women are beginning to take their work lives into their own hands, and they are organizing to help not only themselves but others in similar plight.

In growing numbers, women are establishing and running employment agencies which place women in better entry-level positions. These agencies are designed to assist the young woman college graduate who discovers that she must enter a business as a receptionist while her male counterpart can enter a management trainee program. Women's agencies assist the older woman with years of experience in organizing volunteer groups and activities who now learns that she does not have any experience when applying for a salaried job.

Organizations such as the Denver-based Better Jobs for Women and Washington, D.C.'s Wider Opportunities for Women are forming throughout the country to help women in every life situation find jobs that pay them what they are worth and give them the respect they deserve. One such organization has placed more than 400 women into more than sixty skilled trades in only six years. Women need to seek out the resources that are already available to them.

In addition, newly formed agencies tend not only to help women find better-paying jobs but also jobs which permit women to combine the need to work with the demands of family care. These agencies seek positions for women in companies which offer flexible time scheduling. (Such scheduling is becoming more available.) Or the agencies locate part-time positions for women which are both well paying and professionally challenging. Eleanor Hoskins established a nonprofit agency in Los Angeles. In addition to providing counseling in career planning, her agency actively contradicts the policies of conventional employment agencies which regularly send women only to interviews for pink-collar positions. Her agency and others like it have already had considerable success in placing women into upwardly mobile positions with higher pay, greater challenges, and room for growth.

Many women's centers throughout the United States have career-counseling and job-placement services. A large number of these centers are also running training programs in assertiveness and consciousness-raising regarding issues women face in employment. Hardly a major American city does not have a women's center. If the women's centers are not currently dealing with the issues of working women, they need to be assisted to do so. The Women's Bureau of the Department of Labor has a wealth of free information available on techniques and tactics which have been successfully used in various women's centers. Other valuable resources are the national or local chapter of the National Organization of Women, the American Association of University Women, all organizations of professional women, and the adult education departments of local-school systems.

Organizing Politically

There are many groups of women interested in common goals, activities, and issues. A small but well-organized female task force with expertise on the subject of women and work can inform these various groups. A task force should first identify all groups and organizations in the community which might be receptive to hearing messages and issues of working women. Then it should systematically convey its messages through every available means.

One means of obtaining free or inexpensive publicity is via the public media. Strategies a task force can employ are writing editorials for local newspapers, getting an apprentice reporter from the local television to do a story on working women, calling the producer of the local morning women's program and offering an interview. Such strategies are important tools for placing the issues before the public. Of course, many of the media donate space or time as a public service, but these donations are heavily sought after and difficult to acquire.

A task force on working women can try to initiate an article or a series of articles in trade or popular publications. Many periodicals run short of copy and require a backlog of material to fill space that suddenly becomes available. A well-written article on the subject of women and work may be picked up in this manner in a variety of journals and magazines with large readerships.

Forming a speaker's bureau is an effective method of reaching target groups. A task force which concentrated on addressing women's groups concerning the subject of women and work could build a constituency for women's issues. Also regular speaking engagements to groups with other interests not only informs about women but may stimulate the growth of membership in women's groups.

It is important to work for legislation at all levels of government. Small, special-interest groups often have enormous impact on legislation. In reality, the stronger the constituency, the more likely the change. Thus use of media, speakers' bureaus, and other means of public communication can be influential in gaining political changes in the legislatures. Women need to testify in public forums, to provide proposals for legislative consideration, and to actively court their congressional representatives to initiate or support positive legislation on behalf of working women. Existing laws need to be strengthened or challenged (the Equal Pay Act and the Social Security Act, respectively); new laws need to be drafted and passed (laws regarding flexible time workdays or occupational health).

Education and Training

Approximately 80 percent of American women who work outside the home hold low-paying, low-status jobs in service industries, clerical occupations, retail sales plants, and factories. Opportunities for advancement are few. Education, training, and counseling often can improve a woman's chances for advancement. The National Commission on Working Women sponsored regional dialogs with working women and developed the following recommendations as education and training strategies.

Recommendations of the Council

I. The Council recommends to the President and the Congress that:
    1. Federal antidiscrimination laws (including age discrimination laws) and regulations be enforced more thoroughly by all appropriate agencies to assure that women and girls are afforded educational as well as job equity. Such enforcement should cover career counseling, curriculum selection, classroom training, and postsecondary preparation so that in the future women can be better equipped to avoid the problems of today's working women.

    2. Effective programs of public information concerning citizens' rights and responsibilities under antidiscrimination laws be undertaken.

    3. The Departments of Labor and Health and Human Services undertake a demonstration program to establish the costs and benefits of stimulating, by tax and other incentives, employer subsidies for employees' education and training. Such a program should cover both job-related and other education, should be designed to facilitate usage by lower level workers, and should analyze the results in terms of productivity and upward mobility.

    4. The Departments of Labor and Health and Human Services undertake a joint effort to provide funds and technical assistance, under existing legislation, to augment local counseling services for women, within both educational and community

settings. Such programs must offer information and assistance concerning the job market, nontraditional occupations, education and training opportunities, financial aid possibilities, child-care and other supportive resources, and individual goal-setting and career planning. They should seek out both employed women and homemakers needing their services.

5. The federal government support with funds, tax incentives and consultation the establishment of locally controlled child-care centers for all children, including night and summer services.

6. The federal government extend and publicize its programs for flexible working hours and part-time employment, which could permit women to train for new fields of work.

7. The federal government establish a policy of hiring paraprofessionals whenever appropriate.

8. The Department of Labor encourage all employers to formulate and distribute career path manuals for all employees.

II. The Council recommends to the Secretary of Health and Human Services:

1. Legislative definitions be sought which would make less-than half-time students eligible for federal student assistance programs.

2. State education agencies and institutions be encouraged to publicize the possibilities for adult students to receive academic credit for lifelong learning experiences, including academic credit based on demonstrated abilities acquired at work.

3. Educational institutions be encouraged to make it possible for all degrees to be earned in classes with flexible hours such as evenings and weekends.

4. Funds be provided under discretionary programs to support additional efforts, such as the NCWW Regional Dialogues, intended to foster self-confidence and networking and career-planning skills among working women.

III. Finally, because the needs and problems disclosed by this limited number of working women present major implications for society, the Council urges that the Departments of Health and Human Services and Labor allocate funds for more comprehensive research on the "80 percent."[58]

Conclusion

In addition to addressing the issues and strategies previously described, women individually and collectively must develop strategies to change the present system of employment inequality.

Economic independence is essential to the emotional and social well-being of women. To lack economic strength in a monied economy is to be almost powerless over one's own life and the lives of those one is responsible for. Women must begin to look at their problems in economic terms and must start to plan for change around economic issues. Our culture understands the language of economics; it does not understand the language of social equality. Women need to begin to fight for economic recognition both inside and outside the home. The labor that women put into the care of home and family is worth thousands of dollars per year. Yet this worth is seldom viewed as work which warrants compensation. The injustice of this fact and the lack of economic independence which women face make social equality and social viability often seem too-distant goals. Men too need to understand the critical role they have in their daughters' development. In *The Managerial Women*, Hennig and Jardin point out that the single most important variable in the development of the girl toward success as a top manager was the role of the father. If he encouraged and expected her to have a career, and shared his work experience with his daughter, her chances of succeeding were greatly increased.

An overview of the problems working women face points out strategies women can use to deal with these issues and problems that are common to them. Using fundamental principles of CO to develop plans and goals for changing the policies and practices which hinder their progress, women can begin to systematically make changes in their future lives as workers. Table 3-1 shows examples of strategies developed by Kathleen Fink for women to penetrate the scientific and engineering fields. Such strategy breakdowns as education, reeducation, political, legal, institutional, accommodating, and support group are excellent models for other occupational categories.[59]

Novelist-essayist Tillie Olson wrote, "The oppression of women is like no other form of oppression. . . . It is an oppression entangled through with human love, human need, genuine (core) human satisfactions, identifications, fulfillments."[60] Women often experience this oppression where they work, because they work. This chapter described some of the details of women and their work. To understand these details is to begin to organize for social change.

Table 3-1
Examples of Programs to Increase the Participation of Women in Scientific
and Engineering Careers

Strategy	Target Group	Possible Sponsor
Education and reeducation		
Nonsexist career guidance materials	High school, college	American Personnel and Guidance Association
Publicity in mass media	Public	Recent articles in *Harper's, Scientific American*
Workshops on women in science careers[a]	High school up	National Science Foundation
Programs to combat math avoidance	Math avoiders	Rutgers, Wellesley, Mills College, Math Center, D.C., Educational Development Center, Mass.
Studies of labor market projections for women in various careers	Those interested in careers	Department of Labor
Programs to relate courses to career requirements	Teachers and school Administrators	Mills College, Calif.
Reentry programs for unemployed women with training in fields	Unemployed women	Wellesley
Political		
Women involved in powerful establishment groups	Professionals, students, lobbyists	Deborah Shapley (editor, *Science Magazine*)
Influencing legislation	Professionals, students, lobbyists	Senator Kennedy's proposals
Influencing federal agencies	Professionals, students, lobbyists	HHS' Women's Action Program influenced policy in employment in agency. HHS task leadership in eliminating sex discrimination
Legal		
Laws to enforce equality in employment, promotion, education, salaries	Schools, government, employers	Those organizing around ERA, and so on
Influencing policies within institutions	Schools, employers, government	HHS
Institutional change		
Voluntary affirmative action and recruitment of women	Employers	General Electric
Cooperation: schools and employers to inform, train, and recruit women	Schools, employers	National Science Foundation's Visiting Scientist Program

Table 3-1 – *(Continued)*

Strategy	Target Group	Possible Sponsor
Accommodating work/family		
Day-care centers at workplace	Working mothers	ABT. Associates, Cambridge, Mass.
Housework service teams	Working women and men	Various local agencies
Support groups	Students, professionals	Boston YWCA plan for club; Association for Women in Science, Society of Women Engineers, Purdue; geographic support network in the Bay Area, Calif.

Source: Kathleen Fink, Examples of Programs to Increase the Participation of Women in Scientific and Engineering Careers, Unpublished paper for Women's Course, Boston College, Massachusetts, April 1978.

[a]Funding for such workshops has been provided by Carnegie Corporation, General Electric, and the Alfred Sloan Foundation.

4 Woman as Eve

Introduction

Since the time of Adam and Eve, women have been penalized because of their sexual nature. They have been forced to take a secondary position relative to men. Because of Eve's historical position, she and women in general have been cast in the role of the seductress. And it is as wanton seductress that society tends to view and thus justify punishment of women. This chapter discusses the various forms this societal posture has taken. It presents the traditional view that female sexual pleasure consists of the vaginal orgasm through the penetration of the penis and the denial of the clitoris as the sexual female organ. It also discusses some societies that advocate female circumcision. The importance of this sexual issue as a power conflict between men and women needs to be appreciated. The struggle of women is thus limned not only as political and economic but also sexual.

The divorced woman and the displaced homemaker become victims of the traditional female sexual role which did not succeed. Birth control, sterilization, and abortion are further extensions of this subject. The tradition of blaming woman for her original sexual nature has resulted in the tragic role of the divorced or displaced homemaker as well as the mother who bears children not out of her choice but that of a man's or society's.

Strategies for working with divorced women and displaced homemakers and for advocating the birth control-abortion issues are presented. The basic issue here is woman as Eve in a power struggle for sexual equality. When woman attacks the power of the penis she takes on a formidable foe. No wonder women have been passive, submissive, and receptive to the traditional role of housewife and mother of many children. As women break free of these restraints because of their own desire or circumstances, many support groups as well as services will be needed.

Historical Perspective of Eve

The Book of Genesis describes the creation of man and woman, the garden of Eden, the forbidden fruit, Eve's successful temptation of Adam, and the dire punishments visited upon them and their progeny for time eternal. But it is the nurturing female who must suffer both childbearing and submissiveness.

"In sorrow shalt thou bring forth children, and thou shalt be under thy husband's power, and he shall have dominion over thee."[1]

Eve has been presented again and again as the source of evil, original sin, the sinning creature who brought sorrow to the world. Adam is consistently presented as having been seduced by Eve, as if he had no responsibility for his own behavior.

Aristotle on his philosophy of woman said: "the woman is as it were an impotent male."[2] Thomas Aquinas contends that: "Women should have been created at the beginning of creation as a helper to man for the sake of pro-creation, not for any other work, because, for any other work, man could be better helped by another man."[3]

In spite of the negative picture of Eve, "we see in Eve the woman who is superior to the man. She takes the initiative and does not consult Adam,"[4] moreover, she nobly takes all the blame for her husband's weakness and comes through as being the stronger of the pair. This is in contradiction to the purpose of the myth which is to degrade the woman and to paint her as a troublemaker. It is interesting to note that in the *Legends of the Jews*, Eve is said to have remarked late in her life: "I promised him that I would protect him from God. And so he blamed me when we were ejected from the garden."[5] This implies that the woman was expected to be the protector, the stronger of the two, the communicator with God.

Traditionally, Eve was blamed for the expulsion from the garden. Their (Adam and Eve) loss of the Garden of Paradise was her fault. Sin, sickness, and death were supposedly the results of one woman's action with one man. The history of manhood and womanhood has accepted this translation: the apparent contradiction in the Biblical version is that on the one hand woman is only a rib of man created to be his companion and on the other hand she had such persuasive power over him as to cause him to break his word. This is not faced or even addressed by Western religions. This initial presentation of woman as seductress meriting punishment has been an historical staple. To gain an appropriate perspective of women in society in relation to their sexual role and the responsibility they have had to bear, we must see it in relation to the Garden of Eden.

Sexual Roles of Man and Woman

Men for the most part have historically and traditionally believed that inter-course is required for a woman to achieve an orgasm. Although the clitoris is known to produce pleasure for the woman, it is not seen as the primary organ or as being able to produce an orgasm to match that which was commonly believed a result of vaginal stimulation by the penis. In some cultures the clitoris was seen as providing pleasure for the woman and serving no other useful purpose. It did appear that women were able to receive stimulation and pleasure without men, and it was not necessary to have a man participate for the woman to achieve an orgasm. Apparently this was threatening to men: the fact that the penis was not as valued as they thought or believed it to be.

The patriarchal theorists were Mill, Engles, and Veblen. The theory bases society on the biological physical strength of the male and the debilitating effects of pregnancy on the female. The theory became the major force for the organization of the monogamous family away from theorists who advocated group marriage or polygamy. It was during the patriarchal takeover that some extreme patriarchs devised a method of reducing women's pleasure in sex without affecting man's. If the clitoris afforded pleasure to women without male participation, man must not only obviate this pleasure organ but must ensure woman's reliance on man for sexual gratification. The result was the clitorectomy or female circumcision. Another result was a more perverse form of control of men over women. Engels contended that women constituted the first property.

The anthropologist Montegazza in 1885 said that female circumcision was practiced in Egypt because "Egyptian men do not care for any sensual participation on the part of the women in the act of coitus. The circumcised women are therefore left with the desire for pleasure that must go forever unsatisfied. . . . It would be hard to imagine a more selfish form of perversion."[6] Other societies offer different reasons for circumcising their women, such as concern for female chastity and unfaithfulness to the husband. Although female circumcision is not a worldwide practice, some societies still engage in this practice. As evidence of current practice of female circumcision, the World Health Organization conference held in Khartoum, Sudan, in March 1980, included it on its agenda.

The clitoris is often equated with the penis; it is a mysterious appendage seemingly designed for women's pleasure. Unlike the penis, it is structured for neither urination nor seed deposition. It is a purely gratuitous sexual adjunct which causes no discomfort or humiliation, but is capable of producing a great deal of pleasure for women.

Sigmund Freud's philosophy on women has played a significant part in effectively slowing women's efforts to separate themselves from their male-defined identity. Freud's *Three Essays on the Theory of Sexuality* formulated his basic ideas concerning female sexuality: for little girls the major erogenous zone is the clitoris; in order for the transition to womanhood to be complete the clitoris must abandon its sexual primacy to the vagina. Women in whom this transition has not been complete remain clitorally oriented. Freud contends that women are not whole human beings but mutilated males who reconcile themselves to live without a penis.[7]

The idea of the superiority of the vaginal orgasm over the clitoral orgasm was useful for categorizing women. Clitoral women were labeled as neurotic and masculine. Women who had vaginal orgasms were feminine, mature, and normal. The clitoral versus vaginal orgasm dispute continued until 1966 when Masters and Johnson published *Human Sexual Response*. After interviewing 487 women they arrived at the following conclusions:

1. The dichotomy of vaginal and clitoral orgasms is entirely false. Anatomically all orgasms are centered in the clitoris, whether they result from direct manual pressure, indirect pressure (during intercourse), or stimulation of other erogeous zones such as breasts.

2. Women are multiorgasmic.

3. Women's orgasms vary in intensity.[8]

The Masters and Johnson findings were revolutionary and liberating in terms of expelling certain myths. Prior to Masters and Johnson, female sexuality was defined in a male-oriented manner. If pleasure for a woman was achieved through the vagina, she was dependent on male participation to experience an orgasm. If pleasure for a woman was achieved through the clitoris, woman's self-derived sexual pleasure was a threat to the male, his masculinity, and his ego.

The Hite report published in 1976 reconfirms what was proved in 1966. Interviews with 3,000 women aged 14 to 78 confirmed clitoral orgasm was the orgasm and vaginal orgasms were for the most part faked for the benefit of men.[9]

Women's sexual response is culturally conditioned. This conditioning has helped shape the vaginal orgasm as a symbol of the male system of values. In many cases no regular orgasm occurs. At other times there may be an orgasm but the sensations can be dulled by the presence of a penis. Some women who think they are having an orgasm during intercourse are probably not. In any case an orgasm with or without intercourse, thought it may be perceived differently, is the same basic orgasm. Orgasm is always due to clitoral stimulation in some form and always follows the same physiological pattern. Therefore the term *orgasm* always refers to clitoral.[10] With orgasmic physiology established the human female now has the undeniable opportunity to develop realistically her own sexual response levels.[11] The sexual problems of our society will never be solved until there is a real equality between men and women. If society allows the Masters and Johnson and the Hite material to filter into the public consciousness, hopefully to replace the Freudian myths, the woman will be able to enjoy, define, and express the forms of her sexuality.

Women: Married, Divorced, Displaced

Traditional American societal norms allude to the belief that marriage is usually a culmination of events that has brought two persons together as a result of mutual attraction for each other and a desire to bind the relationship for a more permanent or long-term period of time. Ideally people marry for love and see the "happily ever after" as the way it will be. This is rarely the case. Fewer and fewer marriages last for a lifetime, and seldom are these marriages trouble-free.

Women under the most desirable circumstances should marry for love. They also marry due to an expectation that is placed on them by society, and they marry for emotional and financial security. Men marry for emotional and sometimes financial security. Women who marry but do not or are unable to educate or prepare themselves to be self-sufficient become dependent on their husbands for support in order to live and to survive. In many instances, marriage can be seen as the most available if not the only survival option in a world which has narrowly defined a woman's position in society. Women are conditioned to accept fewer options than men and commonly choose marriage as the path to what is hoped will be a comfortable life and decent existence.

Men have established and maintained an economic imbalance which has kept women financially dependent. The independent husband who disclaims any liability for the problem is still part of the ruling sex. He is the same person who says, "no wife of mine is going to work, or I won't have my children raised by a stranger, or our clients won't accept women handling their accounts."[12]

Until the nineteenth century women had very few legal or property rights. The female identity no longer existed once the marriage took place. If the marriage dissolved, the woman commonly was left with nothing. The laws for divorce and support in this country have improved but continue to be less than desirable. If a woman thinks that she is entitled to something from the husband (such as retirement benefits), she usually has to fight for them in court.

Divorce laws differ from state to state. However, an overwhelming majority of legislators and judges are men. They write, interpret, and enforce the laws at all levels of government, and as a result the laws tend to be male-oriented. Women are provided compensation, but in most cases not adequate enough for the time and effort they have put into running a household and raising children.

Divorce is a common occurrence in our society today and is much easier to get than it was in the past. The most common type of divorce today is the no-fault divorce. This term refers to a broad class of legislation including irreconcilable differences, irretrievable breakdown, incompatability, and so on, as grounds for marital dissolution or divorce. Relatively few states allow divorce only on the grounds of the fault of one party.[13] Though many other terms define the reason for divorce, the result is always the same.

Economic fault exists within a no-fault system of divorce with regard to the awarding of alimony, maintenance, and support payments. Although it is now easier to get a divorce, it can be difficult to get support from the husband after the marriage has been dissolved. Even if a woman is awarded a monthly allotment to be paid by the husband, seldom is it enough for the woman to live on especially if there are children involved. A divorced woman lacking both the ability to adequately support herself and alimony, soon realizes that she has devoted her life to satisfying the needs of others and paid little attention to ensuring the satisfaction of her own needs.[14]

A woman who has devoted her life and made a career of being a home-maker and a housewife, though it is an honorable career, will be prepared for little else if divorce occurs and in many cases if the spouse dies. Few women who have been homemakers for many years have the skills necessary to compete in today's marketplace. An earned but unused college degree offers little assurance for employment to the job-seeking former homemaker; the value of the degree is measured against its utilization in the business com-munity.

Legislation and bills have been introduced into Congress to hopefully protect and compensate a homemaker or housewife if divorce occurs. The basic idea behind the legislation is to make amendments in the Social Security Act that will give the same benefits to women who maintain households as everyone else is entitled to who is gainfully employed. Being a homemaker will be considered as being employed and earning a wage (even if not actually received). The amount of earnings for services rendered will be equal to the national average monthly wage for a person who is employed in another occu-pation.[15] If a woman gets divorced, at the present time she is not automatically entitled to any of the benefits that the husband has earned over the years. Although she has kept the household and at times entertained her husband's clients enabling him to make the big sale or land the large contract, the woman comes out empty-handed. This is usually the case unless she takes the spouse to court in hope of being awarded a percentage of his retirement benefits. An important set of bills introduced by Congresswoman Patricia Schroeder from Colorado calls for a portion of the military retiree's pension, the Foreign Service retiree's pension, and the federal civil servant retiree's pension to be awarded to a divorced wife based on the number of years of the marriage. These bills need the support of women's groups because millions of women would be helped and the legislation could be the lead for other state and private industry pension plans. The inequity of the system is seen in that community property states 50 percent of the pension is awarded because it is seen as prop-erty not income. For women contemplating divorce it is important they under-stand this issue before filing in a certain state. A community property state would be to the advantage of many women filing for divorce.

Other legislation has also been introduced that will provide for direct old age, survivors and disability insurance, and medicare benefits for homemakers.[16] Some states have also introduced or enacted legislation designed to benefit the divorced homemaker. One such law states that "deductions of alimony and child support shall be made directly from the husband's paycheck, similar to union dues, checkoff or tax withholding."[17] Although this type of legislation is significant, it only covers one state and therefore only reaches a limited number of women. Introduction of legislation is a start, but the process is not complete until it is enacted and becomes law. These laws must also apply nationwide and should cover all women who have made careers as homemakers and housewives.

The term *displaced homemaker* refers to that group of women who due to divorce or widowhood are thrust out of their role of running a household. They become displaced through dissolution of the household following divorce or loss of the husband's income to maintain their status. The displaced homemaker has made a career of her homemaking abilities and as a result has developed no other technical skills that qualify her for a decent position in a competitive work-oriented society.

Following divorce or widowhood, a woman suddenly finds herself alone and must fend for herself. Some women have two careers: one as a homemaker and the other in a paid profession. In this case, adjustment may not be as difficult because they will continue to generate an income. Women who have no professional education and a minimal amount of formal education are finding it increasingly difficult to blend themselves into the mainstream of the work world and soon learn that the positions they would like or the ones they need to earn a decent salary or continue the standard of living to which they are accustomed are out of reach because they do not possess the necessary skills or schooling that the position requires. Displaced homemakers of middle years have difficulty finding a job because of their age. Although they may have many productive years left, the younger employee is usually picked over the older candidate for the jobs.

A partial solution to the predicament of the displaced homemaker has been the formation of the Displaced Homemakers Network, Inc. The program is designed for middle-aged women whom divorce or widowhood has left in economic straits.[18] Displaced homemakers themselves are banding together to make the program a reality. The Displaced Homemakers Network will work closely with the U.S. Department of Labor in seeing that pertinent issues are aired. The network will offer advice, support, and materials both to present members and to new centers that will be set up across the country under legislation passed by Congress. Another purpose of the network is to have a voice in the way legislation is carried out. The new legislation gave the Department of Labor $5 million for fiscal year 1979 to set up multipurpose programs. This would include job training and placement, peer counseling, and creation of new jobs for displaced homemakers within the programs.[19] The network will also concentrate on other issues that affect the displaced homemaker. Among them are health insurance, revision of social security legislation discriminatory to women, and nursing homes: 80 percent of whose inhabitants are women.[20] There are also other organizations that share a concern in preparing and moving women into a work environment and looking out for the rights of displaced and middle-aged women. The Alliance for Displaced Homemakers, a predecessor to Displaced Homemakers Network, and the Older Women's League Educational Fund are a few. The Business and Professional Women's Club also offers support to these groups.[21]

The need for these types of efforts on behalf of displaced homemakers is evident. They need the opportunity to acquire new skills, polish old ones, and receive training that will adequately and appropriately prepare them to enter a competitive work environment. Displaced homemakers also need the support, both moral and emotional, that will enable them to cope with the anxieties and pressures that may arise with a transition of this nature. These organizations can also help instill a sense of confidence and self-worth that what these women have to offer both inside and outside a home is still a valued part of our society.

Birth Control and Abortion

Birth control and abortion as an alternative choice are major moral and social issues in our society today. Opinions on what is right or wrong and who should have the power to choose is argued and debated worldwide. Is it a legal issue, a religious issue, or a woman's issue; should it be an issue at all? One of the most fundamental rights of women is the right to choose whether and when to have children. Only when women control that choice will they be free to be themselves, for their children and their spouses. Birth control is the single best method for implementing this choice. Although birth control may allow the woman to choose when she wants a child, it is not effective enough to prevent an unwanted pregnancy.

Society's attitudes toward sex education, sexuality, and health care make it hard for many women (especially the very young and the poor) to choose, obtain, and use methods of birth control that will work for them. At present, a second indispensable tool to control fertility is abortion, the termination of pregnancy by medical means.[22]

The antiabortionists sometimes argue that abortion violates an age-old natural law. But for centuries abortion in the early stages of pregnancy was widely tolerated. In many societies in Europe and later in America it was used as one of the only dependable methods of fertility control. Even the Catholic Church took the conveniently loose view that the fetus became animated by the rational soul, and abortion therefore became a serious crime at forty days after conception for a boy and eighty days for a girl. (Methods of sex determination were not specified.) Apparently, it was condoned if done within this time frame. English and American common law dating back to the thirteenth century, shows a fairly tolerant acceptance of abortion, up until the quickening, the moment sometime in the fifth month when the woman first feels the fetus move.[23]

Most laws making abortion a crime were not passed until the nineteenth century. In 1869, Pope Pius IX declared that all abortions were murders. By the 1860s in this country, new legislation outlawed all abortions except those necessary to save the life of the woman. Abortion is now legal in the United States, though there has been legislation introduced in an attempt to make it illegal again. The Hyde amendment strictly limits funding of Medicaid abortions.[24] Hyde is taking his antiabortion crusade even further in hopes of having abortions outlawed. In 1973, after several years of research and pressure at all levels by women's groups, family planning organizations, and civil liberties groups, the U.S. Supreme Court legalized abortion performed by doctors up through twenty-four weeks of pregnancy. Today any woman who chooses should be able to end an unwanted pregnancy with a safe and relatively inexpensive abortion in a clinic, hospital, or doctor's office. Unfortunately, this is not always the case. In many parts of the country abortion is still less available, more expensive, and more negative than it should be. The Supreme Court decision is also under attack by a small but powerful antiabortion movement.[25] Hyde is a part of this movement to get the Supreme Court to reverse its decision.

Although there are alternate methods of birth control available, some successful and others not so successful, abortion is the world's most common birth-control method, chiefly because billions of people still have little access to other methods.[26]

Most people seem to think that there are no laws against contraception in this country, but that is not the case: only 40 percent of the states have no laws limiting the distribution or display of contraceptives.[27] The rest forbid young people or unmarried people access to contraception, or say that distribution to anyone must be through doctors or licensed pharmacists. Massachusetts at one time turned down approximately $30 million in federal aid because it would have had to comply with federal stipulations that age and marital conditions be no barrier to the receipt of birth-control service.[28] Numerous cases have gone through the courts that disputed the legality of a single person's access to birth-control products; some ruled in favor, others against. The overall outcome is that the rights of single people were deemed of no legal consequence, and young women go on lying about their age and their marital status in order to get what they need providing they know where to go in the first place or what to ask for.

Some people believe devoutly that the the pill is 100-percent effective, for women who can use it safely. Because it is easy to accuse a woman of not taking it when she should, failures are explained away as the patient's fault. Even the drug companies admit that there is a failure rate of anywhere from 0.1 percent to 1 percent.[29] With approximately 6 million women taking the pill in the United States, they have at least 6,000 surprises every day and probably more. What is of more concern today is the possible harm to women's bodies that may result from taking the pill. Recent research indicates possible blood clotting, severe skin eruptions, and heart problems; women over 35 are warned against taking it. Women have en masse accepted a modality for birth control only to find their bodies may be affected for life because of it.

Although the pill appears to be the most effective method of birth control, it does have failures and reported side effects and many women do not trust it. For this reason, many have gone back to using the diaphragm with cream or jelly. They know it does nothing odd to their body chemistry, it lasts quite a while, and there is a curious psychological advantage (usually considered a drawback) to the fact that they can exercise choice each time they use it. Women who do not have access to these methods fall back on withdrawal, some form of rhythm, or pure luck.[30] It is a surprising fact how few women know what contraceptive foam, another method of birth control, is and that it can be bought over the counter. Condoms are also available and if used correctly are quite effective; in fact, a condom and foam used together are very safe and are a quite readily available combination.[31]

The intrauterine devices (IUDs or loops) are another method of birth control. Although quite effective, they fail 1.5 to 3 percent of the time.[32]

Another significant mode of birth control that is worthy of discussion is sterilization. It is interesting to note that most people do not seem to know that only a few states have even the mildest laws restricting access to sterilization, and that in thirty or more states Blue Cross-Blue Shield and Medicaid programs will even cover some of the costs.[33] To sterilize a man is a simple office procedure, called a vasectomy; to sterilize a woman can sometimes be a major abdominal operation, but increasingly is becoming a simpler procedure. Because of the automatic identification of reproductive matters with the woman—an identification reinforced by the woman today usually being the one responsible for contraception—and because a majority of men confuse fertility with potency, somehow an operation on the woman is thought of first when a couple is considering sterilization and knows little about it.[34]

Women in America and in other countries should have freely available to them some form of birth control. As noted earlier, abortion is the most commonly used method worldwide because women do not have access to or have not been informed of other methods of birth control, some of which have been discussed here. Abortion should not be a regular method of birth control. Other methods are quite effective and to a certain degree quite safe. Although there are safe methods of birth control available, statistics indicate that none is 100 percent immune to failure. Therefore some women who practive a proven method of birth control will become pregnant. Some women may choose to complete the pregnancy. Others may choose to terminate it. Still others may not have any choice at all and are forced to bear a child they did not plan for, may not want, and in numerous cases cannot afford.

Having access to abortion as an alternative, if conventional birth-control methods fail, allows women freedom to choose and freedom to limit their own reproduction. It also gives women power over their own bodies. Access to birth control and the freedom to choose abortion if necessary will put the controls in the hands of women where they rightfully belong.

Conclusion

As women develop organizing strategies to solve the sexual dilemmas posed in this chapter, it may help to realize that the value system to be changed started in the Garden of Eden. As of late 1980, the Republican Party has disclaimed the woman's right to choose abortion. It is only when the historical impact of the sexual struggle can be seen in the context described here as a power issue does it make sense that abortion becomes one of the major political issues for the presidential election in the United States. It also shows how well planned and organized the strategy to accomplish the goals of sexual issues needs to be. Abortion is not the issue alone, nor is birth control, nor is the vaginal orgasm. Central to all these issues, is woman's right to her own body for pleasure and for or not for reproduction. This is Eve's issue.

5 Woman as Victim

A victim is one who is destroyed, injured, or sacrificed. Woman as victim is seen clearly when studying such subjects as rape, battering, alcoholism, and drugs. In the first two she is a victim of men, in the second two of society.

This chapter discusses each subject from both a descriptive and historical approach and pictures the myths that have grown around each. The extent of the problem as well as the resources available are explained. Most relevant is the attempt to show how strategies need to be designed. The organizational systems dealing with these problems are analyzed.

Even though there are strategies for each of these areas, it is critical to remember that women as victims need an overall strategy. Women need to organize against this helpless picture of themselves. They need to develop strength and confidence so as a group they are not victimized by men or society. The way to this end is by only one means: gaining power. Even though this sounds simplistic, the consistent aiming at access of power as the target can be the first critical step for women to take. David did it with a slingshot. Women must first learn to realize the necessity for gaining power, as a group. Then they must be constantly alert to the opportunity to use the slingshot and, lastly, have the courage to do so.

Rape

Definition

> By anatomical fiat—the inescapable construction of their genital organs—the human male was a natural predator and the human female served as his natural prey. Not only might the female be subjected at will to a thoroughly detestable physical conquest . . . but the consequences of such a brutal struggle might be death or injury, not to mention impregnation and the birth of a dependent child.[1]

The crime of rape in this country is steadily growing until today it constitutes one of our major criminal-justice issues. An estimated 250,000 women will be raped next year.[2] According to the Federal Bureau of Investigation, one rape occurs every ten minutes.[3]

The legal definition of rape is that it is "an act of sexual intercourse . . . with a female . . . where she resists but her resistance is overcome by force or violence . . . or where she is prevented from resisting by threats of great or immediate physical harm, accompanied by apparent power of execution (such as a weapon of some sort)."

Increasingly, the act of rape is being defined as any unwanted sexual activity. Martin Symonds, director of the Victimology program at the Karen Horney Clinic, states that "it is crucial that we consider rape as a crime of violence and not a sexual act. Most women, particularly victims or rape, have accepted the violent nature of the crime of rape, but many men still perceive rape as a sexual act and consequently have difficulty in properly assessing victims' reactions."[4]

The following facts destroy some of the myths about rape:

1. Rape happens to babies, elderly women, teenagers, and young women. Every woman is a potential victim.
2. Ninety percent of all rapes are intraracial. Most women are raped by men of the same race.
3. About 50 percent of all rapes are committed by an assailant known to the victim.
4. About 50 percent of rapes are committed in the home. Women have the right to be anywhere without the fear of rape.
5. No one has a right to tell women how to dress. If a woman wears a certain outfit (for instance shorts and a tank top), it may be because of hot weather. There is no outfit that says "rape me."
6. Women do not ask to be raped. Women who do not act fresh or provocative get raped also.[5]

Organizationally, the issue of rape for women can be divided into two major categories: the legal system composed of the laws and statutes in each state, and the larger, more global issue of social and psychological services for victims of rape.[6] At the roots of both categories, however, is the fundamental question of women's social roles and the way that role has been constructed in a male-dominated society. In addition to discussing these subjects, this section also addresses change strategies.

Rape and the Criminal-Justice System

In her book, *The Rights of Women,* Susan Deller Ross points to four major assumptions underlying this country's laws on rape. The first assumption is that women are basically untrustable and that they will lie if given the opportunity. Closely related to the idea of lying is the appendage assumption that women are really scornful creatures who will punish innocent males by accusing them of rape. In this way, the laws were necessarily designed to protect the males from these vindictive, dishonest women.

The second assumption is that women secretly want to be dominated and raped, that they somehow ask for it either overtly by hitching rides from strangers and wearing "suggestive" clothing or more subtly by a glance, a walking style, or even taking a job at night. In this way, laws are designed to help men escape responsibility for their criminal offenses by placing the major portion of the blame and responsibility on the rape victim.

The third assumption upon which these rape laws are based has to do with the concept of "good" women and "fallen" angels. The laws subtly assume that only the good women can really be raped or sexually invaded. Bad women, defined in this case by women's sexual past and current practices, cannot really be raped because they have somehow consented. If the rape victim has had an active sex life, and, according to Ross, especially if she has slept with her assailant in the past, the male criminal-justice system will pass judgment on her charge of rape on the basis of her sexual activity rather than on the criminal action of the rapist.

Ross's final point involves the concept of women as the property of men. As Brownmiller discusses in her investigation of rape and war, women have been the spoils and the reward for victorious soldiers. The ideology of women as the property of men can be seen in the laws concerning rape. "Ideology number four is that women are chaste, delicate creatures belonging to particular men (some man's wife, mother, grandmother, girlfriend), and that rape is thus a particularly heinous crime since it involves a violation of both the woman's unique purity and the man's property rights."[7] The combined effects of these cultural assumptions result in laws designed in such ways that the conviction of a rapist is nearly impossible.

Rape is the only criminal act where, in a court of law, the victim is required to convince the judge and jury that she tried to fight off her attacker. No victim of armed robbery faces this requirement.[8] It is an interesting requirement in light of the fact that many police officers all across the country tell women not to fight their attackers—that the struggle required by her to prosecute is the action the police tell women will get them severely injured or killed.

According to DeCrow, today's Model Penal Code on rape contains another requirement that makes the prosecution of a rapist nearly impossible. That requirement is known as collaboration.[9] There is no other violent crime where the victim is responsible for this requirement.[10] "The word of the victim is not enough as it is in other crimes. Thus, in many states to convict a man the prosecutor must prove through evidence independent of the woman's testimony that she was penetrated, that force was used, and/or that the man accused was the actual person who did it."[11]

The problems with the collaboration requirement are many but the most striking involve the realities of how these laws so totally misunderstand or ignore the nature of the crime of rape. To be collaborated, one almost always needs an eyewitness and few rapes are committed in the presence of other people. In addition, the penetration requirement can be extremely difficult to prove. Women who wait to report the crime or those who have taken a bath or douched (which is an extremely common occurrence) destroy the sperm and with it the evidence that could meet the requirements of penetration. It is also known that many rapists do not have the ejaculatory response and leave no evidence even if penetration has occurred.[12]

Collaboration is nearly impossible to comply with when the woman has delayed reporting the crime to police. This makes her suspect. This is the dishonest woman, the scornful woman accusing the innocent man. Some states have a way of finding this out. They actually allow the defense attorney to order a psychiatric evaluation made on the victim, the results of which may be made public and presented to the jury.[13] In no other crime is the victim subjected to these kinds of invasions; but in the crime of rape, the woman is somehow the central participant and the major focus of all activity.

The last legal issues surrounding the successful prosecution of rape involves other evidence beyond collaboration requirements and the requirement that the woman must prove that she struggled and resisted. The rules of evidence in court cases are such that they allow the victim herself to stand trial. Over and over again in the literature on rape, this trauma is described. The woman's sexual history is not only accepted in the rules of evidence, her sexual past often becomes the whole basis upon which the defense builds their case. This relates back to Ross's assumption that only the pure women can really be victims of rape. Not only is this common practice embarrassing and humiliating to the woman, but stunned by the trauma of being raped she is verbally abused by forceful lawyers and made to describe the most intimate parts of her life publicly. The added insult is that this humiliation could become the weapon that sets her assailant free. Women's rights groups all over the country are trying to change these rules of evidence that allow the victims of rape to continue being victimized. But as long as there is a single state, a single courtroom that allows the woman's sexual history into the question of a rape incident, women will continue to be victims.

The Social and Psychological Victimization of Rape Victims

There is not a female alive in this country today who does not fear rape. They have heard about rape from parents, teachers, and television ever since being cognizant of the fact that they were female. They learned that there was something unique and some different and dark threat simply because they were females. Social actions and mobility are affected by rape and by the threat of rape every day of a woman's life. They do not walk in certain neighborhoods, do not go out at night alone, and do not talk to men in bars whom they do not know, especially if they have seen or read *Looking for Mr. Goodbar*. On the most basic psychological level, each woman is a rape victim.

Rape victimizes women in other important ways. The threat of rape actually affects women economically and has been used against them in the labor market. On the one hand, many women will not take jobs at night or certain kinds of jobs such as the night manager of a convenience store because of the threat of rape. But this unique form of discrimination also works in reverse; employers use rape as the excuse not to hire females in certain positions. "Rapists perform for sexist males the same function that the Ku Klux Klan performed for racist whites; they keep women in their place through fear. The threat of rape is used to keep women out of jobs—for example, the *Pittsburg Post Gazette* has used this as a reason not to hire women reporters; it is used to keep women off the streets at night; it keeps women passive and modest for fear that they will be thought provocative."[14]

The emotional awareness of rape by every woman renders each a victim on some level. But what of those women who have actually experienced the nightmare in reality. In the late 1960s and early 1970s Ann Wolbert Burgess and Lynda Lytle Holstrom identified the rape trauma syndrome. Pioneering researchers in this area they are professors at Boston College. For one year they followed all rape cases reported to Boston City Hospital. In recent years, these two women have identified two forms of the rape trauma syndrome and have connected these two variations with the kind of rape the women experienced.

The "blitz rape," according to Burgess and Holstrom, is "out of the blue." There has been no previous contact between the victim and the assailant. The woman is selected at random by the rapist as his mark. A mark, as defined by Burgess and Holstrom, is the person selected to become a victim of some form of illegal expectation.[15] In the blitz rape, the victim cannot understand why she was selected to become the mark. The other form of rape is called the "confidence rape." It occurs between two individuals who have had some previous contact relationship or association. The confidence rape is more subtle; it is a setup which has involved some planning on the part of the rapist to victimize someone he knows.[16]

There is one other form of rape that has not been discussed as much in the literature. This is the gang-rape involving two or more males committing a confidence rape against some woman they know or a blitz rape involving someone they simply picked out.[17] In any form of rape, the most common outcome is that women suffer significant degrees of physical and emotional injury.

Essentially, there are two phases in the rape trauma syndrome: the acute phase and the long-term phase. The rape trauma syndrome is all-encompassing: it involves the physical, the emotional, and the behavioral reactions of a victim of rape, reactions which occur as a direct result of having been faced with a life-threatening event.

As Brownmiller so thoroughly convinces us in *Against Our Will, Men, Women, and Rape*, rape is not an act of sexuality but it is totally and assuredly an act of violence. It should not be surprising then to learn that victims of rape are often battered, broken, torn, and physically traumatized. There is usually a great deal of soreness in their bodies. Often their throats, chests, arms, and legs are particularly sore as a result of their assailant's force and violence to those areas.[18]

Beyond the physical, there are generally disturbances in the victim's sleep patterns which occur in the acute stage. Also in this immediate stage, there are often disturbances in the eating patterns with a marked decrease in appetite. Some victims of rape complain about stomach pains in this stage as well.

On the emotional side, the rape trauma syndrome is characterized by tremendous fear; a fear of death is mentioned more than anything else as well as a fear of bodily harm and physical injury. Along with the strong fear reaction, the rape trauma syndrome also involves feelings of humiliation, guilt, shame, and embarrassment. Burgess and Holstrom recognized that because there are such strong first reactions on the part of rape victims, there are often severe mood swings in this initial, acute stage of the syndrome. There is visible nervousness, then sudden withdrawal. There are tears and then sudden rage and anger. Many rape victims deny the terrifying experience. These women are at-risk for permanent disruption.[19]

The long-term process of recovery for a rape victim can be just that: long term. Many victims Burgess and Holstrom followed up reported that normal daily occurrences would upset them. Many victims reported being able to function at minimal levels. Some women coped with their feelings of fear and vulnerability by simply staying at home.[20] Another typical response was for the victim to turn to family and friends for support and for safety. Victims of rape often continue to be victims long after the rape has past. Theirs are the actions of people in fear. They move, change their phone numbers, stay indoors, buy huge locks or elaborate protection devices. They are people who have lost the sense of control over their lives and they are trying hard to regain some portion of it.

Strategies: A Beginning

In the work that Burgess and Holstrom have done over the last few years, one thing emerged more than anything else: rape trauma syndrome is very real and those experiencing it need comprehensive care.

Rape crisis hotlines and centers have sprung up all over the country in the last several years. People and professionals are becoming more empathetic, more responsive to the needs of rape victims. But the problem is immense and complex and the work has only begun. The helping professionals who come into contact with the victims of rape must be trained and sensitized to the needs of these people. Police, medical personnel (especially those in emergency rooms), physicians, district attorneys, lawyers, all play important roles in the recovery of nonrecovery of rape victims.

The following list of services are provided by the Rape Crisis Center. They run outreach and education and counseling services around rape and are a striking example of strategies to combat this terrible crime which victimizes women.

Victim Advocacy Services. Center members will assist a victim of sexual assault according to her needs and desires. If a victim wishes to report the incident to the police or pursue legal action, she may obtain information, advice and support from the Center. If she chooses not to report to the police, the Center will aid her in choosing another form of action.

Crisis Counseling. Each Center member is specifically skilled in short-term counseling of victims of sexual assault, provided free of charge.

Referrals. Referrals to legal, medical, and counseling facilities and resources (including free clinics) may be obtained from the Center.

Information. The Center can provide information on all aspects and implications of rape such as medical, legal, social, psychological, and political.

Speaker's Bureau. The Center offers presentations for audiences of all ages and interests on a variety of topics related to the problem of rape, as part of its community education program.

Self-Defense and Prevention. The Center gives self-defense demonstrations and classes, disseminates lists of prevention tactics and other prevention literature, and designs and implements local prevention programs.

Publications. A variety of publications, including articles on rape and a book titled *How to Start a Rape Crisis Center* are available.

Consulting. Center members can help anyone design rape workshops, and seminars, prevention programs, educational programs, and counseling programs. The Center consults with groups setting up rape crisis centers.

Media. Members of the Center are available to provide information to journalists and to speak on radio and television.

Training. An eight-week training program is provided to volunteers who come to work at the Center. The Center also has available programs for training hospital emergency-room staffs, hotlines, and security staffs.[21]

There is much to do before rape victims can be assured of nonsexist adequate medical care that will not only doctor their physical wounds and injuries but will consider the possibility of venereal disease or unwanted pregnancy. Police and attorneys need to be aware of the damaging and sexist nature of their questions and of their rather hostile attitude toward the woman, the victim. Judges should be sensitive to the sexist nature inherent in their rules of evidence regarding the prosecution of rapists and the impact that experience can have on the entire life of the rape victim. There should be a reshuffling of evidential procedures that put the victims on trial in our courts and not the rapist. There has to be a new willingness to look at the kinds of assumptions Ross pointed out that form the foundation for our laws on rape.

Because the laws and the institutions dealing with rape were so blatantly inadequate, biased, and unjust, the National Organization for Women created a special task force at their Sixth Annual Conference in 1973. The mandate for this task force was and still is, "To define the crime of rape. To research existing laws covering rape and related crimes against women and children. To propose a model guide for state legislatures, for adoption into their criminal codes. To research and recommend follow-up procedures, that is, psychological assistance, to help victims of rape. To explore effective forms of resistance."[22]

Other groups have formed on college campuses, in women's centers, and in clinics all over the country. They organize services, using both professionals and volunteers who may themselves have been victims of rape. Many of these rape crisis programs come into the emergency rooms on the call of an emergency-room staffer, provide comfort, empathy, and support to the rape victim from the first moments through the long court process. Some programs in the recent past have started to think about helping the family members of rape victims, something that is vitally important if full recovery is going to occur.

A fuller realization of the problems of rape was recognized with the establishment of the National Institute of Mental Health's Center for the Prevention and Control of Rape, in Rockville, Maryland. Various research and demonstration projects have been funded by this office.

Rape is a complicated and frightening issue. It is a major social problem. It is a problem women have to face. It is a woman's problem. At some point in the near future, when minimum services are in place and state legislatures have changed the laws that continue to victimize, and when there is sensitizing of the players and participants to the realities of rape, then there needs to be a closer look at why there is rape at all in this society. As Hilberman states: "The eradication of rape is contingent on educating and sensitizing our society to the meaning of the crime and the context in which it occurs. Innovative and empathetic services to victims will serve as a deterrent to the crime by facilitating reportage and thereby apprehension and prosecution of the assailants. Ultimately, however, the elimination of rape will require a massive reconsideration and restructuring of social values as well as a reorientation of the relations between the sexes."[23]

Battering

Battering (previously referred to as *battery*) is the unlawful use of force against a person without that person's consent. Female victims of outrageous beatings are often blamed for their maltreatment by a kind but disinterested tribunal. "I have been listening to the victim-blamers and pondering their thought processes for a number of years. That process is often very subtle. Victim-blaming is cloaked in kindness and concern, and bears all the trappings of statistical furbelows of scientism; it is obscured by a perfumed haze of human-itarianism."[24]

The Myths of Battering: Understanding the Problem

Some relatively new terms have been added to our legal lexicon: battered wives, wife beating, wife abuse, battered spouse, battered women, abused women, and domestic violence. They are the new symbols of a rising consciousness about women and about women as victims. This new language serves both to illuminate the issue and to color and distort it with myth.

The truth is, battering women is nothing new. An eighteenth-century English proverb tells us that "a dog, a woman and a walnut tree, the more you beat them, the better they be." While the pearls of wisdom from our folklore tint our thinking, it is not difficult to see that thinking like this stems from the conception that woman is the property of man. It is far more difficult, however, to uncover the subleties that Ryan speaks of. It is more difficult to truly define the spiraling forces that allow the physical and psychological abuse of women to be defined as a social problem and yet remain thoroughly unrectified and untouched.

As with all the issues and problems of women identified in this book, blaming the victim is not an event; it is a process and an evolution of concepts, of thought about the way the world works and about the players in it. As Ryan so articulately points out, blaming the victim evolves as an ideology" from the collective unconscious of a group or class and is rooted in a class-based interest in maintaining the status quo."[25] While the terminology of battered women defines it as a social problem, the real issues center around the action that terminology provokes and the reality is that those forces that could impact and change the conditions of the battered woman syndrome have an interest in maintaining the status quo—and so the condition never really changes. It gets patched.

Lenore E. Walker writes an intuitive and in-depth discussion about the myths surrounding battered women. One of the most blatant myths centers around the notion of "who" the battered wife or women is: she is not middle class; she is not healthy; she is not educated; she is not independent. In other words, she is a woman we hear and read about but she is not anyone we know. She is not at all like me.[26]

Myths are often born from fear; a kind of fear created solely from some automatic feeling of identification with the victim. This fear, subtle and quiet, develops the need for women to define the differences between themselves and the victim. The visible and statistical differences fulfill their need to detach and remove themselves from the groups at-risk and will rest in the false safety of not themselves becoming one of those victims.

But according to Walker, if you are a woman, there is a 50 percent chance that you will be a victim of battering.[27] Battering is not defined as a sado-masochistic relationship between two consenting parties. Rather, it is a physical, sexual, or psychological action inflicting harm by one person upon an unconsenting other. Battering in the true sense of the word involves any woman in any kind of personal relationship; it is not limited by the boundaries of marriage certificates.

Battering occurs in every geographical area, in all age groups, and at all socioeconomic levels. While statistical reports lead one to conclude that battering is more prevalent in the lower socioeconomic strata, empirical and subjective evidence suggests a bias in the reporting systems and not in the actual phenomenon of battering.[28] "Most previously recorded statistics of battering have come from lower-class families. However, lower-class women are more likely to come into contact with community agencies and so their problems are more visible. Middle- and upper-middle-class women do not want to make their batterings public."[29]

Another preconceived myth about battering is that it occurs most often in minority groups. The evidence points to the contrary. According to Walker, battering does not occur more often in minority groups but minority groups do have fewer resources/recourses to deal with their batterings than the Anglo-Saxons do.[30]

Once one understands how widespread and pervasive the problem of battering is, the task of understanding why becomes critical. Why does the male in the relationship beat the female in the relationship? Why does the female in the relationship tolerate the beatings and batterings? Why doesn't she leave; why doesn't she seek help; why doesn't she report it to the police? Why does it continue past the first beating to become the pattern and cycle of battering?

Batterers

Batterers often were battered themselves, and, almost without exception, there was battering in their childhood homes.[31] Also, according to Martin, batterers often have records of past violent behaviors. Many have police records for assault.[32] While no hard evidence exists, the character of the batterer is stereo-typical male-macho and Martin suspects from the experience in the shelter for battered women in Oceanside, California, that many batterers are military men.[33]

Walker provides a more psychological perspective of the battering male. She describes them as a very mixed group but having the following set of similar psychological characteristics.

1. Low self-esteem
2. Believes all the myths about battering relationships
3. Is a traditionalist believing in male supremacy and strong, traditional sex-role stereotypes
4. Blames others for his actions
5. Is pathologically jealous
6. Presents a dual personality: one to the outside world and one in his inter-personal relationships
7. Has severe stress reactions and low-coping skills
8. Frequently uses sex as an act of aggression to enhance self-esteem in view of growing doubts about his virility; may be bisexual
9. Does not believe that his attacks or violent behavior should be punishable or have negative consequences; feels justified in his actions[34]

The Battered

The battered woman's psychosocial makeup is surprisingly isomorphic with the psychosocial makeup of the batterer. She too tends to believe in the traditional sex-role stereotypes.[35] "The victims may exemplify society's old image of ideal womanhood—submissive, religious, nonassertive, accepting whatever the hus-band's life brings. They may exercise no independence of income, ideas, or movement, be anxious about housekeeping, and develop devotion to home and family to the exclusion of outside friends and interests."[36]

In other words, the battered women bought the fairytale notions of Snow White, Cinderella, and June Allyson that someone would take care of them and that they would be safe placing their very survival in the hands of their mates. This phenomenon is often referred to in the feminist literature as "learned helplessness." Learned helplessness is not only accompanied by the myth of interdependent security, it is characterized by the failure to develop adequate coping skills in adult life. The social and psychological presence of learned help-lessness leaves the door to victimization wide open. Learned helplessness both invites attack and renders one defenseless in the event the attack occurs.

But the battered syndrome goes farther than mere sex-role stereotyping and the psychological characteristics of the players. Battering, more than anything else, is a process. It has a beginning, a middle, and often a tragic and fatal end. It is an interplay between two people that jets and jumps, submerges for a time, and then resurfaces on cue. Here lies part of the reason why the battered remain to be battered again.

Myths abound about the secret, deep-seated psychological pleasure the battered woman gets from being beaten and dominated. According to Del Martin, nothing could be farther from the truth. Think about it. What human, what organism derives pleasure from pain? If the women described above are stereotypically normal in their devotion to and adoption of the "total woman," how is it possible that this dreamer, this believer gets pleasure from nearly getting killed, from having a miscarriage as a result of a beating, from being broken and stitched? In one's wildest dreams, this woman could not stay in a battering relationship because she gets pleasure from being battered; what then? It may be easier for society to want to think this because it removes the battered woman from the mainstream. She is abnormal. When one realizes the prevalence of the battering, however, this myth collapses. What makes this traditional Eve stay, and stay, and stay?

There have been several hypotheses surrounding the issue of personal resources and battered women. The idea put forth was that women did not have the financial stability or independence to leave and start out on their own, especially with dependent children. Given the psychosocial profile of the battered woman described above, this may in part be valid. If there is a total submersion in home and family, the chance of having an independent income, job skills which are reasonably marketable, self-confidence, and knowledge about the workplace appear to be extremely unlikely. Certainly in the planning of any shelter for battered women, these barriers need to be taken into consideration. The reasons battered women stay in the battering situation, however, go far deeper than mere economics.

Del Martin asked battered women why they returned to their husbands and got the following answers: he threatened/performed further acts of violence; she had nowhere else to go; the children were still in the marital home; she felt love or sorrow for the batterer.[37]

One of the real secrets and tragedies of the battered wife lies in that last comment: that she felt love or sorrow for the man who beat her. Battering does not occur all the time. In fact, evidence suggests that battering occurs in a very definite cycle. And while there is predictable violence, there can also be great emotional tenderness and closeness to such an extent that the battered woman may actually believe the promise that the beatings will end and may feel and believe the remorse in her mate's face and words. From the outside looking in, it is difficult to understand this forgiveness, this innocence. And because it is difficult to understand, it is difficult to accept. But the time space between beatings is often long, the pain forgotten, replaced by the image of the man and the relationship the battered wife longs for. She heals physically;

psychologically she often forgives and moves to the promises of the future. It is this hope that binds and chains the battered woman to the batterer and it is not until that hope is gone or real fear for life creeps slowly in that the woman seeks help and refuge, if such refuge and aid exist.

Strategies for Change

One is back full circle to the issue of victim-blamers and the collective consciousness that roots its self-interest in maintaining the status quo. Inherent in this collective consciousness are two important factors at two totally different levels; the first has to do with resources allocated to aid these victims and the second, with changing the attitudes about the sexes that allow battering to happen in the first place.

Women's groups all over the country are taking the cause of battered women and wives into their own hands and are starting shelters for battered women. An excellent list of existing women's shelters can be found in Terry Davidson's book, *Conjugal Crime, Understanding and Changing the Wife-beating Pattern.*[38] For the most part, shelters for battered women are short-term emergency. Long-term care requires resources beyond the reach of most women's groups. Legal advice exists at most shelters as does some sort of short-term supportive therapy, often peer counseling or small group therapy. Again the more professional therapies require more dollars, dollars which are beyond the reach of these women's groups.

The other reality is that there are simply not enough of these shelters available, even on a short-term emergency basis. "The need for facilities and counseling for battered women and their children is overwhelming. You will undoubtedly be confronted with a 'full house' most of the time, and much of the discouragement and frustration you will encounter will be the result of not being able to provide adequate services to all of the women who seek you out."[39]

Of course, providing the necessary care for those needing it requires dollars and resources which are unavailable and out of reach at the current time. This scarcity of resources for the battered woman relates strongly to the collective consciousness Ryan speaks of and its striving for the status quo. Nowhere can an example of blaming the victim be seen more clearly than in the case of the battered woman. As with the rape victim, the battered woman is suspected to be responsible for what has happened to her: "she provokes him; she knows better than to nag at him when he is drinking; what man could tolerate that kind of nagging?" Somehow, in our cultural mind, one is able to take the case of a man beating a woman and turn it around so that it becomes her fault and her responsibility.

On another level, the battered woman is blamed for remaining in the situation. If she did not somehow get bizarre and masochistic pleasure from his beatings, she would simply leave. Of course, this explanation makes no mention of the fact that there are so few shelters available for her to go to, so few alternatives open to her, because society refuses to provide assistance. And lastly, the victim is blamed because society refuses to see the attitude that creates the sanction for battering to even exist. That women in this situation really should not be helped that much—because they are women and because something in that means that being battered is part of the pie and really is not that dreadful. It is important to realize that there is much lip service to solving the problems. The mental-health field provides terminology for those problems and holds seminars and conferences describing and defining them. In the end, the collective consciousness really does not want to find the remedy. If society took the problem seriously, there would not be a great need for more shelters, better services, more holistic services. There would be more services for the batterer. The society would work to develop an intolerance for the stereotypical roles that create the kind of inequality conducive to dominance-subservience, that is, battering.

Change in the growing problem of battered women involves much more than starting emergency shelters, though no one would deny that such resources are mandatory. Change in the case of the battered woman must be attitudinal— attitudes that have become most basic—the attitudes about men and the attitudes about women. And this kind of change takes tremendous courage, from men, and especially from women.

In some ways victimization can and should be thought of in terms of "survival." Bettelheim points out that survival has to be divided into two aspects: (1) what the victim can do to survive (what he can do for himself and what others can do for him), and (2) what the outside world can do to change the structural conditions that encourage victimization. In other words, we need to concentrate on individual and societal/structural variables.

It is clear that in public policy there is a need to recognize that victimization may require some types of services that have not been conceived of for other persons or for other problem areas. Some initiatives, as suggested from various sources, might include:

1. Developing outreach programs to deal with the victims of whom we may not be aware. This is a particularly important area, and perhaps the most fundamental concern behind the delivery of services to victims. In this society, we are accustomed to people applying for services, such as going voluntarily to law-enforcement officers. Consequently, many persons are hesitant or ashamed to actively seek help when they need it. Vigorous outreach efforts are required to identify these victims and their families without stigmatizing them in the process, and to provide them with an appropriate and humane range of services.

2. Victims have, in the past, been served almost exclusively through the

criminal-justice system. The mental-health system must become integrated with these efforts in order to provide for the psychological needs of victims.

3. Training prosecutors, police, and hospital officials to be more sensitive to the needs of victims.

4. The creation of advocacy in victim assistance service and continued funding support for these programs. For this society services are provided when they are demanded and when effective constituencies ensure their provision. This reality is not likely to change. Advocates for victims can help to ensure the delivery of appropriate services.

5. The provision of compensation/preparations, and provision of free crisis intervention and the long-term care for victims.

6. Support for the family members of victims.

7. More attention should be paid to delayed psychological disabilities that victims may suffer.

8. Public education to change victim-blaming that still is current in our society and its law.

Both the immediate and longer-term needs require a different type of public policy than presently exists. Developing new policies that must be met by public officials, as well as scientific research, which needs to be rearticulating the realities of the victim is also necessary.[40]

Women and Alcohol

Women drink alcohol and men drink alcohol. When women drink alcohol there is another set of variables associated with them that affect their drinking habits, their own feelings about themselves, and the treatment they receive. These variables include the double standard applied to women by men drinking, the class distinctions among women themselves, and the negative sexual associations with a woman who drinks. These added factors foster more hidden drinking and more vigorous denials. The treatment network and the research system study women alcoholics in the traditional manner. This exacerbates rather than relieves their sickness. Worse yet, many female alcoholics are simply not available for treatment because of the system's limiting viewpoint. The following section presents the subject of women and alcohol from a historical viewpoint and traces the evolution of the double standard. After presenting the variables associated with women drinking, it presents an organizational approach to the problem.

History

Even though women have been drinking alcohol since recorded history, serious study of the subject by scientists is new, most of the literature being generated within the last eight to ten years. There is a great deal in the literature of today about the double standard of alcohol and its relationship to men and women. This double standard, so the literature goes, imposes more restrictive, more punitive, more severe sanctions on the drinking behaviors of women and has been identified as one of the major barriers for women getting or seeking help for drinking problems.[41] This double standard is so pervasive in the literature on women and alcohol that it warrants taking a close look at its developmental history. How did this split in social prescription between ancient Babylonia, Egypt, and the nineteenth and twentieth centuries impact the double standard that prevents today's woman from getting treatment?

Of course, the history of alcohol and women goes back even farther than the last ten years. Women's involvement with alcohol has been documented as far back as ancient Babylonia (5000 B.C.) when women were the caretakers of fermented wines and spirits and it was women, not men, who determined when, where, and how much beer people would drink.[42] Women were probably the world's first professional brewers. Ancient Egyptians believed that the gods gave fermented drink through woman, that it was woman who gave this particular gift to man.[43]

But the history of women and alcohol changed dramatically in the nineteenth and twentieth centuries. No longer were women in control of alcoholic beverages. No longer were women revered for their involvement with fermented spirits. Now the reverse was true. Women who drank alcohol were not the high priestesses, they were the low-life prostitutes that threatened the family and home of the good and respectable women. Today's double standard of alcohol and women probably had its roots in the Victorian era of England. No doubt, these values and attitudes were transplanted to American soil along with many others during the late-nineteenth and early-twentieth centuries.

While the explanation of the double standard is complex, a simple explanation emerges from the investigations. For the first time in the history of the Western world, the image and concept of the "lady" was born during this time out of a new social structure and a new economy. Industrialization carved out the world's first working middle class and with that middle class was born this new creature the economy and social structure could afford: the lady of the leisure class. It was during this time that woman became more closely associated with her sexual nature and her social role became inextricably intertwined with the physical and psychological nature of her sexuality. Here too was born the distinction between classes of people and classes of women. While the male's social class was tied with his profession and his earning power, woman's social class became associated with her sexual morality. The new image of lady, or woman, became the model to which people aspired and that lady was sexually pure, morally beyond reproach, and alcohol-free. It was here that woman's use of alcoholic beverages became associated with her sexual practices.[44] Lower-class women drank alcohol more openly; they also were considered sexual beings breeding too many children and even spreading venereal disease. These women threatened the home, family, and morality of the middle-class women and when the first march for prohibition began, it began with middle-class women attacking prostitution and demon rum with equal force.[45]

It would be incorrect to say that middle-class women never drank. Middle-class women drank a lot of alcohol and took a lot of opium but they took these chemicals for medical and not social purposes in an era when female sickness dominated the life-style and leisurely days of these women.[46]

Alcohol did have important medical uses at the time. It was used often in childbirth, to alleviate discomfort during pregnancy, to calm women during menstruation, and even to help soothe the nervous young mother who was nursing her new infant.[47] It was not that ladies did not drink alcohol, it was that they did so in the privacy of their homes and they did so for the right reasons: medical reasons.

Today, the remnants of the Victorian lady are with us. We are in an era where we medicate for emotional as well as physical pain. Horn and Wanberg discovered that women still self-medicate. In their survey, these two researchers discovered that men and women drink for different reasons. Men drink for social reasons; women drink to calm nervous tension, to ease depression, for the psychological rather than the social effects.[48]

Women today are notoriously isolated rather than social drinkers. While more and more women are venturing out to bars and taverns after work or are feeling free to order wine at lunch, more women than men drink in their homes or in friends' homes rather than in more public places.[49] (National Clearinghouse for Alcohol Information, Strategies for Reaching Women with Alcohol Problems, Special Projects, by Susan Bower, 1979.)

As did their Victorian sisters, today's woman tends to drink alone rather than with others. One of the differences between men and women alcoholics that emerges most consistently in the literature is the fact that alcoholic women are isolated drinkers, be they upper-class or skidrow dwellers.[50] This has not changed in over 100 years.

The barrier of the double standard that exists today also has its roots in the connection made between women, their sexuality, and their use of alcohol. One can see this connection in the literature of women and alcohol of the 1970s and 1980s. The very nature of the questions asked in scientific investigations into women and alcohol are sexual in nature. One would be hard-pressed to find similar research questions asked about male alcoholics.

One finds that alcoholic women are promiscuous, and, at the same time, that they are sexually frigid and ridden with sex guilt.[51] There may be serious infertility problems, gynecological problems, excessive miscarriages, painful menstruations, and a variety of other biological feminine difficulties.[52] Joan Curlee and Sharon Wilsnack found alcoholic women have serious sex-role conflicts, that they drink because of unconscious feelings of masculinity. Much of the research around women and alcohol issues still centers around woman's biological, psychological, and social roles as females. Alcoholic women are thought of in association with their sex and their reproductive functioning which is also related to sexuality. It was only when the fetal alcohol syndrome research showed a relationship to pregnant women drinking and their unborn fetus did investigators show a major interest in the subject of women and alcohol. There have been few investigations into the nature and scope of alcoholism and women that view women outside their confined and predetermined gender role and this, perhaps, is a more serious form of the double standard than research and scientific investigation, under the veil of objectivity and self-proclaimed neutrality, exploring the problems of women and alcohol wrapped in cultural bias and submerged double standards. It perpetuates in a subtle form the double standard in the public's consciousness and attitudes and in the alcoholic woman's consciousness.

Size of the Problem

The ratio of alcoholic men to women has narrowed in recent years. Lisansky found this ratio to be approximately 1:5;[53] Cahalan, approximately 1:3;[54] While there are arguments about the ratio of men to women alcoholics, there is no argument that the gap between the two is rapidly closing. Some would argue that there are indeed more women alcoholics today than there were twenty years ago. This argument states that women are drinking alcohol more often and that, by exposing them to alcohol, women are at-risk for alcohol problems and more women are becoming addicted. The other argument states that there have always been large numbers of women with alcohol problems but that, as public becomes educated to the nature of alcoholism as an illness and with the emergence of the liberated woman, women are coming forth to seek help for their alcohol problems and are simply less hidden. The truth probably lies somewhere in between; there are both more women experiencing problems with alcohol and women are becoming visible with these problems and are willing to seek help.[55] By any count, there are an estimated 1 million to 3 million women in the United States with alcohol problems. "Changing lifestyles and mores have undoubtedly had an effect (on women's drinking behaviors), but singling out a single cause for increased numbers of alcoholic women may be an unrealistic goal."[56]

Anyone would agree that alcoholism is a complex set of signs and symptoms with many components and multiple causes. No one has been able to disaggregate all the etiologies and causal and associative factors involved. This is true of both men and women alcoholics.

Psychological Differences

Some important research has looked at the psychological aspects of alcoholic women. It must be realized that most research in this area has been done with women already in treatment for alcoholism and that this group may or may not be representative of the universal population of alcoholic women.

In her review of the literature, Lindbeck found that alcoholic women have a greater tendency to come from homes where there was alcoholism, particularly in fathers. While this is true for alcoholic men, it is the degree of difference that is important. Alcoholic women come from these families more often than do alcoholic men.[57] In addition, alcoholic women came from homes where there was a high incidence of depressive or affective disorders in the mothers.[58] Mark Keller, one of the foremost researchers in the field of alcoholism, states that the incidence of depression in alcoholic women is very high. Knowing this, it is important to view findings of depressive mothers with some question. Alcoholism may have been present in the mothers of these alcoholic women as well but may have been misdiagnosed or may have been a secondary diagnosis after depression. One of the major problems facing women with alcohol problems is the reluctance or failure of physicians and other helping resources to identify alcoholism and, instead, identify affective or depressive disorders.

Lindbeck and Gomberg also found that the homes of the women surveyed were highly disruptive, being riddled with divorce, separation, death of a parent, and major illness. This would be consistent with what is known about alcoholism generally: alcoholics tend to become ill at three or more times the rate as non-alcoholics, early death is common in alcoholic people, there is a high incidence of divorce and marital disruption among the alcoholic population, and domestic disturbance is associated with problem drinking in the home.[59]

The differences in psychological factors between men and women with alcohol problems may be related to other psychological disorders since men and women exhibit different forms or kinds of psychopathology in relation to their drinking.[60] None of these psychological factors influencing drinking patterns appear to be stronger than that of drinking behavior in women being associated with affective disorders. In investigation after investigation and in self-reports of women alcoholics themselves, depression has stood out. Winokur, Clayton and Reich[61], and Schurkit[62] all found strong associations between the onset of alcoholic or heavy drinking and depression.

Indeed, these findings also relate to Gomberg's findings that there is a high incidence of precipitating crisis events prior to the onset of heavy or alcoholic drinking in the research on women and alcohol. Women, more so than men, appear to be able to pinpoint the onset of their problem drinking to some specific life-crisis event such as death of a child, divorce, death of a parent, or even what is commonly referred to as the "empty nest syndrome."[63] Excessive drinking associated with a definite life situation has been found by many researchers.[64]

Whichever way one looks at the problem of women and alcohol, there appears to be some important psychological factors playing a part in the development of problem drinking among women and these psychological factors seem to be associated with affective or depressive disorders related to specific life situations. In this way, one could argue that alcohol abuse and alcoholism among women could be a form of coping, an adaptation to the situations and gender roles in which women find themselves.

One hypothesis advanced by Klerman views depression in just this way: an adaptation to a "helpless" situation. If women with alchohol problems exhibit depression as frequently as appears in the literature, the adaptive view of coping and depression and alcoholism among women may be extremely valuable. Klerman views depression as an evolutionary adaptive process: social, physiological, psychodynamic, and subjective. "The depressive episode may be initiated as a response to helplessness and fallen self-esteem, but attempted adaptation fails. It does not prepare the organism to meet environmental contingencies. It causes a misperception of self."[65] Klerman suggests that this form of depression is an imbalance between the external levels of stress and the individual's vulnerability.[66]

The model of learned helplessness for depression and for women and alcohol could be an important component of the puzzle. Seligman and other investigations in this area of learned helplessness have shown that symptoms of learned helplessness in animal laboratories and in patterns of clinical depression found in women using mental-health clinics were extremely similar. The most significant characteristic was a form of what researchers call "passivity," whereby the women or the laboratory animals are unable to exert control over external forces harming them and develop an inability to demonstrate voluntary responses toward those external forces.[67] "If the animal (or woman) undergoes multiple trials of inescapable shock, the helplessness persists longer. In humans, a single catastrophic incident such as the death of a child produces this sense of depression."[68]

The fact that women themselves, in treatment for alcoholism, have been able to identify these kinds of catastrophic incidents and have related them to feelings of depression prior to the onset of problem drinking could be significant. The other significant variable operating here is that of helplessness which is learned in relation to the catastrophic incident and other feelings of powerlessness over the events and situations the woman finds herself in. With few supports coupled with a sense of personal powerlessness exacerbated by a life-crisis event, women turn to alcohol for relief. Thse factors have important implications for secondary prevention efforts in this area. Problem drinking, for many women, could be a function of negative coping that would yield to support systems and responsive helping professionals and resources.

Sociocultural

Sociocultural investigations in the area of women and alcoholism are concerned with social learning and social response to the problem rather than with the etiologies of alcoholism. One of the most significant findings in this area involves the denial and protection mechanisms that work to prolong the woman's problem drinking and result in her getting either the wrong kind of treatment or no treatment at all. This denial manifests itself in the individual woman, in her family, in the would-be identification agents such as employers, police, judges, doctors and hospital emergency-room personnel, and unfortunately the mental-health and social work professions. The concept of denial and protection is rooted in that of gender-related mental health and illness as defined by culture. There are acceptable illnesses and unacceptable illnesses and these acceptability factors are cut according to gender roles. There are some kinds of illness that are acceptable for women to have and there are illnesses that are more acceptable for males to have.[69] Alcoholism and alcohol problems have always been more male-acceptable.[70] As Morris Chafetz, first director of the National Institute of Alcohol Abuse and Alcoholism, stated in 1976, "No one likes to think that the hand that rocks the cradle is a shaky one." The stigma associated with the female alcoholic reinforces the denial system. The double standard is so strong in female alcoholism that her own denial which is inherent to the disease is seen throughout her societal systems that should be confronting her and insisting she get treatment. Thus, she is often sicker than the male when treatment is sought and recovery then becomes more difficult.

Because of these and many other complicated factors related to social stereotyping, only 30 percent of the estimated 1 million to 3 million women with alcohol problems ever get treatment for those problems.[71]

Treatment Resources

Treatment needs to be viewed from two perspectives: modality and resources. Under the former the field continues to apply the same criteria in treating women as men. Dr. Jean Kirkpatrick, herself a recovered alcoholic, founded a national organization, Women for Sobriety, as well as wrote the book *Turnabout*.[72] In this book she put forward a new approach to treating women's alcoholism problems. It is bold and forthright and includes the following thirteen psychological steps. (See chapter 10 for full details on Women for Sobriety.) These steps, which a woman progresses through, explain the philosophy of the organization and show the awareness of women in recovery.

1. I have a drinking problem that once had me.
2. Negative emotions destroy only myself.

3. Happiness is a habit I will develop.
4. Problems bother me only to the degree I permit them to.
5. I am what I think.
6. Life can be ordinary or it can be great.
7. Love can change the course of my world.
8. The fundamental object of life is emotional and spiritual growth.
9. The past is gone forever.
10. All love given returns twofold.
11. Enthusiasm is my daily exercise.
12. I am a competent woman and have much to give others.
13. I am responsible for myself and my sisters.

Even if the identification factors were corrected and women with alcohol problems were "uncovered" and referred to treatment for alcoholism, there would be few referral places. A critical aspect to the problems of women and alcohol centers around the response of the helping community: mental health, drugs, medical, and alcoholism. Resources to help women with alcohol problems are skimpy and scattered. Even in treatment programs available to women, women are grossly underrepresented. Women have not had the benefits of treatment because they have not had access to the resources available for treatment of alcoholism. In 1978, there were only fourteen treatment centers for women in the country. Only one of these treatment centers had child-care components so that women with children could go to the center. The problems are lack of resources generally and of treatment programs that are unresponsive to the unique needs of women, such as child care, depression, and dual additions common in women. It is important to bear in mind that researchers have consistently found that physicians prescribe drugs as treatment for alcoholism. James found 35 percent of female Alcoholics Anonymous (AA) members surveyed reported they had abused drugs, and almost all the drugs had been prescribed by physicians.[73] Morrissey and Schuckit found a drug-abuse history in one-fourth of 300 alcoholic women.[74] The subject of alcoholic women in treatment has recently been investigated by Eileen Corrigan. She challenges many former concepts and clearly shows the need for more research to clarify previous assumptions.[75]

Organizational Structure and Solutions

In 1976, the National Council on Alcoholism (NCA) founded the first national Office on Women and Alcoholism. Its purpose was to serve as an advocate for women with alcohol problems. The NCA is the largest private, voluntary health organization in the country which has alcoholism as its main focus. The Office on Women received the director's salary, office space in the NCA Washington office, and a part-time secretary. Along with student interns and female volunteers, the first director was able to do several important things.

1. Identified women in each state concerned with alcoholism who would be willing to work in a national network.

2. Formed the National Women's Coalition from this group.

3. Sponsored for the first time a women's tract at the NCA's regular conference.

4. Identified philosophically the need to link alcoholic women with the feminist movement. This was crystallized in the first women's tract meeting when Susan B. Anthony, recovered alcoholic and reknowned feminist, and Ruth Abrams, executive director of the Women's Agenda (an organization of women's groups), spoke to a standing-room audience of over 300 people. Since the first director's departure over two years ago (1978), the Office on Women and Alcoholism of the NCA has been absorbed by the Minority and Family office in New York City. Unfortunately, it has no separate office that women can easily identify as they did previously.

An attempt was made to assign a women's advocate within the National Institute on Alcohol Abuse and Alcoholism (NIAAA) as far back as 1976. The woman assigned to this position also had other responsibilies. She recently resigned from the NIAAA and went to work for a different government agency in a different field. There is currently no individual in NIAAA specifically assigned to women's concerns at the director's level.

The political status of women in the field of alcoholism is not much better at the state level. According to Jacquelyn Hall at the National Institutes of Mental Health, some states are making an effort to pay special attention to program development for women but these efforts consist of more rhetoric than action. About one-third of the states will report to have nothing or very little in the way of women's services.[76] Hall identified a number of deficiencies in women's programs at state levels. The state plans for alcohol and drug services in the majority of cases did not include:

1. Adequate needs assessments of in-depth analysis of available data from alcohol, drug, or criminal-justice tracking systems.

2. Development of strategies to meet the special needs of women who were in treatment within the state.

3. Identification of needs of special populations of women within the state (minority, poor, older, working, or single mothers).

4. Educational or prevention projects geared specifically toward women.

5. Information on the ratio of male to female administrators, treatment staff, counselors, and salary discrepancies between professional personnel.

6. Information on the role, activity, responsibility, or authority of existing women's task forces in the state.

7. Demographic description of women with polydrug or prescription drug

problems. The former is defined as more than one drug. It usually means alcohol with another drug.

With the resignation of the two key staff representatives for women in alcoholism (NCA and NIAAA) the women and alcohol movement suffered a severe blow. There was not a strong enough women's network to have developed in two years to push for the replacement of these positions. It is noteworthy from an organizational perspective that both positions after two years were abolished. One could postulate that the women who had them were too effective. As women in general have been ignored in alcoholism, special groups of women have gone totally unnoticed.

Employed Women

With 48 percent of American women in the workplace, the occupational alcoholism field has failed to develop workable needs assessments, program development strategies, program components, or effective identification plans to reach and help employed women. The recognition of the need of special strategies to reach women in the workplace has only recently occurred. The traditional model of confrontation, male counselor-administrators, and referral to AA was being applied. Slowly as caseloads continued to reflect low numbers of women, the need for alternatives became apparent. The model presently being tested under an NIAAA contract includes the following components and are described in the film *Alcohol and the Working Woman:*[77] (1) women counselors, (2) women support groups, (3) outreach programs directed at women, (4) polydrug education, (5) special training for supervisors in confronting women, (6) prevention programs in the workplace and day-care nurseries, and (7) treatment facilities aimed at women's needs.[78]

Black Women

If the plight of women generally is critical in the allocation of alcoholism and drug resources, the plight of black women and other minority women is even more severe. There is evidence that the black population is significantly different in their use of alcohol and other drugs to warrant special attention.

1. Social indicators and factors associated with problem drinking among the black (male) population include poverty, failure in school, lower-education achievement, and domestic instability.

2. Blacks with alcohol problems tend to be younger than whites with alcohol problems and the onset of alcoholism in blacks tends to be earlier.

3. AA has not experienced the success with blacks that it reports for

whites, and surveys indicate that blacks have indicated different perceptions and expectations from AA than have whites.[79]

Knowing these basic and important differences exist between blacks and whites, the differences between black women and white women and those between black women and black men could be crucial in reaching and treating black women with alcoholism or alcohol and drug problems. According to Gains, black women are dramatically underrepresented in treatment populations.[80]

Other Victims

Josi Couture recently founded an organization called The Other Victims of Alcoholism, Inc. An other victim is defined as someone who is affected by someone else's drinking problem. There are, of course, varying degrees of harm done to other victims depending on the relationship and the strength of association. An employer of a problem drinker may be impacted through monetary loss associated with alcoholic employees; coworkers may become disconcerted trying to cover up for an alcoholic peer in the work setting and may suffer their own loss in job performance as a result. But spouses of alcoholics can suffer severe emotional disruption, broken families, beatings, loss of esteem, and myriad other devastating effects from an alcoholic partner. There are some special needs of female victims of alcoholism and these needs go largely unmet save for a few treatment programs that treat the family as a whole. One occupational program, Kemper Insurance Company, targets other victims and the organization Al Anon reaches out to them. The tragedy is that the bulk of the helping resources for women who find themselves victims of someone else's drinking problem is that the focus is on the alcoholic and not on the alcoholic's victim. The family of the alcoholic is enlisted to help the alcoholic recover, get help, stop drinking. The wife with her particular needs is often ignored. Given the social structure and the current construction of the nuclear family, being the wife of an alcoholic carries different implications than being the husband of an alcoholic. Gomberg points out that husbands of alcoholic wives are ten times more likely to leave the spouse than are wives of alcoholic husbands. More often, the wife continues to live with her drinking mate and continues to be victimized by him. This spousal difference needs to be accounted for in treatment for alcoholism and in mental-health care for victims.

Final Strategies

The issue of women and alcoholism is an important one. As the numbers of women with alcoholism and alcohol and drug problems continue to grow, the needs increase and the resources must be developed to meet those needs. As more sensitivity to the existence of other groups of people requiring help develops, it is imperative that a strong and powerful voice expresses their needs, ensures allocation of resources, and assists afflicted populations to receive the necessary and requisite treatment.

Applying CO concepts to this area, it is clear the alcoholism field is male-dominated. There is no group with power to advocate for the needs of women. In every private national alcoholism agency (NCA, ALMACA, and ADPA) chief executives and presidents are males. Women should seek executive positions. As a group, women need to organize in order to effect change. The potential could be there in the present national coalition if appropriate funding and staffing could be obtained. Prominent and influential women affected by the disease need to speak out and use their power to help other women still suffering from alcoholism.

As we reflect on the problem, it is clear that applying much of the CO framework could have relevance to this area. Women alcoholics have been victims of the stigma and double standard. They have been victimized by lack of services. Worse yet, as spouses of alcoholics they are victimized even further by remaining in intolerable situations. Lastly, alcoholic women compete with alcoholic men for dollars to help alcoholic women. The struggle then becomes more complicated and the strategy needs to be more carefully designed.

Drug Addiction

Extent of the Problem

The issues surrounding drug abuse and addiction among women has generated a great deal of discussion but little has been done to disaggregate the factors leading to these problems. Few substantive solutions have been suggested.

Historically, women have used some drugs more than men. Tonics and assorted patent medicines (often containing opium) were obtained from physicians or purchased over the counter by and for women. The link between the medical world and women's drug use continues today. Where nineteenth-century women found solace and relief in Lydia Pinkham's Tonic, today's women have access to a wide variety of mood-altering drugs, especially the psychotropics.

Research on today's drug use indicates that women differ from men in the amount, kind, source, and pattern of that use.[81] It is fairly clear that, at least in reference to licit drugs, women's involvement is much heavier.[82] Women use a wider spectrum of psychotropic chemicals.[83] Recent surveys indicate that 60 percent of all psychotropic drugs used in this country are used by women; 70 percent of all antidepressants are used by women; women use 80 percent of all amphetamines.[84]

The National Institute on Drug Abuse (NIDA) estimates the following figures regarding the use of prescription drugs in the United States: 32 million women as against 16 million men have taken tranquilizers, or 42 percent of adult females as compared to 21 percent of adult males. Whereas 16 million women have taken some kind of sedative, only 12 million men have, or 21 percent of women and 16 percent of men. While 12 million women have used stimulant medications (for weight control or physical or emotional fatigue) only 5 million men have ever used prescription amphetamines, or 16 percent of women and 8 percent of men.[85]

In a study of 4,000 New York women as reported by Dr. Carl D. Chambers, the director of research for the New York State Narcotics Addiction Control Commission, women account for 80 percent of diet-pill users. The proportion of women users of actual antidepressant drugs, those camouflaged as diet pills, was 76 percent. The use of minor tranquilizers by women was 72 percent.[86]

Causes: Role of Medical Profession and Drug Industry

The factors associated with the massive ingestion of mood-altering chemicals by American women are complex and complicated. Globally speaking, much of the drug-taking behavior can be associated with the growth and expansion of the medical model since the 1950s. Where once the practice of medicine focused on physical illness and complaints, today's physicians are also treating emotional illnesses and complaints resulting from what social scientists refer to as problems in living. The revolution in the drug industry added fuel to the medical trend with the discovery of meprobamate (Miltown and Equanil) in 1955 to treat depressions (a common female complaint) followed by the discovery of chlordiazepoxide (Librium and Valium) in the 1960s.[87]

Drug Industry

Drug companies align themselves with the theories and ideologies the medical profession subscribes to regarding women and their health. In 1978-1979, the industry spent $3 billion advertising its products. This is equal to almost three-quarters of the combined annual budgets of all medical schools in the United States.[88]

Screening drug-industry advertisements and approaches to marketing these new drugs shows that the women were targeted early as major consumers. Not only were women singled out but the drug industry capitalized, even generated, negative, stereotypical images of women; an image that requires treatment by medication.

"It has been my impression, after intensive study, that many advertisements for psychoactive drugs as presented to psychiatrists and other physicians portray women in a bad light and are sometimes seriously demeaning."

1. Is the woman to be drugged because the husband or male friend is upset?
2. Is a woman to be drugged because her husband is beating her?
3. Women might be drugged not only for annoying husbands but also doctors.[89]

The American Medical Association (AMA) is aware of the strong, sometimes subversive advertising practices of the drug industry but has taken few steps toward developing policies to prevent the rise of advertising pushing mood-altering drugs for women. "The AMA's board of trustees admits that it leaves much of what is advertised in their periodicals to the discretion of the manufacturers. Advertisements of drugs are fully accepted even though the claims made for them do not conform to the findings of its own monographs and AMA Drug Evaluations: Even *Good Housekeeping* and *Parent* magazines do better in protecting their readers-consumers."[90]

What is important about the drug industry's advertising practices in regard to women is that they are aimed at developing an agent for drug distribution—the physician. Clearly, physicians are the main sources of drugs for women, especially drugs with abuse potential such as the psychotropics. The fact is that physicians are our society's main (legitimate) drug dispensers and the more one comes into the contact with the service the more likely (the more at-risk) one is of getting drugs. Some 80 percent of prescriptions for psychotropic drugs are written by obstetricians/gynecologists, internists, and general practitioners. Not only are these the physicians women see most often, they are also the physicians with the least amount of training in pharmacology.[91] Statistically, women go to physicians of all kinds twice as often as men do.[92] By mere virtue of their greater exposure to the source, women are at greater risk, twice the risk.

But the problem of drug use and abuse is deeper than the exposure factor; Linda Lindell suggests that, not only are women seeing doctors more than men, when this is controlled for, doctors still prescribe a disproportionate number of drugs for their female patients. This, Lidell suggests, could have much to do with the nature of the interaction between physicians (90 percent of whom are male) and female patients. There is an implied double standard held by physicians in treating women and men. They are far more likely to prescribe drugs for women than men. "Citing research in medical school . . . physicians with more pessimistic attitudes toward treatment outcome are more likely to prescribe tranquilizers for women, because they feel women need not be as mentally alert as men and because they hold the same pessimistic view about women's role in this culture."[93]

Not only does the predominantly male medical profession have its own sexism and sex bias but this bias is capitalized on by the drug industry, depicting women as either hyperactive shrews or as weeping, depressive, helpless puppets. The message is clear: do not recommend counseling, positive actions, or constructive changes; the solution lies in the drug. "Librium rather than liberate; instead of new vistas, Luminal."[94]

Women too may play into the trap largely because they have been trained, socialized, to do so. Women have been acculturated to be more open and more expressive of their feelings, to be emotional beings rather than rational ones. There is some indication that this ability to recognize feelings and to express those feelings places women at high risk for prescription drug abuse in the doctor's office. So stereotypically, not only do physicians expect their female patients to present emotional or psychological complaints but women in fact live up to this expectation.[95]

This model is consistent with findings from other surveys. Substance abuse in women has been associated with life situations and life crises. Women at-risk for drug abuse are:

1. Women in later years who experience what psychologists call "the empty nest syndrome"; the children have grown and gone and a feeling of uselessness settles in.

2. Working women who feel the stress of a double standard: discrimination in pay, opportunity, status.

3. Single mothers who feel trapped by their responsibilities and guilty because they feel trapped.

4. Divorced women forced from dependency to independency with few supports and little time to develop strong coping skills. They are unsure of themselves, uncertain about their futures, and often alone and lonely.

5. Elderly women living with the pressures of fixed incomes and diminishing health, often alone and lonely and feeling physical vulnerabilities, medication is the easiest escape, the solution.

6. Women offenders, who for the most part have been involved with illicit drugs rather than prescription (licit) substances, have drug problems that are well entrenched but not identified and almost never treated. A study done by the Law Enforcement Assistance Administration (LEAA) showed heavy use of tranquilizers and mood-elevators by female prisoners as high as 98 percent in San Francisco jails.[96]

Polydrug Abuse

Women with alcohol problems or alcoholism are also at high risk for drug abuse or polyaddiction. It is well known in the professional alcoholism community that Valium is one of the treatments of choice for alcoholism. Because women are not supposed to be alcoholics, women themselves hide or disguise the problems and physicians are reluctant to diagnose it. Instead of referrals to alcoholism treatment, prescriptions are written. One study on alcoholic women indicated that as many as 80 percent of these women used one or more prescription drugs as often as they did alcohol. Polydrug abuse and cross-addiction in alcoholic women is common.[97]

Drug abuse, especially polydrug abuse, and the abuse of alcohol with other drugs is dangerous and frequently fatal. Surveys of emergency-room patients indicate that as much as 90 percent of drug overdoses involve women using legal substances.[98] Half of all drug-related deaths in the state of Virginia are white women, the majority middle-aged, who died of overdoses of barbiturates and tranquilizers. This group represents only 17 percent of those in drug treatment in the state.[99]

Solutions and Strategies

Part of the problem of women and drug abuse lies in the huge gaps of knowledge about the problem, its causes, the women at-risk, the signs and symptoms relating to outreach and identification of women in trouble with drugs or drugs and alcohol. Intervention techniques are seriously lacking as are effective or adequate treatment facilities geared to meet the physical, psychological, emotional, and social needs of women. Not only is there a serious dearth in treatment options for women, there are significant barriers to the treatment that does exist. For unemployed (no insurance) or for the underemployed (lower income and inadequate insurance) financial restrictions abound. The treatment network is politically divided so that many alcoholism treatment programs will not take drug abusers and drug treatment programs will not take women with drinking problems. Many women simply fall between the cracks in the system. Too, women sense the double standard, fear the added stigma of being labeled "drug-addicted" or "drug-abuser." Consequently, women either hide their own problem or are protected by family, boss, and friends until the problem has reached crisis proportions. A very real problem for women who have dependent children is the possibility, if a drug problem is admitted or help is sought, that they might lose their children by being declared unfit.[100]

Women's treatment needs go far beyond crisis hotlines, emergency-room care, or detoxification. Yet the knowledge about the needs of these women (what treatment modalities would be effective) is so rare, so sparse, that few modalities exist. Funds to build and operate good treatment centers for women drug-abusers are rarely available even if the models for care were developed.

The woman drug-abuser/addict evokes little sympathy or empathy from her society. No one cares what led her into heavy-drug use, what happened in her life that made her vulnerable, how much fear and suffering she is experiencing. She is looked down on, as an object of disgust. She is "fallen" and "sinful." She is in the truest sense a victim of her own culture: the medical profession that gives her the drugs, the employer who forces economic dependence, the husband who ignores and denies, the society that refuses to develop and expand to meet her needs and to help alleviate her daily pressures. But most of all, she is a victim of ignorance, a victim of public apathy.

In addition to providing the appropriate treatment facilities women must be instructed on the dangers of drug use. Even if the physician prescribes it, women should question its value and even refuse medication. Physicians too should be instructed on the dangers of drugs and the potential usefulness of counseling and referral services.

The federal agencies need to become more involved. The NIDA gives little priority to women and legal drugs. Traditionally NIDA has placed its interest and research in heroin. It is timely for NIDA, whose special mandate for the country is researching drug problems, to take a leadership role in this area. In addition, there are federal regulations covering prescription-drug advertisements which are supposedly enforced by the Food and Drug Administration (FDA). FDA warns that advertisements must not be false or misleading. There are a total of twenty-two specific practices in the Federal Register (section 1.105 (6) 27 June, 1968) related to prescription-drug advertising which come under the watchful eye of FDA. In addition to federal laws relating to this subject, the AMA has developed principles governing advertising in the AMA scientific publications. These principles follow rather closely the FDA guidelines. Only the pharmaceutical products approved by the FDA can appear in the AMA journal. The AMA also warns that the advertisement should not be deceptive or misleading. It is evident that despite FDA and AMA regulations and principles these bodies have been unable or unwilling to prevent advertisers from spreading a fallacious message in the area of psychiatry. It would appear that the FDA guidelines and the AMA principles give mental-drug advertisers a free hand in extending their products and thereby shaping treatment.[101] The result is that women continue to be identified as nervous, distraught, complaining, and unable to cope with the tensions and pressures that accompany daily life. They also continue to be made the victims of the drug industry and the medical and psychiatric professions. A massive national educational effort is critical to stop this continued drugging of women.

Woman as Bureaucratic Object

Bureaucracy is the formal organization by which a task is to be accomplished. It includes a pyramidal structure of authority as well as supposedly rational efficient means to accomplish a goal. One of the major organizational developments in this century has been the growth of bureaucracies. As they grew, they became more impersonal, wasteful, and difficult to hold accountable. More importantly, their growth seems to be related to speed or lack of it. As a result, getting something done can take an incredible amount of time. This is often due to the decision-making process which seems to lodge everywhere and nowhere simultaneously.

For women the growth of bureaucracies has particular importance. In the social welfare bureaucracies, for example, tradition has grown up over the years. Trying to change the system becomes very difficult. Regardless of how much society might be willing to alter toward women in any of the three institutions described below the bureaucratic structure works against it. Women in prisons, women on welfare, and women being treated in the mental-health systems are excellent examples of the way systems are using women to maintain themselves. Women caught up in these three institutions need more than rescuing from the system. The institution itself must be reshaped completely and rebuilt. Women should see these systems as adversaries. The bureaucracy needs its clients, its objects, and in these cases women are much easier to use than men. These institutions use women for their own survival. In addition, because of the bureaucratic nature real change is difficult if not impossible to achieve. The women's movement needs to understand the power of the prison, mental-health, and welfare bureaucracies over millions of women. It needs to combat this by an organizational, massive approach to change. The institutions of prison, welfare, and mental health hold the traditional view of women pictured in this chapter in their very fiber. This needs to be clearly perceived. Otherwise there will continue to be women in prison, on welfare, or in mental institutions far out of proportion to their numbers.

Prison System

Statement of the Problem

There are more than 15,000 women in our nation's prisons.[1] There are probably many thousands more in our 4,000 local, city, and county jails.

127

Experts in criminal justice warn that crime rates are rising every year. They also warn that women are committing more crimes. More than 1 million women were arrested in 1978, which represents 15 percent of all adult arrests in that year.[2] It is true that more women are being arrested and convicted than ever before. It is also true that women are receiving longer sentences. Between 1960 and 1972 the arrest rate for women rose three times higher than the arrest rate for men.[3]

Professional researchers in the field of female crime posit the theory that the nature of criminal behavior is changing and is becoming more violent. This would account for the fact that the number of women sentenced to federal prisons has increased by 81 percent in the last ten years. While approximately 21,000 women were arrested for violent crimes in 1977, this represents a mere 5 percent increase over ten years.[4] Freda Adler's theory as reported in her book *Sisters in Crime: The Rise of the New Female Criminal* is that women are becoming more aggressive, their crimes more violent, because of the women's liberation movement.[5] While part of this theory may have some validity, the idea of increasing violent crimes by women does not hold up in the statistics. There is, however, a new kind of female crime, not different in gravity and scope, that could be attributed to the changing role of women. Between 1960 and 1972 embezzlement by women rose 280 percent. During that same period, male embezzlement rose 50 percent. Larceny for women rose a staggering 303 percent, for men 82 percent.[6]

It is certainly valid to assume that much property crime is based on opportunity. One must have access to a computer to commit a computer crime, one must have access to financial books and records to embezzle large sums of money. Certainly, as women enter positions and professions in the labor market that give them access or opportunity, the crimes they commit will differ. But women, for the most part, have always committed crimes against property. They still do. Only shoplifting, bad checks, and petty theft are gradually expanding to become forgery, grand larceny, and embezzlement. "Shoplifting is still a popular means of getting extra cash for men and women alike, but many of today's hustlers have moved onto higher levels of sophistication. Women have found that forgery, embezzlement, and fraud bring in more money than a stolen typewriter or fur coat."[7]

There is a rise in white-collar crime among women and these crimes are committed largely by middle-class women. The vast majority of women in jails and prisons, however, are not middle class. They have been and remain today poor minority women who do not have access or opportunity to commit the bigger, more expensive crimes. These women have not been part of the feminist movement and liberation cannot have caused some nebulous new aggression that led them to crime. Still, the impact of feminism affects them but more indirectly.

The criminal-justice system is still operated and run by males: male police who decide to make an arrest; male prosecutors who determine the charge and decide whether or not to drop charges, prosecute, or plea bargain; male judges who determine guilt or innocence and the sentence. What may have been liberated is not these women but the attitudes and willingness of the male decision makers to arrest, convict, and incarcerate them. With bad-check writing and shoplifting having been and remaining the number one and number two offenses of female offenders, the nature of crimes women commit has remained fairly much the same; the ramifications of committing those crimes is what accounts for the dramatic increase in arrests, convictions, and numbers of women in jails and prisons.

The bulk of female crime is economic. These women are not zany Bonnies of the Bonnie and Clyde milieu who gave up waitressing to become bank robbers. The profile of the female inmate is that she is 25 or 26 years old, a member of a minority or ethnic group, from a poor background, usually having lived in an inner city. She is nonviolent, often having experience with drugs or narcotics.[8] Seventy to eighty percent of these women are mothers of small children and the vast majority of them are heads of households, single parents. Almost all have experienced severe economic pressure. Crime against property was an easy way of elevating those economic pressures. ' "It was so easy,' said Julie Veltoren, a twice-convicted check forger now at Goochland County. 'I hit every bank from Richmond to Alexandria (Virginia). I was writing those checks eight hours a day . . . I could make $9,000 in one morning.' 'But,' she said, 'I always got caught.' "[9]

Once caught, convicted, and sentenced, female offenders arrive at institutions. There, they find a system designed to "break them." They are forced to live with officials who have a certain attitude about women and certain attitudes about women lawbreakers.

> "They're grown up, but they act like they're in kindergarten . . ." and then pointing to a 50-year-old woman quarreling with another inmate, "She is my problem child." Lieutenant Archibald, Riker's Island.

> Marjorie T. Ward, director of the Women's Division at Arizona State Prison: "They don't have that much time to lollygag around. They're generally busy . . . we keep them busy . . . plus we're constantly watching them."[10]

Women are children in jails and prisons. Privileges and parole depend on how compliant one can appear, how docile one can become. Lack of spunk or spirit will keep one out of what prison officials refer to as "solitary reflection," "peace and quiet," or the "adjustment cell"; cells that are housed in buildings C-cells inmates refer to as the "hole" or the "rack."[11]

They must not only cope with guards (the bulk of whom are male) and administrative attitudes, highly structured routine, and backbreaking, dull work but must also learn to survive (passively) with other inmates in an environment packed with tension, anger, and frustration; where rivalry flares between short-termers and long-termers; and where bad-check writers bunk beside murderers.

While most female offenders are heterosexual before incarceration, 60 to 80 percent of them will enter into homosexual relationships while doing their time. Some of this can be attributed to loneliness and need for warmth and intimacy, but a large part of homosexuality in female prisons has to do with fear and survival. The studbroad is usually a leader in the prison community. She is often large and strong, with hardened, curt laughter, rough talk, hair slicked back and cropped, long pants, and frequently wears male underwear. In exchange for "favors" and sometimes as much as $20 a week, the studbroad protects one or more lovers from the others. These groups become families of sorts with the studbroad as matriarch. Unlike homosexuality in male prisons, however, homosexual relationships in women's prisons are almost never forced; there is almost never inner fighting among inmates over these relationships. And once a woman is released, she returns to heterosexual preference.[12]

By far, the most difficult problem for women in prisons and jails has to do with children. With 70 percent of all female prisoners being mothers of an average of three small children, there are more than 21,000 children who have mothers behind bars.[13] And these children are also punished: "Punishment has traditionally been targeted against the individual offender. In the past, it was extended to the family through confiscation of rights and property. More subtle ways of punishing the children of prisoners endure. Frightened by the sudden removal of a parent, these children are left to face the imprint of stigma, the mockery of peers, the enforced isolation, the sense that those placed in physical charge of their lives do not really want or love them, and the uncertainty about their future. This punishment is beyond measure."[14]

Women prisoners know the anguish of their children. They know the torment of not having the time to explain the separation of being far away, perhaps for as long as ten years or an average of four or five. "For mothers who care, part of the anguish is knowing the children have suffered alone, frequently from when the mother was arrested, and taken away without ever having the opportunity to explain what was happening. The situation can intensify with courtroom drama."[15]

Most children whose mothers "do time" are left with relatives: fathers, grandparents, sisters, aunts. Many of these relatives have serious problems. Other children are split up and farmed out to foster homes. Often the mother loses track of where her children are. Children rarely visit their mothers during incarceration. Many institutions discourage or even forbid it, saying prisons are no place for children. Some women do not want to subject their children to the humiliation of a body search or to the prison itself. Some do not want their children to see them behind bars. When there are so few facilities for women, as in the state of Virginia, some women are just too far away to have their families visit them.

After years of separation, a woman is suddenly thrown out with little or no preparation for a reunion with her children. They no longer know each other. There is guilt and anger that have built up over the years. There are jealous grandparents who want to keep the children they have raised. There are families who do not want the children subjected to the negative influence of a criminal mother. There are women who fight courts, welfare, and foster parents for years to get their children back. There are women who cannot even find their children.

Some women's prisons have begun programs (Nebraska, Minnesota, Tennessee, and California) to help women make this difficult transition and rebond with their children. In a Santa Clara, California, facility an apartment-type model has been set up where children live with their mothers and go to a day-care center while their mothers are on work release. With rent charged on a sliding scale, this program almost pays for itself. The Federal Correctional Institution at Pleasant has started a Pregnant-Inmate Program, probably the only one in the nation, where women and their newborns can live together for six months. In most prisons, infants are taken from their mothers within minutes, hours, or days of birth. The consequences of this policy for the emotional bonding between newborn and mother could be tremendous but no research has been done on the subject.

Little is being done to put programs, let alone meaningful programs, in women's prisons. With few exceptions, women's prisons do not offer realistic employment training. In jails, such programs are nonexistent. The little training available is useless; machinery is outdated and not used in the commercial world. Women are trained in sex-role-stereotyped skills and in obsolescence. Few prisons have staff trained to help with the emotional or the physical needs (obstetrics and gynecology, for example) of their populations. Practically no attention has been paid to the inmates who are mothers. The efforts to get funding to develop useful and meaningful programs for women in jails and prisons have been turned down by legislators and sheriffs because, they say, "They are not running a Holiday Inn" and "because these women broke the law and need punishment, not prizes."[16]

The public is apathetic or antagonistic, or believe that prisons could not really be that bad because, like Goochland described below, they look so good with their tennis courts and putting courses. As a result, for many women offenders, getting out of prison is as horrifying as going in. "A man released from prison usually has a home and a family to return to. Not so for most women behind bars because the average female offender is single yet responsible

for some children, she has to re-establish a home and family. . . . Some women
fresh out of prison are afraid to make change at the drugstore, to rent an apart-
ment, let alone face a potential employer who may take a dim view of hiring
an 'ex-con.' "[17]

Inside the Prison System

The following visits were done by Deborah Millikan, a professional worker
for the Offender Aid and Restroration (OAR) Association. OAR is a national
organization dedicated to assisting prisoners, with headquarters in Charlottesville, Virginia. She visited the two facilities for incarcerated women as part
of her work. This is her unique and vivid description of the prison scene.

> Jackie was smart, striking with her strong but slight body. She had grown
> up in a family splintered by the stresses of poverty. Her father had only
> stayed long enough to molest her sexually; she had been 9 years old.
> Jackie's mother had never known about that or, if she did, she never let
> anyone know she knew. She grew up in a town that grew up around the
> navy. Norfolk, Virginia—in the Tidewater Basin never really prospered.
> Blacks bore the brunt of the dearth in affluence. Jackie learned early how
> to deal with the poverty and the physical, emotional, and economic
> threats that went along with it.
>
> By age 17, Jackie had been arrested and held on charges of truancy, sexual
> promiscuity, petty theft, incorrigibility. By 18, she arrived in the Gooch-
> land Industrial Farm for Women. It would be the first of three convictions
> of felonies. Jackie had written one too many bad checks, too many times.
>
> From the appearance of Goochland Industrial Farm for Women, one
> would think one was standing on the campus of an exclusive private
> Southern women's college. There are no electric-wire fences around the
> women's state prisons; there are white fences and colonial brick struc-
> tures—"dormitories," they call them—settled in rolling, green hills. Enter-
> ing the main administrative building, one is struck by the smiling faces.
> One nearly forgets that one is in the only correctional institution for women
> in the state, that the institution is filled with felons: female offenders.
>
> The male counselor arrives in the waiting room which is full of geraniums
> and other potted plants, some of the healthiest, plumpest plants in the
> state. One is struck at how relaxed he is. He hands over a release form.
> One must sign this form before going on the prearranged tour. The form
> releases the state and the institution from any liability should harm come
> to one or should anyone be "taken hostage" by hostile female inmates.
> One begins to remember where one is and a sense that something is brew-
> ing under the surface—something that cannot be controlled—begins to
> emerge. One signs. As one walks out the door to the beautiful, winding
> road dotted with trees and circled with those white fences, the smell of
> honeysuckle is in the air. There are tennis courts perched at the base of
> the mountain, eight all-weather courts with no one on them.

We are told that the correctional institution was built in the mid-1930s. Jackie, dressed in a white cotton shift she made herself, takes the group to the "Honor Dormitory" where the "girls" who "earn trust" can go to bed at 11:00 P.M. instead of 10:00 P.M. and have many other privileges. What these other privileges were remained unclear. No one was in the Honor Dormitory.

Next stop was the medical building. Complete with its own pharmacy and two physicians for 295 women (Goochland's capacity is 300), the antiseptic odor crept into our nostrils until everyone gasped for clean air. Three women in cutoff jeans mopped and remopped the floors around us. They told us these women had not earned honor dorm status.

"Can honor dorm inmates go on furlough?" someone asked.

"Of course," came the smiling answer from Jackie.

"What if the honor dorm inmates get pregnant?"

"Oh," she answered, "long before we go on furlough the doctors give us whatever kind of birth control we want."

The male counselor seemed surprised at Jackie's answer.

"What if someone gets pregnant anyway?"

"Well," she answered assuredly, "any woman who is pregnant either when she gets here or gets pregnant while she is here has to be separated from the rest of us and so she comes here, goes into one of these rooms in the infirmary, until she has the baby."

"What happens to the baby?"

"We call the welfare department after it is born, or relatives."

"Does the mother get to see her baby?"

"For a little while."

"Is abortion an option that is discussed with a pregnant inmate?"

The male counselor was obviously shaken by this question.

"Why yes," he said quickly. "It is an option for the girls."

And one of the mopping inmates blurted, "Yeah, but by the time you go through the paperwork and the bullshit you're in your last month and it's too late."

Jackie and the male counselor smiled nervously. She was obviously not honor dorm material. (The parole board will hear about this one.)

"Who pays for the abortions?"

"Oh, um."

"The state?"

"Yeah," he answered quietly, "the state. Let's move on to our vocational training." Jackie was quiet for the first time on the tour.

Vocational training at Goochland is designed to teach jobless, underskilled, single-parent inmates a trade that will see them through once they get on the outside. According to Al, the male counselor, 95 percent of the inmate population has never finished high school. Many have never held steady jobs. With the mean age of 25, most prisoners in the Goochland Industrial Farm are there on convictions of property offenses; bad checks reign the number-one offense followed by forgery and, in the last several years, by drug-related offenses.

Jackie and Al say that they are proud of the progress they have made in their employment training programs. They have made inroads in the last five years.

The first stop was to one of the Incentive Work Programs. Here women are paid wages according to their productivity output. The door to the colonial building opened. A female guard led the group to another door which poured steam and heat once the giant lock opened. There, at last were the inmates in the laundry; noisy to the point where one's ears screamed for relief: gigantic industrial washers and driers, large machinery a steam-bath in June's ninety-five degree heat. There were job slots for some forty women in this laundry which contracted for services with the state to do the laundry for state hospitals, work crews, and the male state prison.

"Is this a work program that is sought after?" I asked.

"Oh yes," answered Jackie.

"Why?"

"Because here you can earn up to $100 a month but in nonincentive jobs you can only earn around $50.

Later we learned that the inmates at Goochland often sent monies they earned home to their own mothers and grandmothers to help pay for the care of their children. Yes, the money was important. Even when incarcerated, inmates at Goochland were still single parents.

Other employment training programs for women at Goochland include cosmetology training: women who are accepted to this program become hairdressers and can take the state certification boards at the farm. Of course, employers know where they received their training. If they can get a job when they get out, these women can expect to earn $150 per week.

Industrial sewing: the day of the tour at Goochland, women were making caps, like an assembly line, each woman never making a complete cap, but cutting or stitching the same piece over and over again in a hot, little room built in the mid-1940s. The caps and other garments made by the women in this employment training program were for the men from the state's male prison's work release, road crews. Most industrial sewers earn minimum wage unless they are unionized. Few industries are unionized in the South where these women will be working.

Key punch: there are thirty women sitting hour after hour typing letters onto tapes for the Virginia Employment Commission with promises of secure, high-paying jobs once they are trained and released. With the boredom inherent in the job of key punching, there is a large turnover in the labor pool but key punchers still earn minimum wage on the outside, according to the Virginia Employment Commission.

The commissary: where inmates at Goochland can buy cosmetics, candy bars, sanitary supplies, and greeting cards. Women working in the commissary learn how to stock shelves and run cash registers. Managers of the commissary, the beauty parlor, the key-punch operation, and the laundry are not inmates but state employees.

Women at Goochland have some opportunity to take college courses or can get their GED. Everyone works at least half a day in some job whether it is mopping or key punching or cooking the food for the honor dorm. Classrooms are small. In fact, the smallest building at Goochland is the school, which is some indication of the priority placed on education. The library is smaller still and filled with dime novels, most very old.

After spending two hours at the Women's Industrial Farm at Goochland everything seemed sugar and spice. There was a drama club that had just put on the musical *Annie*. There was the greenhouse that, run by inmates under supervision, provided all the plants for the governor's mansion, public libraries, and official ceremonies. Sweet, smiling faces almost everywhere one went until . . . the group came to the building where women on C status were housed. No one was allowed within 100 yards of this building.

The June 1980 issue of the *Virginia Guardian*, an American Civil Liberties publication, reported on a woman named Safiya Asya Bukhari who has been locked in solitary confinement in the Goochland facility since March 1977. Ms. Bukhari is a member of the Black Liberation Army; she is a political prisoner. The men arrested with her and housed in the men's correctional facility only several miles from Goochland have been in the general population for some time. There is a law suit pending on the grounds of equal protection. Ms. Bukhari is in solitary confinement in the building the group was not allowed to see.

The contrast of building C to the other buildings on campus is startling. The windows are small with thick-wire netting. The door is thick and gray with large bolts. The bricks are dirty and dark. The building is frightening. It was said that it would not be safe to go into this building. Even though most of the group have worked in corrections and directly in jails and prisons before, they were told that protection was needed from these women. More than likely the institution needed protection from the discovery of the conditions in the building.

Later the group interviewed a woman who has spent time in Goochland's building C. The cells are tiny and dark, she says. The guards, some male, some female, are abusive. There are some cells with mattresses on the floors; there are some cells with nothing on the cement floors. Some cells have toilets, some have only holes. And until the last two years, when the state passed a statute requirement of at least one normal meal per day, inmates housed in building C could actually be forced to live on bread and water.

Despite the putt-putt course, the tennis courts, the theaters, and the schoolhouse, there is no other facility in the state of Virginia that houses women offenders. A large percentage of the Goochland inmates have homes more than 150 miles away in the Tidewater-Norfolk area. Goochland also houses misdemeanants at the discretion of their judges so that minor offenders are placed in the same correctional facility as more serious offenders. The outcome of the lack of other female facilities in the state is that women offenders in Virginia are separated from family and friends by tremendous distances. Unable to visit, families lose touch, ties and bonds are broken during periods of incarceration which range from less than one year to life.

To survive at Goochland, to avoid building C, women must become girls. Streetwise Jackie must pretend she loves to play putt-putt. She must say to the male counselor that she is not worthy of parole. She must join the drama club, take visitors on tours, wear dresses she made for herself, do laundry for male prisoners, discuss at length the flowers to be sent to the governor's mansion. In short, Jackie and other Honor

Dormitory or A-classification women at Goochland must become passive-dependent, visibly demure, verbally grateful for training that is obsolete and demeaning, for labor markets that are flooded and that pay minimum wages.

Jackie was asked why she was a three-timer. She said she knew what her trouble was, it was money; she could not find a job on the outside even though she had passed the cosmetology certification and was now an experienced seamstress. She has not seen her two children in more than a year. The first two times her mother took them but, with her third conviction, the court ordered in the child protective services from the Welfare Department and Jackie's children are in a foster home. She is not sure where. She says she will have trouble getting them back once she makes parole in about a year. This often happens in the lives of female offenders.

The majority of women at Goochland have been in some local jail before they were sent out to the Big House. Knowing this, a visit was paid to the women's section of Richmond City Jail.

Capacity at the Richmond Jail is 600. On the day of the visit, the inmate population was 601. Because of a Virginia state statute, saying that men are not allowed to see or hear female inmates (it might cause a riot), the female section is totally isolated and apa.t from anything else in the jail. The capacity in the women's section is about 100. On the day of the visit, there were approximately sixty-five female prisoners.

Jails are full of a variety of people; mostly poor, minority people. Women, both in the Richmond Jail and at Goochland, are no different from the general population of jail inmates. Ninety-five percent of the female population at both institutions are black. Eighty to ninety-five percent have less than a high-school degree. The vast majority are nonviolent having committed property crimes.

If Goochland was a travesty, the Richmond City Jail is a breathing seething hell. There are three large cell blocks, each crowding thirty beds and thirty women into each block. One of the blocks is designated for misdemeanants but if the cell gets full, it is not unusual for a misdemeanant awaiting trial to be placed in the cot next to a woman waiting to go to Goochland for a life sentence, even though the mixture of misdemeanants and felons is prohibited under a state statute.

Guards talk about how much more difficult the women prisoners are to handle. While there are seldom full-blown riots in women's sections, there are little outbursts of violence, offender on offender. The day before our visit one older inmate badly hurt a younger cellmate by hitting her with the shower head. The young woman was not in the hospital.

The large room where the three cells are is hot and the air is thick and still. Crowded elbow to elbow, cot to cot, two feet apart, women are woken at 6:15 A.M., fed in cell-block sections beginning at 6:30 A.M. No television is allowed until 11:00 A.M. No one is sure why there is this rule. After breakfast, the women go back to their cell blocks and cots to sleep until 11:00 A.M. when they are taken out, block by block, to eat lunch all on the same floor. Women in the Richmond Jail never leave that floor. The television comes on at 11:00 A.M. Arguments break out about which shows will be watched. Some play cards, most sleep because the heat is staggering.

There are two educators employed at the Richmond Jail, but with 500+ men prisoners to teach, they spend one hour in the women's section; but it is sporadic and most days they do not get there at all. Because the law states that male inmates may not see or hear female inmates, women in the Richmond City Jail are not allowed outside to recreation areas. Males in the same facility go out for regularly scheduled exercise; there are basketball nets, large open court yards to move around in. Males too have recreation rooms away from the cell blocks. They move throughout the entire facility. Women remain confined to a small area on the second floor void of activity, movement, education, recreation, with no diversion from the crowded, locked cell blocks. So taxing is the jail experience that many women actually ask for space in the solitary cells across the hall. Be it for safety or solitude. The only reprieve women have in this jail is to move to what should be the most punitive area.

With few marketable skills, the stigma of being an offender, guilt, no money, children, singleness, no job, a poor self-image, few coping skills, small wonder the women offender returns to jail and to prison over and over again.
      "Jackie, do you think you'll stay out next time?"
      "No," she whispered and looked into the eyes of the author, "no."

Strategies

As overwhelming as this subject may be, organizations like OAR can do much to bring the plight of women in prisons to the public's attention. OAR aims to reduce confinement in jail of nondangerous offenders, including misdemeanants, public inebriates, mentally ill and retarded persons, and juveniles. To this end, the Edna McConnel Clark Foundation for 1979 awarded OAR a planning grant for the Alternatives to Jail Project. The foundation followed the initial award with a two-year action grant to establish a spectrum of alternatives to jail in three cities: Fairfax, Virginia; Knoxville, Tennessee; and Lincoln, Nebraska.

OAR/USA has begun to assess each community in order to develop a comprehensive set of alternatives specifically tailored to meet each community's needs. OAR is considering pretrial options such as citations, release on recognizance, and third-party custody; and exploring sentencing alternatives such as restitution, community service orders, increased use of probation, alcohol and drug treatment, and job training and placement and specific needs for female offenders. At the same time the local core groups of the project are nurturing community involvement. They are consulting with local judges and corrections officials and establishing contacts with business, labor, and civic leaders.

Almost a decade of experience working in jails in a wide range of communities has given OAR/USA a clear understanding of the jail crisis, especially in relation to women. Local communities have the resources and power to reduce the number of people confined in jail. Thus, OAR/USA is supporting the alternatives project staff with its extensive experience in community development, use of volunteers, and development of citizen awareness. OAR/USA is also providing technical assistance in creating, funding, and evaluating alternative programs.[18] In addition, the following recommendations developed by the Women's Prison Association clearly delineate some needed strategies:

1. Record-keeping procedures on women prisoners need to be revised.
2. Improved methods of treatment are needed to reduce recidivism.
3. First priority should be jobs and job training.
4. Expansion of diversionary treatment programs.
5. More emphasis on community-based correction.
6. Expansion of work release and school release.
7. More attention should be given to the children of women offenders.
8. Abolish sex-based discrimination in the criminal-justice system.
9. Public education programs to emphasize problems.[19]

All women need to be concerned with assisting this group of women, who in many ways are in the most helpless, powerless position in our society.

Welfare System

The United States, through its federal, state, and local agencies, administers a system of financial and other assistance to certain categories of needy people. This assistance is provided through the public welfare system which consists of two programs: the Supplemental Security Income (SSI) program and the Aid to Families with Dependent Children (AFDC) program.

These public-assistance programs were born out of the Social Security Act of 1935. SSI was established through legislation in October 1972 (P.L. 92-603). It is a program of uniform national, minimum cash income to aged, blind, and disabled individuals. SSI replaced the state-administered programs of Old Age Assistance, Aid to the Blind, Aid to the Permanently and Totally Disabled, and the combined programs of Aid to the Aged, Blind and Disabled which were earlier programs under the Social Security Act. The administration of SSI was assigned to the Social Security Administration (SSA) of the Department of Health and Human Services (HHS) formerly HEW. Within SSA, the Bureau of Supplemental Security Income was given early administrative responsibility. SSI is 100 percent federally funded through open-ended appropriations from federal general revenues. Persons who are age 65 and over, blind, or disabled as defined in the Social Security Act, and whose income and resources are below the limits specified in the act are eligible for SSI benefits. Calculations of the benefit level for an individual or for a married couple in which both spouses are eligible with respect to age, blindness, or disability must take into account both the earned and unearned income of the applicants.[20]

Aid to Dependent Children (ADC) was the forerunner of the AFDC program. In a 1961 amendment to the Social Security Act, the ADC program was retitled and called Aid to Families with Dependent Children. The objective of AFDC as defined by statute is "to enable each state to furnish financial assistance, rehabilitation, and other services in order to encourage the care of dependent children in their own homes or in the homes of relatives with whom they are living to help such parents or relatives to attain or retain the capability for self-support, and to help maintain and strengthen family life."[21] The new focus revised the program and stressed the essential nature of the family in society and permitted the states to include at their option, coverage of families with unemployed parents (AFDC-UP).[22]

AFDC provides cash assistance with funds from federal, state, and local governments to children who are lacking adequate parental support. Federal and state statutes and regulations govern benefit levels, eligibility, and treatment of income. Eligibility for cash benefit is based on several criteria in addition to financial needs. The Unemployed Parents' program, which has never included more than 5 percent of the total AFDC recipients, gives aid to homes in which there is a dependent child (legitimate or illegitimate), younger than 18 or 21, who has been deprived of parental support by reason of death, disability, divorce, or desertion and is fully enrolled in public school, vocational school, or college. At its inception, the program catered chiefly to children in need because of the death of one parent, usually the father. As Old Age Survivors, Disability Insurance (OASDI) programs expanded to meet the problems of dependence owing to death and the family system became more unstable, the chief recipients of AFDC became children who were in need by reason of divorce or desertion.[23]

Statement of the Problem

The general objective of the AFDC program is to encourage the care of dependent children in their homes by their parent and to help the parent maintain the family life. In 95 percent of cases the parent is the mother. Fathers have never been expected to care for children. The children become the mother's economic burden if the father chooses not to support the family. Society has traditionally defined the woman's place as in the home caring for the children. There are increasing signs of change in this ideology. More increasingly women are being urged to work. With this trend has also come changes in the policy of the AFDC programs. The policy has shifted from one of encouraging mothers to stay at home and care for the children to that of getting out and working. Legislation enacted to support this policy was the Work Incentive (WIN) program. The WIN program was designed to encourage women to work. Although this policy could have been an asset to welfare mothers, it did not provide other needed benefits. If the welfare mother did get a job, she could seldom get ahead because no day care was provided. If she had to pay day-care costs out of her earnings, she usually had less than what she would have had gotten from AFDC. In essence, the WIN program was a disincentive to work because of its inequities. Day care was not the only issue involved in the WIN program. Program participants had their earnings deducted from their AFDC checks. This further discouraged women from working because there was little chance for any of them to come out ahead.

The transfer of the administration of the adult welfare categories (blind, aged, and disabled) to the SSA under the SSI program has profound implications for women. This program is routine and federalized and has minimal regulations. There is no stigma to being on SSI. The result is that AFDC has the only large category of economically dependent people who can clearly be considered as "undeserving" that is, (welfare mothers).[24] The institution of welfare now has a caseload that is 95 percent women. They become an easy target and are branded as "chiselers" and "lazy." In reality they are the most vulnerable and least powerful group of women in our society, hardly an economic threat as politicians often brand them.

Overall, the policy decisions regarding the welfare system have played an important role in further stigmatizing and dehumanizing welfare recipients. The lack of adequate policy has also added to the financial burden of women on welfare in other ways. For example, though there are laws that require fathers to contribute support to the family unit, in many instances the laws are not adequately enforced. A father deserts the family and becomes unreachable. He moves away, refuses to answer summons or letters from the Welfare Department, or just drops out of sight. Enforcing the laws and developing more stringent guidelines will eliminate some of the stress and pressures to which women are subjected. Fathers need to be tried and fined and jailed for breaking the law. Why the legal system has let them get away so easily is a shocking indictment of a double standard toward certain crimes by our law-enforcement officials.

Social Workers and Welfare

The public-welfare system historically and in more recent times can be characteristically identified as a social work institution. The social work profession has its roots in the nineteenth-century charity groups. The groups established a position as protector of the poor and downtrodden. The protective relationship implies inequality, meaning one group protects the other. There exists here an underlying assumption that there is a deficit in the ability of a person or group to protect themselves. They therefore needed some assistance in looking out for their interests.[25] With a striving toward professionalization, social workers identified a discrete body of knowledge which was appropriate for a client group whose main characteristic was an inability, due to numerous circumstances, to live independently or without financial assistance from an outside source. As the social work profession developed, they assumed an increasingly active protectionist role. The protectionist philosophy has encouraged women to strive to be traditional homemakers. The protectionist view argued that men and women were not equal and could not be compelled by industry to perform and produce as if they were. This ideology was the foundation on which the social work profession was built. The concern was for the less fortunate, particularly poor women and children unattached to economically secure men. Their link to economic security had been cut and their defenselessness left them in need of protection.[26]

As society progressed over the decades, so did the social work profession and the welfare system, though the social work profession still assumed the protectionist role. Through welfare reform, the public-welfare system was shaped and reshaped, mostly through the influence of social work and social policy professionals. Unfortunately this was congruent with the values of the larger society that could use women as scapegoats and blame the economic ills of the country on the welfare costs. An example of the reshaping and changes that occurred can be seen in the AFDC program. The program was based on the ideology that woman's role was that of child rearer and homemaker. Through development of social welfare policy the ideology changed and began endorsing mandatory work requirements, all the while harassing the recipients and pushing them toward conforming to this ideology.[27] It is apparent now that there were no mechanisms built into the policy design that would provide an incentive to the recipient to work (arrangements for day care, provide training, and remove financial penalties for working). The failure of the policy to work implicated not the designers of the policy, the social workers, but the AFDC women instead. They were seen as defective not only in maintaining a stable family relationship but also in lacking the abilities to hold down a full-time job that provided an adequate income on which to live. The ultimate outcome of the protectionist viewpoint was the segregation and stigmatization of women on welfare.[28] In essence, the AFDC women were victimized by the social work profession as well as society. The system of values in social work advocated assisting those who were unable to contend with the injustices of society on their own. Part of this value was the importance of the family unit and a child's need for close ties with parents. Women were urged to stay home with their children. As a result, they were made dependent on the welfare system. For the most part, they were uneducated and had very few if any marketable skills. Unconsciously, but with honorable intentions the social work profession helped create the plight of welfare women in today's society.

Role of Women in the Welfare System

This section might be more appropriately titled if the prefix *non* were attached to role because it more adequately describes the position of women on welfare. AFDC recipients, particularly women, are controlled almost totally by the welfare system. They are deprived of taking much initiative on their own for fear of repercussions by the welfare worker, or they are unable to do anything in terms of self-advancement because they lack the skills and the education. A study of the typical AFDC family revealed an average of 2.6 children, one of whom is a preschooler. There is no father in the home. The mother has not completed high school but has had some prior work experience, most likely as a service worker.[29] This pattern applies to about two-thirds of all AFDC households.[30] Economically women fare worse than men and as a result are sometimes discouraged from working. For example, statistics indicate that (1) earnings of all full-time year-round workers over age 18 in 1973 showed the median income of men to be \$10,201; for women the median income was \$5,970 or 58 percent of the males' earnings; and (2) the median annual income for women with eight years or less of education were much lower; \$4,303 but still 57 percent of the earnings of men with a similar education.[31]

Data on women in AFDC and female-headed families in poverty is even worse: (1) it is estimated that this group of women would be likely to attain median earnings of \$5,037 a year if fully employed; and (2) 20 percent of all AFDC women have eight years or less of education and could look forward to a median income of \$4,300.[32]

AFDC can be described as the poor women's institution.[33] There is an implication that women on AFDC are, as a class, poverty-stricken because of a voluntary decision. They have deliberately disrupted a traditional and an honored source of income: dependence on the male breadwinner. Implied here is that as a class, they can now be described as having left the normative standards and can in fact be labeled socially deviant and in need of society's control.[34] This is exactly what happens to a woman who is a recipient of assistance from the welfare system.

A recent in-depth study of a group of thirty-five women who had received AFDC benefits depicts the various measures the welfare system uses to control women. It should be noted that the figures presented here represent respondents who mentioned this information in the course of a wide-ranging open-ended discussion. Information from such open-ended interviews probably underestimates the number of women who actually experienced these things. The percentages are offered only as rough guidelines to the frequency of each experience and opinion. Respondents in the study indicated the following:

1. Fifty-four percent of the women reported that they were not given enough information about the benefits and programs available to them.

2. Seventy percent felt that the welfare system had control of their lives in more ways than one. This was related to privacy and things they owned.

3. Thirty-four percent of women felt that they had little control as consumers. They were limited in choice of housing and were unable to get credit.

4. Sixty-three percent of the women felt that they had little control over their economic security. They were not told how decisions were made which related to their allotment, and benefits were cut or terminated at any time.

5. Sixty percent reported experiencing occasional derogation from their caseworkers. They also said that the bad attitudes toward them were also dehumanizing and demeaning.

6. A majority of the women also expressed their feelings on how stressful it was to receive benefits from a welfare system that was inadequate and could not meet their needs. Instead of paying a recommended third of their income for rent, some were having to pay half. There was never enough money for school clothes for the children, or busfare, or all the other expenses that are a part of daily living.[35]

It is evident by some of the responses that the welfare system and AFDC are doing an injustice to women. Welfare, in all its efforts to assist an impoverished population, has fostered dependency and helplessness.

The Welfare Experience: Breaking Away

Throughout the history of the welfare system, it is evident that there have been a shortage of programs that encouraged and assisted women to seek independence from welfare. Programs have been implemented but they simply have not been adequate. Studies suggest that women who do attain independence do so mainly through their own efforts.[36] The following excerpts and insights on the welfare system were taken from interviews with two women who were AFDC recipients and who through their own efforts achieved independence from welfare. They are presently social workers with MSW degrees. While students in schools of social work neither felt able to come out as a welfare mother. Even there the stigma of welfare was felt by them and by the enlightened, so to speak, social work faculty and classmates. For confidentiality purposes, the two women will be referred to as Ms. A and Ms. B.

Both women experienced long-term involvement with the welfare system. Ms. A was a recipient for eight years and Ms. B for approximately fifteen years. The circumstances that brought them to the welfare system were different, but the need was the same. Ms. A is a black 26-year-old woman with one child. She became pregnant while in high school with the child being born shortly after graduation. Her parents were not in a position financially to take care of her and the child. She became a welfare recipient six months after the child was born. She continued in a relationship with the child's father and later married him when the child was 3 years old. She remained married for less than one year. After the separation, she had the father adjudicated as the biological parent which required him to make child-support payments. These payments were made directly to the welfare department with the amount of child-support payment being deducted from the recipient's monthly income. Ms. A went through five social workers in the eight years that she was on welfare.

Ms. B is a 42-year-old white woman. She was in her early twenties when she became a welfare recipient. She has three children who at the time were 1, 3, and 5 years old. She had separated from her husband (later divorced) who provided no financial support. He was issued a court order to support her and the children but he ignored it. When Ms. B first received welfare she saw it as a blessing because it helped her get by.[37] Ms. B now felt that she was victimized by the welfare system. It took her one year to get on the welfare rolls. They denied her assistance when she first applied because there was a court order for her husband to provide support. The fact that he never did was not considered by her welfare worker. Ms. B reported that she finally had to get the police to convince the welfare department that she was in need of assistance. She took her children and went to the police station to get help. The welfare program finally accepted her.

Both women felt that the welfare system provided little encouragement or incentive to get off the AFDC roles. Ms. B felt that the welfare workers wanted to keep them on to save their own jobs. The WIN program was available, but Ms. A considered it as almost useless in meeting her needs from an economic or work-related viewpoint. One question that both women were asked, was whether or not the welfare system had victimized them as women. Ms. B felt that she had been made a victim because she was placed in a position that allowed her no chance to ask questions. She felt that to get her check, she was to do as she was told. She indicated that she disliked the way she was treated. She said the welfare workers came into her house to look around and that they were always asking questions about what men she was seeing. Ms. A reported that the welfare worker would sometimes come to her home while she was away and ask her neighbors about her activities.

Both women were asked to describe what it was like being a welfare mother. Ms. A's response: "Being a welfare mother is like being a welfare child because of the paternalistic flavor of a system that takes care of you. You never feel like you're an adult or can make decisions because you're attached through an economic umbilical cord. Road blocks are put in your way at every turn. It perpetuates your being a liar and a cheater because they can track you through your social security number to see if you are working and getting extra money. It's difficult, very difficult."[38]

Ms. B's response: "Terrible. It's hard trying to bring up kids when other people around you have things that you and your children don't. People on welfare don't live, they exist. Welfare people aren't future-oriented. They can't be. They're always planning for today and what's for supper. The system forces you to do things that you wouldn't usually do. I feel that the system is there to keep you in your place."[39]

Both women felt that they were stigmatized by being on welfare. Ms. A felt that there was the stigma of not working in a work-oriented society. You are not supposed to accept money without working for it. Ms. B felt the stigma when she paid for her groceries with food stamps. She always felt like people were looking at her. Ms. B said that there was also a stigma attached to living in public housing. "If you live in public housing everybody knew you were on welfare." Ms. A reported that she felt no stigma attached to using food stamps because she shopped at a local grocery store. The people in her home area were equally poor and also used food stamps.

As mentioned previously, both women through their own efforts freed themselves from the control of the welfare system. Neither woman's parents were welfare recipients. They were not born into the welfare system but sought its assistance at a time when they had no other resource. Both women were able to get off welfare by getting an education. Ms. A got her bachelor's degree in three years and went on to get her master's degree. Ms. B also got a master's degree. Both of them became professional social workers (specializing in CO and planning). Ms. B reported that the welfare system does not encourage education. They do not gear women to enter colleges and universities but urge them to take vocational courses. She feels this is a short-term solution. Ms. B said that she feels that education is the only realistic way of getting off welfare and economic independence is best for the mother and the children. "If parents stay on welfare, the children usually do too. The mother is an important role model."[40] At the present time, all three of Ms. B's children are attending college.

Ms. A said that she had always been motivated educationally. She received no help from the welfare system in going to school. She financed her education through loans and awards. The schools in granting awards did not question the welfare status. As a result, awards were based on ability and economic level. In essence, one institution, the educational, was responsible for helping these women fight the other institution, welfare. Her parents were very supportive of her going to school and took care of her child while she did. Ms. A said that she had one of the best welfare workers when she was going to school. When asked to elaborate on this, she replied that she was the best one because: "She did not hinder or interfere. She didn't help too much, but she didn't hinder me."[41]

Both women were asked about alternatives and strategies they would use to change the welfare system. They were unanimous in recommending a way of finding the fathers and making them accountable. They felt that the welfare system did an inadequate job of tracking down the fathers and making them pay child support. They also felt that the system should provide more economic stability and should give the recipients more viable alternatives to what welfare currently has to offer. These two women were also unanimous in their belief that the only way to get off welfare permanently is through education.

Strategies for Change

The welfare system is in need of change. The changes can be made through reform and development of policy that will favor AFDC women. Although the social work profession has contributed to the plight of the poor and AFDC women, they are the profession that can bring about the needed change and can play a key role in balancing the inequities by which women are judged and treated. The approach should form a social policy perspective that says it is economically wise to work toward removing women from welfare rolls besides being psychologically good. The following strategy recommendations should be developed by society and in particular by the social work profession.

1. Enact and support new public policy that will allow poor women a better opportunity to do things they have been unable to do under the current policy of AFDC programs, that is, work, go to school.
2. Assume an active role of advocacy for women. This advocacy should be apparent by a true commitment to women's issues.
3. Reduce the welfare system's control over the recipients' life. This is aimed at the power issues and the need for the welfare mother to feel she has some control over her life.
4. Provide more information on what is available through the welfare system.
5. Advocate to increase the benefits of the AFDC programs to an adequate living standard.
6. Work to eliminate the stigma that accompanies being on welfare.
7. Design the work programs so they are financially advantageous to the welfare recipient to gain.
8. Provide day care to working mothers; this is critical.
9. Do not penalize women financially when they work.
10. Give them better opportunities for education and training.
11. Staff the welfare system with trained, qualified professionals who have a perspective not of protector but of advocate.

Clearly many changes can and must be made in the welfare system. If changes are not made, the system will continue to victimize recipients. The social work profession could have the knowledge and the ability to bring about these changes. It is its responsibility to enlighten society. It is the responsibility of all citizens to understand that welfare is clearly a woman's issue and the welfare mother has become the scapegoat of society and politicians. The children on welfare are children whether they be legitimate or illegitimate of two parents, mother and father. Society must begin to recognize the responsibility of the welfare father who criminally does not support his children and gets away with this. For every welfare mother, there is a welfare father somewhere.

Mental-Health System

The mental-health institution in our society has inadvertently discriminated against and victimized women. Psychology and psychiatry are male-dominated professions. The result is a sexist orientation with standards with which women are expected to conform. These standards, or norms, were created primarily by men and are therefore male-oriented norms. If women fail to conform to these male-oriented norms, they are labeled emotionally unstable or mentally sick.

This has happened to women because of a supposedly different psychological makeup and society's dictum on how women should act and react. Women have been put in a social position that renders them powerless. They are viewed as second-class citizens and are considered subordinate to men. This sense of powerlessness has been a determining factor in the psychological destruction of women. The mental-health system has failed to meet women's changing needs and in many instances reinforces their powerlessness.

Excluding problems related to drug and alcohol abuse, the following areas related to the issue of women and mental health are specifically addressed: powerlessness of women and its effect on their mental health; utilization of the mental-health institution by women; treatment system (various psychotherapy models); the role of Freud and his effect on women; and strategies for change (feminist therapy).

Powerlessness of Women and Its Effect on Their Mental Health

Lack of power and chronic powerlessness are major contributors to psychological disorders. Many women have little power in our society and the diminished sense of control contributes importantly to their lowered self-esteem. So pervasive is the powerlessness that even women who have high self-esteem, who are assertive and self-confident, are viewed as being different or somewhat abnormal by most of society. This lack of power and inequality impacts on the lives of women with social, economic, and psychological consequences for themselves and their families.[42] The President's Commission on Mental Health (1978) provides some assumptions and stated facts that indicate why women are powerless:

1. More than half of all women are employed outside their homes in addition to being homemakers and caring for their children.
2. Women are clustered in low-paying occupations.
3. Women employed full-time outside the home earn less than 56 percent of their male counterparts.

4. One woman in four lives on less than $4,000 per year.
5. Female-headed families have increased 33 percent in the past ten years to 22.7 percent of all households for whites and 38.4 percent for blacks and other minorities.
6. Forty-four percent of all female-headed families live below poverty level.
7. More than twice as many women as men are treated for depression.
8. More women than men in the general population report feelings of depression.
9. Twice as many women as men use the popular tranquilizers Valium and Librium.
10. Fifty percent more women than men report use barbiturates for medical purposes.
11. While women outnumber men in the health professions, men are clustered at the top of the profession as physicians and administrators.
12. Traditional therapists tend to view women as normally passive, dependent, emotional, and childlike.
13. Women who do not display these characteristics are viewed as abnormal by the traditional therapist.
14. Therapy goals for women are often geared to just a reduction of complaints rather than solving underlying problems; adjustment to traditional roles is stressed.
15. Women who are also racial or ethnic minorities or elderly are particularly at-risk for mental-health problems.[43]

The President's Commission Subpanel on Women and Mental Health continues by saying that there is no evidence to suggest that women are innately more vulnerable to mental illness than men. Stress brought about by life events such as poverty, role conflicts, and lack of social support affect women the same as they do men, but many women are more likely to be exposed to these stressful events and are even more likely to be exposed to several at one time. Some believe it is woman's basic nature to be nurturing, passive, and cooperative which fits her traditional role as mother, wife, and homemaker. These same characteristics, however, are often incongruent with characteristics thought necessary for a job situation. This conflict is an unavoidable source of anxiety for many women who work out of necessity, economic or otherwise.[44] The powerlessness of women is a result of their being placed at an unequal or lower status than men.

Jean Baker Miller, noted female psychiatrist, wrote about women and powerlessness and uses the terms *dominant* and *subordinate* to distinguish the roles of the powerful and the powerless.[45] Once a group is defined as inferior, the superiors tend to label it as defective or substandard in a number of different ways. Dominant groups usually define one or more acceptable roles for the subordinates. These roles typically involve doing things that no dominant group wants to perform. Subordinates are usually said to be unable to perform the preferred roles. Their incapacities are ascribed to innate defects and deficiencies

of mind or body, which are impossible to change or develop. It becomes difficult for dominants even to imagine that subordinates are capable of performing
the preferred activities. As a result, subordinates themselves come to believe
that they have little ability to accomplish any but the minimal of tasks.[46]
Such is the case of women in our society today. Society has placed them in the
subordinate role and has dominated them for so long that many women believe
they can do little to break out of their subordinate position. Hence come the
feelings and sense of powerlessness.

A dominant group, in this case men, inevitably has the greatest influence
in determining a culture's overall outlook in terms of its philosophy, its morality,
its social theory, and even its science. The dominant group then legitimizes the
unequal relationship and incorporates it into society's norms. The social outlook
distorts the true nature of this relationship which is the existence of inequality.
The culture explains the events that take place in terms of such false premises
as social or sexual inequality. In relating this to women despite evidence to the
contrary the idea persists that women are meant to be passive, submissive,
docile, and on a lower level or secondary to men. From this premise, the outcome of therapy and encounters with psychology and other sciences are often
determined.[47] Inevitably, the dominant group is the model for "normal human
relationships." It then becomes normal to treat others in a destructive and
demeaning manner to assure the dominant group's supremacy and the subordinate groups submissiveness.[48]

Women, as the subordinates in this case, are being looked at and treated
according to the ideologies of the dominant group. This not only makes them
powerless but in many instances keeps them powerless. The ideologies of the
dominant group (men) infiltrate every part of our culture. The mental-health
institution is not excluded.

Utilization of the Mental-Health Institution by Women

The mental-health institution in America has been and continues to be a male-
dominated profession. Because of the sexist orientation of men in the psychiatric and mental-health professions, women have been misdiagnosed and considered mentally ill or emotionally unstable because they express discomfort
related to daily living situations that may be stressful. Their response to stress
may not necessarily be abnormal or extreme, but measured against the norms
or standards of mental health it can easily be interpreted as an abnormal reaction.

The result is that the mental-health institution is utilized by women a great
deal more than by men. The following statistics support this contention.

1. About 175 women to every 100 men are admitted to hospitals for treatment of depression.[49]

2. Some 238 women to every 100 men are treated for depression in outpatient services.[50]

3. In looking at all physicians' diagnoses of a psychological nature, women account for 60 percent or more of unexplained symptoms, psychiatric and psychosomatic.[51]

4. The information on first admissions to mental hospitals, psychiatric treatment in general hospitals, psychiatric outpatient clinics, private outpatient psychiatric care, and community surveys, all indicate that more women than men are mentally ill.[52]

5. It has been estimated that more than one-quarter of the population seeing a physician during the year has at least one diagnosis of a psychological nature (though they may have a purely physical diagnosis as well). Looking at these data broken down by sex, women account for 63 percent of all unexplained symptoms category, 61 percent of the psychosomatic category, though they account for only 53 percent of all diagnoses combined.[53]

Table 6-1 provides further insights of women in the mental-health institution. It is evident that women are given some mental illness diagnosis much more frequently than men. An example is depressive disorder which appears to be one of the most common diagnoses. Women are diagnosed as having a depressive disorder twice as many times as men. The following areas of discussion will provide further evidence as to why women make up a larger part of the patient load in mental-health systems than men.[54]

Treatment Systems: Various Psychotherapy Models

As mentioned previously, the mental-health institution has been a male-dominated profession. All the founders and key figures of contemporary counseling

Table 6-1
Five Leading Diagnoses for Admission to Outpatient Clinics by Race, Sex, and Rates per 100,000 Population, May 1975

White Males		*Black Males*	
Adjustment reaction and behavior disorders of childhood	(94.6)	Adjustment reaction and behavior disorders of childhood	(95.2)
Adjustment reaction: adult	(81.4)	Schizophrenia	(87.2)
Personality disorders	(73.0)	Adjustment reaction: adult	(65.5)
Schizophrenia	(64.6)	Alcohol disorders	(55.4)
Depressive disorders	(54.6)	Drug disorders	(54.0)
White Females		*Black Females*	
Depressive disorders	(112.0)	Schizophrenia	(145.2)
Adjustment reaction: adult	(102.2)	Adjustment reaction: adult	(133.3)
Neuroses	(74.7)	Depressive disorders	(128.6)
Personality disorders	(67.1)	Adjustment reaction and behavior disorders of childhood	(61.2)
Schizophrenia	(60.9)	Neuroses	(58.2)

Source: NIMH, Division of Biometry and Epidemiology. 1975.

and therapy models have been men. Psychoanalytic therapy has long been a method of treating mental illness and emotional/behavioral problems. Although psychoanalysis may be the dominant mode of therapy on which the mental-health institution was established, it is not the only one. Traditional counseling and psychotherapy models fit into three general categories: psychodynamic approach; experimential and relationship-oriented therapies; and behavior-oriented, rational-cognitive, and action therapies.[55]

There are eight models of counseling and psychotherapy that fit into the three general categories: psychoanalytic therapy, existential-humanistic therapy, client-centered therapy, gestalt therapy, transactional analysis (TA), behavior therapy, rational emotive therapy (RET), and reality therapy.[56]

Psychoanalytic therapy is based largely on insight, unconscious motivation, and reconstruction of the personality. The founder of psychoanalytic therapy was Sigmund Freud. Historically, psychoanalysis was the first method of psychotherapy.[57] Existential-humanistic therapy was developed as a reaction against behaviorist psychology which the humanistic psychologists assert do not do justice to the study of humans. Key figures in the development of this model were Rollo May and Abraham Maslow.[58] Client-centered therapy, developed by Carl Rogers in the 1940s, was originally a nondirective approach developed as a reaction against the psychoanalytic approach. Based on a subjective view of human experience, it places more faith and gives more responsibility to the client in dealing with problems.[59]

Gestalt therapy is largely an experimental approach which stresses aware-ness and integration. It grew as a reaction to analytic therapy and integrates body and mind functioning. The founder of Gestalt therapy was Fritz Perles.[60] Transactional analysis (TA), founded by Eric Berne, is a contemporary model that leans toward cognitive and behavioral aspects. It is designed to help people evaluate decisions they have made in light of the appropriateness at present.[61]

Behavior therapy applies the principles of learning to the resolution of specific behavioral disorders. The results are subject to continual experimentation, and the technique is continuously in the process of refinement.[62] B.F. Skinner is the founder of behavior modification. Albert Ellis' rational-emotive therapy (RET) is a highly didactic, cognitive-action-oriented model of therapy that stresses the role of thinking and belief systems as the root of personal prob-lems.[63] Reality therapy is a reaction against conventional therapy. It is short term, and focuses on the present. It stresses a person's strengths and is basically a way clients can learn more realistic behavior and their achieved success. Reality therapy was founded by William Glasser.[64]

It is evident here that men have dominated the development of therapeutic methodologies. Since all these therapy models were designed by men the result is bound to be a sexist orientation. The problem with traditional psychothera-pies and the mental-health system in general is the use of male standards to measure female behavior.

Alfred Adler contends that all institutions of this culture and its traditional attitudes have been determined and are maintained by males for the glory of male domination.[65] Even children reared by parents attempting to lead egalitarian lives will be affected by traditional attitudes. Children see privileges of manhood from their earliest days and can sense that women do not believe in their own equality. Because masculinity dominates, boys are urged to be manly and to secure power and privileges for themselves. Girls hear and see that which robs them of any sense of their own value, destroys self-confidence, and eliminates any hope of doing something worthwhile. Consequently, it is not surprising that many appear to retreat from life. The advantages of being a man are clear and cause severe disturbances in the psychic development of women.[66]

When one considers this, it becomes evident what women have to contend with when they seek therapeutic assistance from a profession that is primarily male-dominated and sexist-oriented. Although men in the mental-health profession have been trained to be more receptive and understanding in meeting the needs of their clients, they have been reared in the same culture and have adopted similar societal norms and ideologies as many other men. They traditionally have assumed a position of power, with women automatically becoming subordinate. If there are differences between male mental-health professionals, these differences stem from their values and beliefs about the behaviors of men and women.

There are three models of mental health that a therapist can choose from to express his or her values and beliefs about the roles of men and women. They are normative model, androcentric model, and androgynous model.[67]

The normative model defines mental health as adherence to stereotyped sex roles. This is the model widely accepted by the general public and prescribed by society. Since role prescriptions are different for men and women, the normative model implies a double standard of mental health. Therapists utilizing this model attempt to help men and women accept and adjust to their "appropriate" sex roles and treat men and women differently.[68]

The androcentric model is male-centered. Even though this model presents only one standard of mental health for both sexes, it is a male standard, and women are encouraged to change and become more "masculine," whereas men are encouraged to maintain the "healthy" sex-role behavior. A therapist using this model of mental health would still treat men and women differently by encouraging men to accept their "appropriate" sex roles and women to incorporate more "male" traits such as assertiveness and independence as part of their sex roles. This model of mental health interprets masculine-associated activities and traits as superior and denigrates whatever is considered feminine.[69]

The androgynous model encourages men and women to adopt flexible sex roles that are neither masculine nor feminine but rather an integration and balance of both. With this model of mental health there is only one standard for both men and women, and a therapist using this model would treat men and women as equals and would have as treatment goals the integration of the best of both female- and male-associated characteristics.[70]

It is evident through the descriptions of these three models that the androgynous model of mental health would be the most valuable one for treating women. They are given equality in the therapeutic relationship, which is something they have been denied previously. Under this model they are urged not only to develop characteristics associated with males but also to develop their own female-associated characteristics that are traditionally defined as being a part of the surbordinate role.

All models of psychotherapy in the institution of mental health contain implicit value systems. Therapists' values, both personal and professional, influence value changes in their clients and depend upon therapists' theoretical orientation as well as upon their models of mental health. The values also determine whether therapists are providing sex-biased or nonsexist psychotherapy to their client.[71]

The mental-health institution is built on the values to which the mental-health professionals subscribe. Unfortunately they have traditionally subscribed to the normative model.

The Role of Freud and His Effect on Women

There are a number of psychotherapeutic models that are utilized to treat mental illness and related disorders. Many of the theories and techniques have been criticized as being particularly biased against women. According to many critics, psychotherapy has often reinforced the sex bias of our male-dominated society and has helped maintain the myth that women are innately inferior to men. Most theories of personality are based on the behavior of men and only secondarily refer to women in relation to men as distinctly different from men.[72]

Freud's psychoanalytic theory has been the most criticized of all personality theories. Psychoanalysis provided the first comprehensive theoretical explanation of sex differences and has had the greatest and most continuous influence on our thinking and attitudes about women and men and still continues to affect greatly the process of psychotherapy. Even conclusions that Freud himself described as tentative have been extended and misrepresented as a universal theory of the behavior of women.[73]

Freud's theories of feminine psychology has been well documented but has also been as equally criticized as his other personality theories. His greatest contribution was the recognition of women's dual sexual role. Biologically it is women's first task to attract and have a relationship with a man. The second task is that of assuming the mothering role. Although this theory of femininity is a simple one, it was basically accepted from a biological and anatomical viewpoint.[74]

Freud's other concepts of femininity are more disputed than his simple biological premise. He considered women defective because they were born without a penis. He viewed motherhood as a compensation for this deficiency. Freud took the penis-envy complaints of his patients quite literally and also theorized that women were naturally passive and masochistic and had weaker superegos than men. As a result, the women who were perceived as being mentally ill were marked by aggressiveness, neurosis, and penis envy.[75]

Freud's sexist orientation is evident in a statement he once made while pondering the condition of women. "The greatest question that has never been answered and which I have not been able to answer despite my thirty years of research into the feminine soul is: What do women want?"[76]

The sexist orientation has been carried over and is continually evident in contemporary models of psychotherapy. Psychiatrists and psychologists traditionally described the signs and symptoms of various kinds of real and felt oppression as mental illness. Women often manifest these signs not only because they are oppressed in an objective sense but the sex role stereotype to which they are conditioned is composed of such signs.[77] What must further be realized is that these predominantly male clinicians are involved in a political institution that has taken a certain traditional view of women.[78] In psychotherapy a woman is encouraged to talk by a therapist who is expected or perceived to be superior. The traditional therapist may be viewed as ultimately controlling what the patient says through a subtle system of rewards or withholding rewards, but ultimately controlling in a sense that he is attempting to bring his patients to terms with the female role, which is the admission and acceptance of dependency.[79]

There has been a realization, particularly as a result of the women's movement, that psychotherapy, especially that with a Freudian orientation, is not assisting the majority of women with their problems. In many cases, psychotherapists have harmed women more than they have helped. The women's movement has provided a focus on this issue that was not present when the different therapeutic models were being theorized and developed. The result has been a reassessment of the values of traditional psychotherapy that women have been receiving, and the development of strategies to provide women with an alternative to sexist-oriented psychotherapies and to the inequalities, powerlessness, and lack of control and self-determination that women experience in the mental-health system.

Strategies for Change: Feminist Therapy

This section addresses feminist therapy both as a change strategy and policy development which can bring about change in the mental-health system in regard to women's needs.

Psychotherapy has become a significant issue in the feminist movement. Although the primary target of feminist criticism has been Freudian psychotherapy, all psychology and psychotherapy including social work has come increasingly under fire as being dominated and controlled by males and as adhering to a standard of mental health determined by males. In the early

1970s many professionals in the mental-health field began to respond, sometimes disparagingly, at other times positively to the criticism leveled by feminists.[80]

Those who responded positively began to develop and publish new models for working with women in therapy at about the same time that feminists were developing alternatives to therapy. Some of these alternatives were conscious-ness-raising groups, self-help counseling, transition houses, discovering ways of modifying therapy, utilizing referral services, and calling for a new psychology of women.[81]

As a result of the social activism on the part of the women's movement and in response to the mental-health institution's failure to produce nonsexist modes of treatment, an alternative treatment modality was developed. This new therapeutic model came to be known as feminist therapy. There are five components of feminist therapy which differentiate it from traditional psycho-therapy.

1. An assumption that all roles are in principle open to women.

2. A sociological perspective is used in working with women.

3. Develops within women a new "feminist-ego ideal" with the recogni-tion that traditional theories of identity development have ignored women's development and concentrated on men's development.

4. A striving to restore a balance between the emphasis placed on work and relationships.

5. A reassessment of the value of same sex relationships as opposed to the relationship with the opposite sex.[82]

In April 1973 an advertisement offering feminist therapy appeared in *Ms* magazine. Three years later, descriptions such as "feminist therapist" or "feminist psychotherapist" appeared in half the advertisements listed in *Ms* for therapists and therapy referral services. Feminists in many major cities across the county established referral services for feminist therapy.[83]

Generally speaking, definitions of feminist therapy are just beginning to appear in the literature. Walstedt defines a feminist psychotherapist simply as, "someone who supports and understands the desire for female equality."[84] Silveira explains that feminist therapy is, "counseling which affirms women's liberation and proceeds without power differentials between counselor and counseled."[85]

Feminist therapy provides women with much needed support from other women in their attempt to define themselves in their own terms as opposed to the picture of womanhood as presented by society or to defining them-selves in terms of a man. The contradiction arising from what women feel and experience versus what they are expected to be and do can be dealt with more effectively at an agency whose commitment is to woman and her changing role.[86] The need for feminist therapy is evident in today's society during a period of great changes in woman's roles and expectations. For this reason, it is necessary for women to have therapists who are sensitive to the issues which the women's movement develops. It is equally necessary for women to have therapists who are sensitive to the needs of individual women.[87]

The first assumption of feminist therapy states that all roles are open to women. Although this seems apparent, they do not assume that this principle is accepted by society and the mental-health profession. They recognize that barriers still exist for women. One's gender does not necessarily determine career or life-style. Under this first component feminist therapy also believes that women may have to create new roles rather than take over men's roles.[88]

The second component of feminist therapy brings a sociological perspective into the work with women. They help women sort out which roots of their behavior have been determined by internalized societal norms and which behavior is in response to current societal pressures.[89]

The third distinction between feminist therapy and traditional psychotherapy is the development within women of a new feminist-ego ideal. Feminist therapy sees a special importance in acknowledging and valuing women's assets such as nurturance, sensitivity, and emphasis on relationships previously devalued. Equally important is the development of aggressive and assertive qualities.[90] The fourth component of feminist therapy strives to restore balance between the emphasis placed on work and relationships. Feminist therapy feels that woman's work accomplishments and growth deserve as much attention in the context of treatment as do her interpersonal relationships and growth.[91]

The final component of feminist therapy is the reassessment of the value of some sex relationships as opposed to relationships with the opposite sex. Nonfeminist therapies (psychoanalytic) often stress the heterosexual relationships, taking for granted the real strengths and opportunities for enrichment in the same-sex relationships, or maybe not questioning the scarceness of some sex relationships. Feminist therapy takes the position that a relationship with a man can be enriching, but is not total or even central to a woman's mental health.[92]

If a theoretical orientation to therapy is defined in the traditional sense as encompassing a series of propositions and techniques, a model for problem assessment, or a training methodology, it may be concluded that feminist therapy as such does not exist. However, some therapists have incorporated feminism into their therapy and call themselves feminist therapists. This suggests that feminist therapy must be understood more as a part of a social movement than as a type of psychotherapy and less as a theoretical orientation in the traditional sense than as a belief system and a number of ways in which that system is put into practice.[93]

As feminist therapists describe feminist therapy it seems to be based on three intertwined elements: a belief system composed of feminist humanism and feminist consciousness, a therapist-client relationship that renders the therapeutic process compatible with the feminist value system, and consciousness-raising and placing emphasis on the commonality shared by all women that enable the feminist value system to be utilized not only by these therapists but to be transferred in turn to the client.[94]

Integration is a key word in feminist therapy. This involves making multiple connections, and feminism and feminist theory can be seen as making connections on many levels, between feminism and therapy, between one woman and all women, between one's personal problems and one's social awareness, between one's beliefs and what one does in therapy and how one lives one's life. Thus, unlike most forms of therapy, feminist therapy is not just a means to be used from time to time to alleviate stress but a way of life for the therapist and potentially for the client as well. As more feminists seek to connect feminism with therapy and to remove the sexism commonly found in the mental-health system and the therapeutic setting and remove the traditional abuses of power from therapy, the basic nuances of this form of therapy are clarified. It is becoming easier to identify what feminist therapy is, what the basic areas of consistency and inner congruity among feminist therapists are, what distinguishes one feminist therapist from another. As feminists continue to work toward building common theoretical bases and develop new ways of integrating feminism and therapy, feminist therapy will increasingly emerge as a distinctive therapeutic form.[95]

Other Strategies for Change

If women are to achieve appropriate mental-health care, it is imperative to develop strategies in areas related to the mental-health system. Appropriate strategies can bring about changes necessary to dispel the myths of women as subordinates. The right strategy can eliminate many inequalities with which women have to contend. Women along with the mental-health system can be the change agents in eliminating factors that promote mental illness and interfere with treatment.

The President's Commission on Mental Health, Task Panel on Women, and the Mental Health Association have made recommendations and suggested several strategies that will enhance women's experience with the mental-health system.

1. Public funds for mental-health-personnel training should be awarded to programs which have demonstrated a concern for women's issues and a commitment to nonsexist education.

2. Experts on women's mental-health needs should be included in federal government interagency groups dealing with mental health and mental illness.

3. Representation of women on health-related boards should be in the same proportion as women are represented in the community. At least one of the mental-health representatives should have special expertise in the mental health of women.

4. Current and planned insurance programs should be examined for the effect they have on care-seeking patterns for women, particularly lower- and working-class women.

5. Legislation concerning domestic violence should receive special attention and a network of sheltered protective services established for battered women, displaced homemakers, and the aged.

6. Emphasis should be placed on further research on the mental health of women.

7. A comprehensive education campaign to raise public awareness about mental-health problems of women.

8. As a part of evaluation of mental-health services, special attention should be paid to the treatment of women as patients, including therapists' attitudes, prescribed medications, and treatment plans.

9. Education programs should be designed for family practitioners and other physicians, especially gynecologists, to help them recognize signals of mental illness and take appropriate action.

10. Exploration of situations which produce high-stress levels in women and the development of programs which help women reduce and manage stress should be undertaken.[96]

Developing and using strategies to bring about change is a necessary and important part of social and political action: change strategies are the key to making women equal. They are also the key in making the institution of mental health develop new and more appropriate ways of treating women.

**Part III
Case Studies**

Introduction

These four case studies are examples of women's organizations struggling to provide programs and services for women from a feminine perspective. Each program author was asked to present the case with the following format: identification of need, program development, program implementation, and analysis. Each was willing to have her program examined from a community organization (CO) perspective. They have provided a post facto CO appraisal. They were also willing to share their strengths and weaknesses with other women's programs, displaying their true commitment to women.

There are certain similarities in the four case studies. The Federal Women's Program (FWP) and Women for Sobriety (WFS) are national in scope; the other two are localized. Even so, certain organizational factors emerge.

1. Financial problems. Even the FWP which is mandated under law does not have a line item budget. For women setting up programs it is important not only to secure financial support but to generate the necessary skill and expertise to obtain it. Jean Kirkpatrick's honesty about her ignorance in this area is a lesson to be learned.

2. Three of the agencies had problems of in-fighting among women staff or had inadequate staff. This brings out the importance of having qualified and knowledgeable women who know what they are doing. The need for education and training women in administration, program planning, and fund raising becomes clear.

3. There does not seem to be a systematic plan of evaluation in any of the programs. This can be the most effective means of selling programs. Perhaps evaluation appears as a luxury when the need for service seems overwhelming but may be the element that can save the program.

4. All the programs are young and provide innovative, creative services. Extending help to women in the workplace and to those with addiction or battering problems is sparking new areas for human services. We see some very real examples of original thinking: the FWP's women's network; the nursery care of Women, Inc.; the battered women's program in the suburbs; and the women's support group of WFS. Yet, Marilyn Flynn says there is no other way to be innovative than through trial and error. So in addition to being unique because they are women's programs they are also pioneering new techniques, a risky experience in itself.

In addition to the general lessons to be learned there are also specific experiences that the authors point out. The use of collateral duty assignment, that is, a responsibility given as an extra to one's main job can be crippling to both the staff person and the program. The charismatic figure of Jean Kirkpatrick can be a problem because the program becomes identified with her. This is true of other charismatic figures in organizations. Saul Alinsky's

160

Industrial Areas' Foundation and Martin Luther King's Southern Christian Leadership Conference are examples of organizations that were one-man identified. The use of the police of WPS is important. Rather than assuming they would be hostile, they reached out and a valuable alliance was formed.

There are many other lessons to be learned from these studies. The authors describe them well and provide the readers with some valuable practical lessons.

7

Federal Women's Program

Diane Brasher

Legal Mandates

The Office of the Federal Women's Program (FWP) is located in the Office of Personnel Management (OPM) in Washington, D.C. The FWP was established by the OPM (formerly the Civil Service Commission) in response to an October 1967 Executive Order (11375) which added sex to other prohibited forms of discrimination in the federal government. In August 1969, Executive Order 11478 integrated the FWP into the overall Equal Employment Opportunity (EEO) and placed the FWP under the guardianship of agency directors of EEO.[1]

In March 1972, Public Law 92-261, the Equal Employment Opportunity Act of 1972, brought federal employees and agencies under the equal employment opportunity provision of the Civil Rights Act of 1964 and gave the Civil Service Commission additional enforcement powers to ensure that all personnel actions in government are free from discrimination.[2]

OPM regulations implementing P.L. 92-261 require that federal agencies designate an FWP manager to advise the director of EEO on matters affecting the employment and advancement of women.[3] Public Law 92-261 requires that federal agencies allocate sufficient resources to the FWP to ensure a results-oriented EEO program at headquarters and field levels.[4]

The Task Office of the Federal Women's Program (OFWP) in OPM is to provide policy-level guidance and program leadership for the governmentwide FWP. The OFWP gives advice and assistance to agency FWP personnel so that they can better assist women in obtaining and advising them in federal employment. OPM's OFWP's monitors propose policy and relevant congressional legislation for their potential impact on the federal employment of women. The OFWP also identifies and works to eliminate barriers that affect the employment of women in the civil service system.[5]

The overall goal of the FWP is to improve employment and advancement opportunities for women in the federal sector. The FWP has a set of objectives by which their goal is strived for.

1. Recruiting and hiring women for agency jobs.
2. Placing women in jobs which offer them advancement in line with their abilities and ambitions, and opening up dead-end jobs.

163

3. Counseling women about opportunities and encouraging them to plan a career.
4. Encouraging agencies to expand their opportunities for part-time work and to restructure jobs so women can compete for them on an equal basis with men.
5. Encouraging provisions for child care for children of federal employees.
6. Communicating the concerns of women in the agency, between women's groups and the FWP.
7. Developing and using statistical information, assessing employment trends, and evaluating the progress of agency women.
8. Encouraging women to consider nontraditional fields that in many cases offer better pay and advancement.
9. Promoting continued education for employees by arranging work schedules, by granting leave to allow participation, and by participating in the community.
10. Promoting and building upon the concept of upward mobility at all levels.
11. Reviewing the classification and occupation standards for agency occupations.
12. Monitoring the hiring and promotion practices of agencies as they affect women.[6]

All cabinet departments and independent agencies must designate a person to manage the FWP department. Other agencies and regional or field offices should appoint a person to manage FWP, whenever two or more of the following circumstances are found.

1. Women are substantially underrepresented at higher-grade levels.
2. Few or no women are represented in a large number of agency occupations.
3. There is a significant number of discrimination complaints based on sex.
4. There is a high incidence of complaint counseling due to potential complaints based on sex discrimination.
5. There is a limited movement of women from clerical and other support positions to professional positions.
6. There is a large and continuing gap between the average grades of men and women.

As mentioned previously, the goal of the FWP is that of improving employment and advancement opportunities for women in the federal service. As of 1977, women represented 30.5 percent of the total full-time federal civilian work force. Although there has been an increase in the number of women who hold professional and technical jobs, the goal of the FWP is not yet complete. The increase has been seen in the GS-7 to 11 positions. Women have increased only a small amount in GS-12 through 18 positions. As of May 1977, the average grade of women was 5.85 as compared to 8.15 for men. Women with college degrees were also found to be one to three grades behind men with the same educational levels.[8]

Program Development

At the onset of the program the FWP was located structurally under the Office of Equal Employment Opportunity Program, U.S. Civil Service Commission. In January 1978 Provisions of the Civil Service Reform Act transferred enforcement authority for EEO programs to the Equal Employment Opportunity Commission (EEOC). However, responsibility for guidance in FWP remained with the OPM (formerly the U.S. Civil Service Commission).

There are approximately 60 full-time managers and an estimated 10,000 part-time FWP managers and committee members. There are several levels of authority within the FWP structure. The Office of the Federal Women's Program, located within the OPM, provides policy and guidance nationwide to all federal departments and agencies. The next level is the national-level manager who oversees implementation of a particular agency nationwide (for example, agriculture). The next level is headquarters manager usually located in Washington, D.C. This manager participates in various activities (statistical analyses, career counseling, briefing of management officials) to improve the representation of women in positions within that agency. The next level is the Regional Federal Women's Program coordinator. These coordinators are not full-time, but rather part-time or collateral. There are few full-time managers located in the regions.

As stated previously, the initial conceptualization of the program came from President Kennedy's Commission on the Status of Women. The program is unique in its structure.

Support for the program came directly from the White House because of the creation of the Commission on the Status of Women and continues as a White House initiative. Currently, there is support on the Hill from the Congresswomen's Caucus and other subcommittees. Women themselves supported the idea of removing discrimination by beginning organizations such as Federally Employed Women (FEW). There were strong political, social, and economic forces that pushed to remove discrimination from the federal government. Funding for the Office of the Federal Women's Program comes from the OPM. Funding for a FWP within a particular agency comes from that agency's funds. Funding gives the program additional support from top management within the agency.

Program Implementation

The early years of the FWP were spent making it functional. Many unexpected problems and barriers developed and had to be dealt with to build a foundation for the program to ensure its continuance.

Attitudes that have been held by both men and women regarding the capabilities and contributions of women had to be changed. There has been difficulty in getting top management to make the FWP a priority within the agencies. The success of each individual agency's program lies with the attitude of the top management of that agency. They have the ability to make the program a success. Funding and lack of staff to implement programs' goals has played a critical role in preventing the accomplishment of significant program goals. A solution for these two problems must be found in order to expand the current program.

With the reorganization during the Civil Service Reform all the enforcement power of the FWP was transferred to the EEOC. At this time the Office of the Federal Women's Program provides guidance to agencies regarding program implementation.

The current objective of the FWP is to be results-oriented, that is, to achieve gains in the hiring and promotions of women in the federal government. Many agencies have begun programs which are activities-oriented. The agency might have a woman of prestige come to speak at a brown-bag luncheon or have a workshop on assertiveness training. These activities do help women, but are not meeting the current objective of the FWP which is to achieve employment gains. Some agencies, however, feel that they have a results-oriented program, but do not. Results-oriented programs look at such areas as occupational segregation, how much money an agency spends on the training of women in relation to men, the rate of promotion of women versus men, how many women are selected for the Senior Executive Service, or how many women are sent to Managerial Development programs. These areas address the employment of women.[9]

Another perception is that minority and handicapped women have indicated that the FWP does not address their needs. At this time the Minority Women's Task Force sponsored by the Office of the Federal Women's Program is developing an agenda to address these needs.

The structure of the FWP within the agencies has also caused problems in developing the program. The FWP manager within the agency is usually a collateral person, that is, the person has other major responsibilities for the agency and spends a certain percentage of time on the FWP. Many times the FWP manager does not have the time to get away from her work at the specific time she is needed. The FWP then suffers. The program often does not get the attention it requires to be successful and visible within the agency.[10]

Through the FWP structure a network has been developed to reach women in the federal sector and make this program visible to all women at all levels. The program used its structure to ensure coordination between the policymakers and the FWP managers located in the agency. Successful programs and new ideas for reaching women could be sent over this network. FWP also works closely with other women's organizations, such as FEW, to make the program known. FEW can lobby regarding issues of concern to the FWP.

The FWP also prints a bimonthly magazine, *Women in Action*, to keep communication flowing. This magazine addresses issues of women and problems with employment. It apprises them regarding the policy and programs that have been developed to address problems they face in the government.

Coordination with one critical actor for policymaking has also been established. The EEOC plays an important role in that it has authority to enforce the law. The FWP coordinates ideas regarding proposed policy with the EEOC.

There have been many successes for the FWP. It has provided women with a general awareness of their rights and opportunities for career advancement. It has increased the opportunities to bring women into the federal system. It has had some success in getting women into top management. It has helped women to become aware of skills necessary for mobility in their career. But one of the strongest and most important successes has been that it has brought women together forming a network and foundation to continue to strive for equal rights for women in the future.

There have also been failures for the program. A large population of women have not been able to take advantage of the opportunities which have been made available for women. FWP still has a long way to go in getting top management to realize the necessity for this program. The top management still has not been totally successful in achieving a balanced representation at all levels. Budget restrictions continue and this reduces the visibility of the program in many agencies.[11]

Analysis

If this program were to begin again, several needs should be met at its onset. First of all, there is a need for more financial resources to meet continually rising costs and program needs. Second, there is a need for more staff. It is very difficult at the present time to meet the needs and demands of the large number of women who have problems with FWP's very limited staff.[12]

Several new strategies could be used to increase support for the program. One strategy would be to have communication with the Office of Manpower and Budget (OMB) to see if agencies have included the FWP as a line item budget within the agency's budget. Another strategy is to get agencies to be more results-oriented rather than activities-oriented. A final strategy is to make this program more personnel-management-oriented. The FWP should provide input into all personnel policies. At the present time many FWP managers are unfamiliar with personnel policies and regulations. Proposed classification standards for EEO specialists will enable them to gain a working knowledge of personnel management.

The greatest threat to the FWP, in addition to other special emphasis programs, is the current question being faced as to whether we need special emphasis programs. Ms. Ellis Jones, senior equal opportunity specialist, of the

Office of the Federal Women's Program feels that there is a new direction in some federal agencies for the FWP manager to become a generalist, that is, have a working knowledge of personnel issues and the special problems of the Hispanic, handicapped, veterans, and other minorities. She feels that FWP managers should exert additional efforts to include all women as part of their constituency, particularly disabled women. She states that the end result of EEO programs as well as the FWP is to have it go out of business because the work force is well-balanced.

The FWP is evaluated by the OPM Evaluation Program. There has been no official report regarding the program produced by that office. The individual agencies also have an internal evaluation to determine the success of their own program. Individual agency progress is also reported on a periodic basis to the EEOC.[13]

The task itself of the FWP is enormous, that is, changing the role of women in the federal government that time as well as strategies will be important as the program works toward accomplishing its goals.

8

Women, Inc.

Marilyn Flynn

Women, Inc. is a private, nonprofit community service agency, located in Dorchester, Massachusetts, that provides innovative treatment for women experiencing drug- or alcohol-abuse problems. Women are referred to Women, Inc., by the courts, probation departments, correctional institutions, various social service agencies, and by friends and family members.

Services offered by Women, Inc. include a twenty-four hour Residential Program, a Day Program, and child-care services for both programs. The Residential Program is divided into three phases. The first phase is a one-month orientation period, during which the staff becomes acquainted with the new client and her particular problems. Having familiarized themselves with the problems, staff and client work together to develop reasonable treatment objectives. The second phase, which lasts two to five months, is aimed at developing the client's self-awareness and self-confidence. Each client gradually assumes greater responsibility regarding in-house management. In addition therapeutic methods in the second phase concentrate on consciousness-raising with regard to women's issues. Finally, group and individual counseling programs are used to explore avenues of growth for the clients and their children. During the third or reentry phase of the program, clients work to return to the community. Clients become less involved in in-house responsibilities and spend greater time in the community, in school, looking for employment, exploring housing possibilities, and so on.

The Day Program provides for women who for various reasons are unable to commit themselves to a residential program. The Day Program utilizes virtually the same treatment methods as the Residential Program. An integral part of both the Residential Program and the Day Program is the child-care services. Depending on the age group, Women, Inc. has three in-house activity plans: an infant plan, a preschool-age plan, and a school-age plan. The mother and the child-care specialist work together to arrange the child's activities.

Identification of Need

In the early 1970s, few women were involved in the drug-treatment community. Few women sought drug treatment, and there were few women available to staff drug-treatment facilities. The feminist movement began to have an impact on the drug-treatment community in the early 1970s. As the feminists raised social awareness of women's issues, the problem of inadequate drug treatment for

169

women was noted. In response to the growing need for adequate drug-treatment facilities for women, a group consisting of thirteen women and one man organized and created a nonprofit organization, Women, Inc.

In 1974, the group in Massachusetts was concerned about women in the criminal-justice system and women and drug abuse. Members of the group, primarily women, shared a feminist perspective on women's issues. The founders of Women, Inc. included a program director for Massachusetts Crime and Correction, the director of Drug and Alcohol Programming for the Governor's Committee on Law Enforcement, the director of a Pre-Release Center for Women, a woman on work release from the Massachusetts Correctional Institution, Framingham, working as a secretary for the Prison Health Project, a recruiter for Massachusetts Half-Way Houses, a director of Drug Cause Prevention Planning, an attorney for female defendants and a founder of Women Concerned with Criminal Justice, a director of training for the Division of Drug Rehabilitation, a liaison for the Youth Employment Program for Cambridge, a court screener for the Boston Court Resources Project, and the director of New Professionals.

Women, Inc. was created to design and submit a proposal addressing the problem of inadequate drug-treatment facilities for women to the National Institute for Drug Abuse (NIDA). With the help of the Prison Health Project, a nonprofit organization created to examine the health needs of those incarcerated in Massachusetts prisons, Women, Inc. submitted a proposal to NIDA in February 1974. The submission by Women, Inc. was entitled a Proposal to Establish a Drug Abuse Demonstration Project for a Women's Drug Treatment Center for the Female Ex-offender in the Commonwealth of Massachusetts.

In March 1974, prior to NIDA's consideration of the proposal by Women, Inc. the National Drug Abuse Conference was held in Chicago. This conference proved instrumental in activating the need for better treatment for women. This proved to be the first such conference to separately examine and discuss women's problems. Thus, the conference offered women a means of sharing information regarding their common concerns.

The conference had an impact on NIDA. As a result of the conference, NIDA was made more accountable to the female drug-addicted population. In response to growing demands by women, NIDA created a new office within its organization and a woman was appointed specifically to address women's issues. In addition, in October 1974 NIDA funded four projects for women. Among the proposals granted was that submitted by Women, Inc.

Women, Inc. accumulated the documentation of need from five major sources: interviews with female inmates; the Division of Drug Rehabilitation's Study of Women in Treatment; prison statistics from the Massachusetts Department of Corrections; the Prison Health Project's Study of Massachusetts Correctional Institution, Framingham; and a Probation Department Female Drug Offender Study.

Interviews with female inmates were considered an important factor in determining the need for the project because these women represented potential clients. Thus, an effort was made by Women, Inc. to have potential consumers, not experts, determine needs. Those interviews revealed women who lacked self-confidence. In addition, these women were often distrustful and even openly hostile to men. Moreover, because of their race and cultural background these women did not identify with the white middle class and as a result they were reluctant to enter drug programs.

In addition, a comparative study illustrated that the sketch of the typical female client by the Division of Drug Rehabilitation Study of Women in Treatment was not at all consistent with the statistics provided by the Massachusetts Department of Corrections, the Prison Health Project, and the Probation Department. The Drug Rehabilitation Study revealed that the typical female drug user is a:

> white single woman approximately 16 years old. She has received some high-school education and more than likely is still a student. Her family life has not been disrupted by parental separation or divorce. She has no formal criminal record but has been a drug user for two to five years. She is most likely to be using barbiturates. About 91.7 percent are white . . . 7.6 percent are black. More than three-fourths of the women (77 percent) are between the ages of 14 and 25 with 41 percent 14 to 18 . . . 25 percent are using barbiturates; 24 percent marijuana, and 22 percent heroin; 42 percent are still students; 23 percent are members of the labor force.

Statistics and reports provided by the Massachusetts Department of Corrections, the Prison Health Project, and the Probation Department did not support the Division of Drug Rehabilitation's findings. For example, the Massachusetts Department of Corrections statistics, which outlined the admission characteristics of the inmate population of February 1972 for each of the state's correctional institutions, revealed that:

> of women in prison 71.1 percent are between the ages of 20 and 39 years, and only 7 percent are between 16 and 19; 42 percent had some schooling while, 21.9 percent did not go beyond the eighth grade, but none were still students. Most women have worked, 42.1 percent at unskilled labor, 16.7 percent semiskilled, 17.5 percent general service, and 17.1 percent at skilled or clerical positions.

The Prison Health Project Study also failed to support the Department of Corrections statistics. The Prison Health Project Study was conducted to determine the number of residents who would benefit from drug-treatment services. Medical and psychiatric reports of the total inmate population at Massachusetts Correctional Institution at Framingham were examined for indication of drug abuse. The study revealed that of about sixty women at Framingham in September 1973, thirty-seven had a history of drug problems. Of the thirty-seven with a drug problem 46 percent were black. Moreover, of those incarcerated on drug charges 48 percent were black.

The Probation Department obtained similar results. The Probation Department Female Drug Offender Study found that:

> 40 percent of the women arrested on drug charges are over 22 years
> old. Other than arrests for marijuana which is uniformly the highest
> for both men and women across the state, most women are arrested
> for heroin offenses and these are generally the older women. Those
> with previous drug arrests are disproportionately represented in the
> 22+ age category and are more likely than the total sample to be
> involved in charges involving Class A substances (heroin).

In examining the need for more responsive drug treatment facilities in Massachusetts, therefore, Women, Inc. found a significant discrepancy in the target population as perceived by the Division of Drug Rehabilitation and that as shown by a variety of prison studies. This distinction was significant in terms of the female drug-abuser's race, drug choice, age, criminal history, educational background, and vocational experience.

Program Development

Upon identifying the need for change in drug treatment, Women, Inc. designed a research and demonstration project with a target population of older women who were known to the criminal-justice system. As stated in the proposal to NIDA, the specific goal of the program was "to demonstrate that treatment designed for the female ex-offender addict will significantly reduce both criminal and drug-abusing behavior and consequently lower the recidivism of this population to courts, prisons, and drug-treatment facilities."

Women, Inc. adopted a feminist perspective in dealing with the female offender and drug addict. They saw women as the victims of a sexist society. Women, Inc. believed that the courts and prisons reinforced negative attitudes toward women. This attitude, therefore, greatly influenced the program design.

The system of addiction and prostitution fostered the notion of women as servants of men. In reality, the female addict supported her own habit as well as her boyfriend's or husband's. The female addict, then, was the source of income for her pimp and the drug pusher. Yet, the woman was seen as criminal because she was a prostitute.

Women, Inc. also designed their program to correct the defects inherent in traditional drug-treatment systems. The most common form of drug treatment was based on the Synanon Model. The Synanon concept offered a very rigid and structured environment in which the therapeutic community "broke down" and then "rebuilt" the individual. This method utilized harsh punitive treatment to accomplish its goal of rehabilitation. This method, however, was believed effective in meeting the needs of those women who wanted to be rehabilitated. Women, Inc. did not believe that this drug-treatment method provided women with a positive experience.

Thus Women, Inc. designed their program to meet the needs of the female addict and ex-offender living in a sexist society and to address the problems encountered in the traditional treatment methods. In actualizing these objectives a program was designed which combined a variety of treatment methods. The program consisted of the following methods:

1. A combination half-way house/drug-treatment center
2. A treatment mode that combined three models
   a. A drug-abuse rehabilitation center
   b. A consciousness-raising group
   c. A radical feminist therapy
3. A creative approach to job placement
4. A recreational component
5. A child-care program
6. An after-care program

The combination half-way house/drug-treatment center was included because it was thought to fill a gap in women's services. The Report of the Governor's Commission on the Status of Women noted that half-way house parole facilities for women were virtually nonexistent in Massachusetts, and as a result women eligible for parole spend more time in prison.

The DARE Program, developed by Dr. Joseph Mayer and Dr. A.B. Samaraweera, was the method selected for drug-abuse rehabilitation. This method was drug-free and emphasized the client's constant awareness of freedom of choice. Traditional methods of heavy abusive confrontation were not practiced. Prior to adopting this program, Women, Inc. consulted the Nianter State Farm for Women, which utilized the DARE program. The conscious-raising model was derived from a variety of handbooks on the women's movement. This therapy offered women the opportunity to develop through group interaction.

The radical feminist therapy was adopted after consulting a number of sources including *Women and Madness* by Phylis Chesler, *Women in a Sexist Society: Studies in Power and Powerlessness* edited by Vivian Gornick and Barbara Moran, and the work of Cordelia Schukt, Director of Non Residential Services at Today, Inc., Newton, Pennsylvania. This approach was based on the premise that therapy (drug treatment) is male-oriented and male-dominated and men's ideas about women are based on myths and fantasies. Their therapy reinforces stereotypical roles. Women then must accept themselves and must do this in an environment free from men.

A creative approach to job placement meant considering jobs outside the narrow scope of stereotyped job categories. *Education Training in the Urban Ghetto* by Bennett Harrison was used as a resource to understand how minorities are trapped in an unfulfilling labor system. The notion of recreation as treatment was researched through the writings of Mary Barner particularly *Two Accounts of a Journey through Madness*.

The child-care program was adopted after consulting N.E. Seldin's work, which stated that an addict's way of life may contribute to the delinquency and subsequent alcoholism as addiction of the addict's children. Women, Inc. studied the child-care program at Marathon House in Rhode Island. That program indicated that children are more apt to develop to their full potential if they are brought up by their parents rather than by foster parents. Moreover, the *Report of the Commission on the Status of Women* supported the position that the female client benefits from the responsibility of raising her child. The after-care program selected was based on the DARE model which emphasized reintegration into the community.

To enhance the operation of the program, Women, Inc. entered cooperative arrangements with a variety of other agencies. For example, the Washingtonian Center for Addictions provided detox and emergency services. In addition, Women, Inc. fostered good working relationships with the court system and the Massachusetts Correctional Institution at Framingham. Negotiations were also made with vocational and recreational resources such as the Massachusetts Rehabilitation Commission, the YWCA, Cambridge Women's Center, and local colleges and universities.

Program Implementation

Despite the fact that the founders took great pains in designing Women, Inc. the commencement of the program was fraught with difficulties. The problems encountered by the program included the choice of an ineffective director, lack of initial community support, difficulty in implementing the program as designed, and a high-staff-attrition rate.

Six months after NIDA awarded the grant, Women, Inc.'s board of directors hired a director. The director selected was a white feminist without any connection to the drug-treatment community. Because the director selected was not a member of either the black community or the drug-treatment community, the program initially had problems recruiting black staff members and gaining acceptance in the urban community. In addition, the drug-treatment community was initially skeptical of a program whose director did not come from the drug-treatment field.

The problems created by the board's choice of director were reduced as a result of the director's recruitment of an assistant director. The woman selected as assistant director was a member of both the black urban community and the drug-treatment community. Moreover, having worked in the field for two years, the assistant director brought to her position personal and professional knowledge of the problems confronting women in the area of drug treatment.

The leadership problems of Women, Inc. reached a head in October 1975, when the director resigned under pressure from NIDA. The assistant director assumed the role of director. The new director made two major adjustments. First, the decision-making structure was more clearly defined with the new director being ultimately accountable. To facilitate the decision-making process, the new director created a coordinating committee, which consisted of the director, assistant director, child-care director, research director, and admissions director. The committee met weekly to discuss policy matters. Second, the new director was instrumental in founding the Solomon Carter Fuller Director's Committee, which consisted of the directors of ten drug programs in the greater Boston area. This committee met monthly to share information and resources. As a member of this group, Women, Inc. gained legitimacy in the drug-treatment community.

In addition to the leadership problem and to a certain degree a product thereof, Women, Inc. also faced a problem of lack of community support. Community support was vital to the success of Women, Inc. To attract female clients, the program had to achieve credibility in the surrounding community. Lack of community support was manifested in a number of ways. In addition to the paucity of clients, hostility to the program was evidenced by a series of robberies and break-ins at the facility. As a result, the new director began a campaign to prove to the community that it had the community interest in mind and that the program wanted and needed community support.

The strategy to achieve community support was based primarily on the personal interaction and diplomatic skills of the director. She contacted individuals on the street and in their homes. She also contacted local churches, community groups, social service agencies, and local police departments in an effort to make the program known. The director's efforts were successful in establishing the necessary support relationship. This base of support was essential to the survival of the program.

Although the program was carefully designed, Women, Inc. confronted many problems in putting the program into effect. Because the treatment method instituted by Women, Inc. was novel there was little precedent to guide program implementation. As a result, trial and error proved to be the basis for the program's early functioning. For example, in the program's early stages, house government was slow and cumbersome. In addition, the child-care program was totally innovative, and therefore was slow in developing.

A final problem that faced Women, Inc. was the high turnover ratio of the staff. In its early stages of development, Women, Inc. demanded an extremely large commitment from the staff. The staff was required to totally dedicate themselves to making the program successful. Because of the few rewards that accompanied the enormous commitment at this stage, many staff members did not stay aboard. There remained, however, a core group of women deeply committed to the goals of the program.

Despite the plethora of problems encountered, the program's first year in operation recorded a number of successes. For one, the program located a residence within the community. Because of the lack of community support, the search for appropriate housing was not easy. Through the diligent efforts of the new director in cultivating community acceptance, however, the support obstacle was overcome and a residence obtained. Women, Inc. was also successful in beginning the development of a new treatment method. This was a difficult task that required a continual assessment and reassessment of the goals and priorities of the program.

Analysis

Internal administrative problems proved to be the major obstacle to the smooth implementation of the program. As previously described, these administrative problems were primarily fostered as a result of a poor choice for the first director. Had the first director been either a black or from the drug-treatment community, many of the problems could have been circumvented. Women, Inc. also failed to adequately prepare the community for the introduction of the program. As a result, the program encountered added resistance. Although the resistance could not have been totally avoided, appropriate preparation could have greatly facilitated implementation.

Problems of high-staff attrition could also have been avoided. This could have been accomplished by a more careful scrutiny of personnel prior to selection. It must also be noted that the original board of directors did not adequately represent the community. Gradually, however, the director has recruited members who more accurately represent the community. As a result, the program has fostered greater support.

Having overcome many of its early problems, Women, Inc. has, in recent years, broadened its sphere of influence. In 1978, for example, Women, Inc. joined the Women's Coalition for Battered Women. The services provided by Women, Inc. were greatly enhanced in 1978 when it received a grant to offer services to alcoholic women. Since receiving this grant, the agency has developed contacts with other programs responsible for treating women with alcohol-related problems. In addition, Women, Inc. has obtained a PACE grant to aid in providing more comprehensive child-care services.

Women, Inc. has also worked to create contacts within the political sphere. Although the agency was not originally politically aware, they soon realized that political influence was absolutely necessary to obtain required funding.

Women's Protective Services

Karen Smallwood

Women's Protective Services (WPS) is located at the Boston YWCA West Suburban Program Center in Natick, Massachusetts. WPS began as Women against Violence in October 1977.

The purpose of WPS is to provide battered women with support for change and with alternatives to living in a violence-prone environment. The following services facilitate this change: (1) crisis intervention (24-hour hotline), (2) counseling, (3) support groups, (4) assertiveness training, (5) advocacy (legal, welfare, housing, education, employment), and (6) referral. Volunteer training and community education also contribute to this change.

The administrative and policymaking decisions of WPS are made through the West Suburban Program Center of the Boston YWCA. A significant note here is that the YWCA is a membership organization: all staff members are also members of the YWCA. Therefore, they are directly involved in administrative decisions and are both directly and indirectly involved in policymaking.

Identification of Need

Data about battered women is just beginning to be available as programs like WPS accumulate and examine statistics about their clients. In 1977, only vague estimates were available. For example, the FBI estimated that an incident of wife abuse occurs every eighteen seconds in the United States. There are about 20,000,000 American men who batter the women who are their wives and lovers. That is one-tenth of the population. Another tenth is the children who are battered. With an average of 2.4 children per couple, more than 48,000,000 children—almost one-quarter of the population—witness this violence and thus learn that violence is "normal" behavior between people.

A common myth about domestic violence is that it is a lower-class crime. Like child abuse, wife abuse crosses socioeconomic boundaries. An example of this is the case of a college professor who sought help from WPS. This client was a middle- to upper-middle-class professional career woman. Her husband held a senior executive position in a computer company. At the time she requested assistance, the battering and abuse had been going on for quite some time. The woman had lived and attempted to cope with it until the husband began to abuse the children as well. Only then was she able to reach out for help.

After almost twenty years providing services to women as director of the West Suburban Center, Clara Nickolson saw that the need for a battered women's program was as great in the middle-class suburbs as it was in the city of Boston. It is to her credit that she was able to convince the Boston YWCA and the Marlborough CETA Consortium with only the above-mentioned general estimates available.

WPS serves twenty-four (originally eighteen) towns whose predominantly white, middle-class families had a median income of $14,000 in the 1970 census. Many of the wage earners in the areas served work in the computer industry and change location or company frequently for advancement purposes. This type of transiency results in isolation of the family, especially of the woman who often has no support system when friends and family are far away. It is this woman the WPS tries to reach.

Beyond receiving the stated services to the battered women, it was expected that the communities involved would be positively affected through education and sensitization concerning the nature and extent of the problem of battering. Every agency surveyed in the area voiced a concern for the battered women, but none had a program specifically intended to serve the battered woman and none knew of any other program that did.

Program Development

The program model was developed to utilize the abilities of and to provide employment for fourteen residents of the Marlborough CETA Consortium, which consisted of eighteen suburban towns west of Boston. The first group of seven would include unemployed professionals in the positions of coordinator and counselors. The second group of seven would include unskilled individuals who would be trained by the professional staff as outreach workers and legal advocates. CETA would contract with the Boston YWCA to fund the program, which was then known as Women against Violence.

The West Suburban Program Center had been extensively involved in the planning and operation of employment programs since 1971. The center had already sponsored several other CETA-funded programs as diverse as the Executive Secretary Training Program and the Large Appliance Repair Training Program. Ms. Nickolson was a member of the Area Manpower Planning Board at the Marlborough CETA Consortium and of the Balance of State at the state level. As such, she was able to monitor monies available and the moods of the funding agencies in regard to the feasibility of particular programs. With approval from the Boston YWCA board of directors through its Program Planning Committee, the center submitted a proposal to CETA and subsequently received funding for Women against Violence.

Economic forces were favorable: unemployment was high so federal monies were readily available to CETA to create jobs. Social forces were mixed: the women's movement opened the door and let all sorts of women's problems out of the closet, including wife abuse, but a large part of society could not or would not see the problem. There was also that element that either denied its existence or insisted that the woman deserved—even wanted—what she got. "It must be remembered that enduring social and cultural influences tend to perpetuate violence against women. For example, Soto, a former Prime Minister of Japan, was awarded the Nobel Peace Prize even though he had been publicly accused by his wife of beating her" (*Newsweek*, October 1974).

Traditionally wives and children were considered the property of husbands to do with as they pleased. That tradition survives. Each state has laws that prohibit one person from physically attacking another, but if the assailant is married to the victim, the law is usually not enforced (*Ms.*, August 1976).

Reflecting social and political forces in the development of this program were mixed, especially among women. One of the problems of the original program was the schism between women seeking equality and women supporting the traditionally subservient female role. Another one which proved more important to the molding of the program, was the schism between professionals and paraprofessionals, who were often battered themselves. Although the original members remained aloof from the Boston-centered Massachusetts Coalition of Battered Women Service groups and considered such city shelters as Transition House radical, they undermined the leadership of the first coordinator by creating their own coalition within the organization. These members resisted YWCA direction and resented YWCA efforts to procure funding for a professional to coordinate the program. In September 1978 at the end of the initial funding period, several staff members formed their own group to prevent abuse.

In the fall of 1978, state monies became available for domestic-violence programs through the Massachusetts Department of Public Welfare. However, these monies were limited and were concentrated in the programs which served the Boston metropolitan area. Once again the center turned to CETA. This time, however, the program would be more professional and more manageable. The proposal presented six positions: a coordinator, three counselors, an outreach worker, and a secretary. All positions would be filled by professionals with experience except that of outreach worker and secretary, which were filled by paraprofessionals who were battered women. This program model proved much more successful, especially in relating to other professional agencies in the communities served.

By the fall of 1979, state monies had been increased to provide services to battered women across the state but federal monies were being decreased as CETA concentrated on training programs. Therefore, the center again applied for funding to the Massachusetts Department of Public Welfare, which contracted with WPS to provide services to the twenty-four towns currently served. However, the contracted amount was only half that necessary to keep a minimum staff of one coordinator and two counselors at professional salary levels, so the center sought and received the direct support of the Boston YWCA to balance the WPS budget through the fiscal year 1980.

Program Implementation

One area in which problems were expected was the relationship of the WPS to the police departments of the town served. However, without exception, the police welcomed its help in domestic situations for which they had neither enough training nor time. From the onset WPS has regularly received referrals from the police and has usually received complete cooperation in providing the protection available under the Family Violence Law passed in July 1978 by the Commonwealth of Massachusetts.

The group which had been created by former staff members continually considered itself in competition with WPS. In fact, that group even applied for the same monies. The WPS received the state contract because of its professional status in the community. Other agencies had not had positive experience with that group and considered the members' publicly hostile attitude toward WPS as unprofessional as well as confusing to clients who could use all the help they could get. This antagonism came as a complete surprise to the professional staff who had to counteract the negative effects of the former staff. To this date, that group has resisted all efforts by the West Suburban Branch to have the two groups work together on the problems of domestic violence.

Periodically, press releases and in most cases subsequent press interviews have been done to keep the organization's name and services in the public eye. Radio and television interviews were also done with a public service announcement being made for one television station which was aired repeatedly. However, most clients came either because they heard about WPS from family or friends or because they were referred by other agencies.

WPS averages approximately sixty calls per month on their twenty-four-hour hotline. Of these sixty calls, 75 percent of the cases were battered women in need of assistance. The remaining 25 percent of the calls were from persons who wanted to become volunteers or were trying to get help for someone else. These calls came from mothers who knew that their adult children and in some instances their grandchildren were being battered but were afraid to seek help. Some of the mothers who called did not even live in the state of Massachusetts, but had heard about the center and taken it upon themselves to get some help for their battered daughters. Still other calls were from friends of battered women who were attempting to get them some help. Twenty-five percent of the crisis calls in a given month were from battered women who had previously sought help from the center for the same reasons.

Additional publicity for the program was generated through presentations that were made to emergency medical technicians, policemen, hospital medical staff, and volunteer counselors of a rape hotline. In fact, educational presentations were made to any concerned group and training was done with any concerned women, not merely those who were committed to volunteering. Sensitizing just one person to the issues of domestic violence has repercussions throughout his or her social circle and thus works for the changes in attitudes and behavior that are necessary to break the cycle of domestic violence. Relationships established with other agencies throughout the community were primarily referral and information sharing.

A closer cooperative effort with another agency resulted when, in order to serve the entire geographical area, WPS responded to the needs expressed by two different hotlines (one dealing with health problems and the other with drug problems) which received domestic violence calls, by offering to facilitate support groups for battered women in those towns if the hotline could supply the space. This has worked quite successfully for both clients, who do not have to travel as far from home, and the agencies, whose shared personnel and space saved time and money for each.

A significant and what proved to be a valuable relationship also was established between the WPS and the court system. Within that system, WPS counselors worked closely with the victim-witness advocate, a relatively new position which was created to provide victims and witnesses support through the trial process by familiarizing them with court procedures and legal jargon and by being a liaison for them with the district attorney's office, the court clerk, and other elements of the system.

Another position important to the WPS client is the court clerk, who is literally the court's traffic policeman. Almost always male and traditionally inclined to advise the couple to "kiss and make up," the court clerk was often a roadblock rather than a help. Nevertheless, as the court clerks became more familiar with the Family Violence Law and with the WPS program, they became more helpful. This was also true of the most important part of the court system, the judges. Usually male and again traditionally inclined to give the same advice as the court clerk, the judges at first resented the paralegal advocates until they began to understand their supportive role and to appreciate the information and insight that the counselors could provide.

Although this program has been successful for the most part, lack of direction and responsibility on the part of the original staff members was the major failure during the first year of operation because it contributed to the delay in funding for continuation of program services. Survival despite the disruption in funding was the major success. The clients themselves survived to change their lives as they chose, and the program itself survived at least in name even though that was later changed.

WPS handles approximately 720 crisis calls in a year's time. One example of the types of calls for help that are received was previously given. The following are other cases of other battered women that sought help from WPS.

1. The doctor who beat his wife and would then prescribe pain killers to ease the pain. His prescriptions could not relieve the pain that woman was feeling.

2. The 62-year-old woman whose husband had recently retired from his job. He was unable to cope with the stress of being idle and took out his frustration on his wife.
3. The woman whose children had modeled themselves after their father. If it was okay for their father to beat their mother; it was okay for them too.
4. The young woman who had been married for a short time and became pregnant. The husband felt threatened by thinking that he was going to have to compete for the woman's affection. This is usually the first time a woman is battered.
5. The middle-aged woman, who after being battered through the years while raising a family, decided she had had enough abuse. When the children left home, she did too.

Analysis

If this program was reimplemented, there are several things which would need to be done differently. The original program should have had a distinct structure within the entire organizational structure of the YWCA with its specific channels of responsibility. The program coordinator individually supervised each of the other program participants, and the program planning was done with equal input by all staff members. This turned out to be a time-consuming and irregular process. There should have been a delegation and division of direct responsibility as indicated in the following organizational chart.

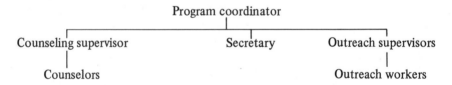

Within this structure, the coordinator and the two supervisors would have developed program planning, which could later be discussed and finalized at regularly scheduled staff meetings, and would have remained in the office as the administrative core with assistance from the secretary.

The basic strategy which was used to increase support of the program when the staffing pattern changed was to emphasize the professionalism of the agency in every aspect of outreach: liaisons with other agencies, interviews, speaking engagements, press releases, and so on. The volunteers were also chosen for their professional attitude and approach to counseling as well as their understanding of the issues of domestic violence, so that everyone representing WPS on the hotline or in person would exemplify the desired professional image. At the same time, however, the clients felt quite comfortable with staff and volunteers in the friendly, relaxed atmosphere of the offices where they received accepting, supportive client-centered counseling. It is felt that these changes did a great deal to further enhance the image of WPS and further legitimize the services provided through WPS.

The greatest foreseeable threat to the program's future is the country's economic condition. In times of tight money, social programs suffer most and women's programs suffer first. The steady rate of inflation has made cost-cutting imperative. The effects are already evident in Massachusetts where women's programs are concerned more with maintaining current funding levels and less with increasing funding in the face of increased need which results from these very same economic pressures.

In addressing the evaluation of WPS, monthly reports are kept which include statistics on the people served and the specific services the client received. The criteria for success is simply that WPS provides the contracted services to physically and emotionally battered women who request help.

10 Women for Sobriety

Jean Kirkpatrick

Women for Sobriety, Inc. is located in Quakertown, Pennsylvania. Women for Sobriety (WFS) is two things: a program for alcoholic women and also an organization. The purpose of the organization is to reach as many women in this country and other countries with a program of recovery from alcoholism via self-help groups. The organization itself was incorporated in July 1975. Prior to that time the program existed in a very rough form and by 1975, it became obvious that to use the program, it was necessary to incorporate and try to become a nonprofit organization within which the WFS program would be administered and put out in some form, probably in the form of literature.

Identification of Need

It is very difficult to talk about this early part of WFS since it is so amorphous. I, Jean Kirkpatrick, am a recovered alcoholic and this organization came about through my way of recovery. My recovery period was from 1971 through 1972-1973 and on upwards. By 1973, it occurred to me that if I could recover so well with the way I was doing it, then maybe hundreds and thousands of other women in the United States could also use this same way of recovery. It is my belief that it is not necessary for alcoholics to be tied to recovery programs for the rest of their lives within the structure of a meeting. I think it is very necessary that recovering alcoholics have a program, a systematic way of changing their lives and growing, but I do not feel it is necessary for all to be committed to weekly meetings.

Early in 1975, I began to think that the best way to show other women my recovery program was to start a group, a WFS self-help group. It was at this juncture, in mid-1975, that the organization was incorporated in our small town of Quakertown. To be incorporated in the state of Pennsylvania as a non-profit corporation, it was necessary to draw up bylaws. This I did. Of course, there was no organization anywhere; there was nothing but what I had jotted down and which was referred to as the New Life Program. The operational facility of WFS was my bedroom.

This procedure continued even after incorporation in 1975 until the end of the year. During this time I was able to have a couple of women use the program. A few groups began to spring up; by February 1976 I had written the first newsletter. By January 1976, there happened to be some publicity on what I was doing and that this program was the first different and new program from the Alcoholics Anonymous (AA) program, which was founded in 1935. The big publicity hanger for the media was the fact that no other program had come along with anything different from AA in all those years. I believe that because the AA program is so successful, everyone felt that nothing else was needed. This simply was not true. Examination of the membership figures of AA shows that only 10 percent of all alcoholics in the United States are in the AA and that less than 4 percent of all women alcoholics are in the organization.

When I wrote my program I knew the AA program was founded by men and that, in the very beginning, women were not permitted to join. I also knew because the WFS program was administered the same way as AA, in the self-help group settings, I would get a lot of backlash about it since AA is held in the highest reverence. To come along with anything else seemed to be rather profligate. The first national publicity that WFS received in January 1976, shocked me to see the headline, Women Form Own AA. And another headline in a New Orleans paper stated that I had said AA does not work and *everyone* needs WFS. I had said AA did not work entirely for me and I felt that I needed something else.

Program Development

By July 1975, WFS was incorporated in the state of Pennsylvania with a set of bylaws. I had received the corporate seal and the notification was published in the newspapers that the sole purpose of WFS was, and is, to disseminate help for women alcoholics to help them overcome their alcoholism.

I was still operating WFS from my bedroom when a United Press International story broke in some fifty-five newspapers across the country. The mail began to reach 100 to 150 letters a day; the highest number received in one day was over 200 letters. Overwhelmingly, the mail was from women who had tried AA but simply could not get sober with the program. Most asked for the WFS program and the location of the closest WFS program group to join. Up to this moment, the WFS program was not established outside the state of Pennsylvania. The first problem was to print the program and to write a brochure about it.

To answer all the letters, I simply had to get help. Everyday five of us prepared 3 X 5 cards with names and addresses of the women alcoholics and we extracted comments from the letters. We would then send the woman our new brochure and explain that there was not a WFS program in her area as of yet, but she would be notified.

Following the publicity of January 1976, I realized we had a great need for money. I found out that each county in Pennsylvania has money from the state and the state gets money from the federal government. At this point I did not know that under the Department of Health and Human Services, there existed an agency known as the National Institute for Alcohol Abuse and Alcoholism. I did not even know that money could probably be had from Bucks County. I received a nasty letter from the person running alcoholism programs in the county and it said that no program would exist in his county without his being informed of it and I was to immediately come to him and explain what WFS was all about and what in the world it was doing in his county. The man has since left office. Nevertheless, I began to get very frightened and was extremely intimidated by this. I began to wonder if it is not possible for some organization to start without having approval given by a county authority. However, I continued to ignore these letters and, needless to say, the relationship with the county and the state was very poor and still is.

I next turned to private foundations, of which I knew nothing. I wrote to all the Philadelphia foundations. Luckily one of the representatives from a Philadelphia foundation got in touch with me and said they might consider funding this operation. Well, of course, there was no operation. All I had was the same thing I had before which was a piece of paper saying we were incorporated; we now had a logo, a brochure, and a single-page program printed. We also had excessive mail coming in and still no staff and no money.

In May 1976, I heard that there was a national conference sponsored by the National Council on Alcoholism and I decided I had better appear. I was still negotiating with the foundation and they informed me they were coming to meet me. I proceeded to assemble a staff. I was the president and Dr. Rapoport, a nonalcoholic dentist, was the vice president. I asked Natalie Shifano, whose husband designed the logo, to be secretary, and Sonja Lowenfish to be treasurer. Now we had officers. I submitted these names to the foundation and still they were not satisfied. They continued to hold the application; they would move it from month to month.

When I returned from the National Conference on Alcoholism I rewrote the entire proposal. For instance, I de-emphasized the fact that Dr. Rapoport was a leading authority as a periodontist. Instead I noted that she was the wife of a prominent lawyer in the city of Allentown. I identified Mrs. Lowenfish as the mother of two children and the wife of a prominent architect in New York. I emphasized the fact that Mrs. Shifano's husband was a successful advertising executive on Madison Avenue in New York. Finally, that of all four board members, I was the only one who was divorced, and that I would be held accountable by them and that we would work closely together.

From the moment I put the emphasis on the husbands and that these women were acting with three very well-established men in their lives and that they would keep control of me, WFS immediately got the money. Although I learned that lesson very early, it has not worked since that time. However, I think that since then we have gotten so much stronger that I fail to use a similar approach because I have difficulty in doing it.

Program Implementation

In May 1976, WFS received $40,000 in funding. This was to pay for two full-time salaries, a secretary's and mine. We finally had some money to begin to operate. The problem was that the money was to be used just for this area of eastern Pennsylvania but WFS was a national organization, and of course we got as many letters from Colorado, Washington, or Texas as Pennsylvania and keeping them separate was difficult.

I was inexperienced in all the ways of fulfilling what I had proposed to do for the foundation. I failed to take into account the fact that, first of all, we were dealing with women. Second, women alcoholics are very difficult to reach and, third, it is very hard to go against an established organization like AA and expect people to welcome you with open arms.

In addition, months passed before I found a person who was willing to act as field representative. It requires special qualifications to get groups started, and I never did find the person who was exactly right for the job. The first person I hired was a woman who was very capable and very able at self-management. She would operate in Philadelphia and surrounding areas for the work-week, but on Friday she was on her own. Her job was to discover effective methods of meeting women alcoholics and setting the time and place for her to meet with them to start a group. Then she would meet with the group until it was established enough for her to move on to start another group. We were unable to say that X number of women had already recovered using the program. In fact, except for myself, there was no other woman who had recovered with the WFS program. In any event, the woman I hired to get the groups started encountered numerous problems. After about four months, she decided she was wasting her time.

The second person that took the job of field representative to start WFS groups was a woman I thought would work out. She was a beautiful person to see; she was bubbly and had an assertive kind of personality. She was a long-time member of AA and had wonderful sobriety. Recently widowed, she was just married to a man who was very big in AA. Immediately, she began to run into some flack as to why she wanted to be associated with WFS when it jeopardizes her with AA. She lasted one month.

We searched another eight weeks before we found a woman who was a recovered alcoholic and a Ph.D. candidate. She also seemed exactly right and began to make some progress. With her, we began to run about three good groups in Philadelphia. I felt secure about this and thought our problems were solved only to find that she began drinking again. So it became necessary to let her go. By this time, our one year of funding had ended and we had really failed in what I had set out to do.

The thrust of the proposal that I had presented to this Philadelphia foundation was that, in one year's time, WFS would be able to put the program solidly into the city and the surrounding areas. I told the board of the foundation that I would have at least six groups started, and probably ten, and that those ten groups, at the end of the funding period would go on and on, self-perpetuating, and in time be able to take care of at least 100 women within a five-year period.

Well, we did have some women in groups, but the results were very, very disappointing. We failed because I did not know enough about how to implement it. In addition, I failed to take into account the skepticism and sometimes the absolute prejudice and criticism that came from the alcoholism community about the new WFS program.

The WFS program is now five years old and we are just beginning to be accepted in the community of alcoholism. There is still a great deal of prejudice and a lot of harassment. Many of our groups folded because of the harassment they got from some members of AA groups. I hasten to add that this is not the official AA position. I received quotations from their founder, Bill Wilson, which stated that AA is not the only way to recover, that there are many other programs, and that AA members should not criticize other programs. Unfortunately, many AA members believe that the AA program is the only way and they refuse to see that if it is not working for women, other options must be available.

We have survived the first five years and, since that initial funding, we have never had additional funding, despite having written to 500 foundations. Possibly one of the greatest barriers has been our inability to achieve funding at the federal level. I think we must have funding at the federal level because we are a national organization. The fact that we are a national organization has really worked against us. It has cut us out of funds from our county and from Pennsylvania, even though the corporation is registered here. It has hurt us in applications to foundations, because foundations are interested in local giving. A foundation like United States Steel will give money to organizations in Pittsburgh or wherever it has a large plant. If there is a plant in Gary, Indiana, they will give money in that area. There are a few foundations that give to national organizations, some of which are Ford, Rockefeller, and Carnegie, but these particular foundations do not give to alcoholism programs. It is their assumption that alcoholism and its treatment are taken care of with funds from the federal government.

The federal government itself could be criticized for discrimination. Just in the year 1975 alone, out of the $75 million that went into alcoholism only $2,500,000 was for women's programs. Money for women's programs has been increasing but ever so slowly and certainly not to a point where it is equivalent to money for men's programs. I have failed to provide an effective proposal to the federal government.

So the program evolved into its current form, to be used in self-help groups across the country and internationally. Its conceptualization came out of my being able to examine myself, to discover my own needs for recovery.

Our income derives from the sale of literature, collections from the groups, my speaking engagements, and the profit from my book. We are beginning now to enlarge our line of literature as much as possible and we are beginning to sell books written by other persons. Prior to this, we were unable to do that because we did not have the capital funds to invest in other books.

In 1979, our fourth year of operation, we were able to produce $68,000 from these sources. Unfortunately, we need approximately $100,000 a year at the very minimum. WFS is located in a house owned by me. Because of this, WFS does not get evicted when it cannot pay its monthly rent. Luckily, we are now beginning to get some very large contributions from persons who are committed to our cause.

Perhaps one of our greatest difficulties as an organization is that we are constantly compared to a national organization of great prominence, one that has certain well-known traditions and establishments, and that of course is AA. AA's strength lies in the fact that it is there, that it has a continuity, and the program remains unchangeable. This is also true for WFS.

It was my belief that professional women in the community of alcoholism would welcome this program, that we women have our own national program. As an organization we have encouraged every woman to become a part of it, and emphasized that WFS is not a one-person, one-woman organization. We have encouraged women to get behind it, so that all of us can work together to bring this program to all women alcoholics in the United States. I hate to admit it, but in the five years that I have been working with women, I can honestly say that perhaps it is from our cultural training and our cultural forces that most women have many problems when it comes to working with each other, having a commitment, assuming responsibility, and even working cooperatively. We have met a lot of resistance in the fact that women do not cooperate with each other, that they continue to have feelings of jealousy and tend to stab one another in the back.

Analysis

If I were to ask myself what I would have done differently if I had to do it over again, I really do not know if I would have done anything differently. Because of no funding, it has been a matter of a few of us doing everything and there has never been time to really think about what could be different. In a week's time, we receive a minimum of approximately fifty requests for help. Whenever there is a TV show or a newspaper that mentions our work, we will get as high as 500 letters a week but, unfortunately, that does not happen too often. Every woman who writes us gets a copy of our program, a sample copy of the newsletter, and always suggestions on how to use the program if she so desires. We are trying to develop new strategies to increase support for the program. I think this can only be done by our board of directors, who are becoming increasingly active in the organization.

It is most definitely an uphill fight, and I think it will continue to be for the next several years; but whenever I do a workshop, I always ask the group assembled how many in the room have heard of WFS. Now, without fail, every hand goes up. Five years ago I was very lucky if one hand was raised.

In summation, I can only say we work at it day by day, we work away at resistance to change and try hard to help women who seek our help. Each day we are getting more and more women to help us and a more positive attitude from the community. It will take time, but we are prepared for this. We have been down a long and thorny path, but I feel that things are changing and I know that the WFS program is here to stay.

Notes

Chapter 1

1. Murray Ross, *Community Organization* (New York: Harper & Row, 1955), p. 39.
2. Charles Grosser, *New Directions in Community Organization* (New York: Praeger Publishers, 1973), p. 10.
3. Ralph Kramer and Harry Specht, *Readings in Community Organization Practice* (Englewood Cliffs, N.J.: Prentice-Hall, 1969), pp. 8-9.
4. National Association of Social Workers, *Defining Community Organization Practice* (New York: NASW, 1962).
5. Robert Perlman and Arnold Gurin, *Community Organization and Social Planning* (New York: John Wiley & Sons, 1972).
6. Neil Gilbert and Harry Specht, "Process vs. Task in Social Planning Social Work" (New York: National Association of Social Workers, May 1977).
7. Perlman and Gurin, *Community Organization.*
8. Ibid., p. 273.
9. Richard Means, *The Ethical Imperative* (New York: Doubleday, 1969), pp. 6-10.
10. Harnie Lune, "The Community Organization Method in Social Work Education" (New York: Council on Social Work Education, 1959), p. 27.
11. Phyllis Chesler and Emily Goodman, *Women, Money and Power* (New York: William Morrow & Co., 1976), pp. 245-246.
12. Saul Alinsky (unpublished speech given at Washington, D.C., 1966).
13. Roland Warren, *The Community in America* (Chicago: Rand McNally & Co., 1963), p. 20.
14. Roland Blythe, *Akenfield* (London, England: Penguin Press, 1969).
15. Robert S. Lynd, *Middletown: A Study in American Culture* (New York: Harcourt, Brace & Co., 1929).
16. Robert Seidenberg, *Corporate Women: Corporate Casualties* (New York: Avon Books, 1975).

Chapter 2

1. Eleanor Flexner, *Century of Struggle: The Women's Rights Movement in the U.S.* (Cambridge, Mass.: Belknap Press, 1959), p. 8.
2. Alice S. Rossi, ed., *The Feminist Papers* (New York: Bantam Books, 1974).
3. Ibid., p. 5.
4. Robin Morgan, ed., *Sisterhood Is Powerful* (New York: Random House, 1970), p. 8.

5. Rossi, *The Feminist Papers*, p. 308.

6. Flexner, *Century of Struggle*, p. 47.

7. Ibid., p. 54.

8. Rossi, *The Feminist Papers*, pp. 247-249.

9. Ibid., pp. 416-422.

10. Ibid., p. 418.

11. Ibid., pp. 426-429.

12. Interview with Susan B. Anthony, niece of Susan B. Anthony, February 1980.

13. Flexner, *Century of Struggle*, p. 109.

14. Ibid., p. 111.

15. Ibid., p. 185.

16. William O'Neil, *Everyone Was Brave: The History of Feminism in America* (Chicago: Quadrangle Books, 1971) p. 96.

17. Ibid., p. 97.

18. O'Neil, *Everyone Was Brave*, p. 104.

19. Flexner, *Century of Struggle*, p. 268.

20. Jo Freeman, *Women: A Feminist Perspective* (Palo Alto, Calif.: Mayfield Publishing Co., 1975), p. 446.

21. Vivian Gornick and Barbara Moran, eds., *Women in Sexist Society* (New York: Basic Books, 1971), p. 674.

22. O'Neil, *Everyone Was Brave*, p. 273.

23. Ibid., p. 277.

24. Ibid., p. 283.

25. Ibid., p. 335.

26. Betty Friedan, *The Feminine Mystique* (New York: W.W. Norton, 1963), p. 13.

27. Ibid., p. 95.

28. Ibid., p. 74.

29. Ibid., pp. 368-370.

30. Maren Lockwood Carden, *The New Feminist Movement* (Washington, D.C.: Russell Sage, 1974), pp. 61-65.

Chapter 3

1. Women's Bureau, Office of the Secretary, U.S. Department of Labor, Bureau of the Census, U.S. Department of Commerce, Washington, D.C., August 1978.

2. Louise Kapp Howe, *Pink Collar Workers: Inside the World of Women's Work* (New York: Avon Books, 1978), p. 1.

3. Jeanne Mager Stellman, *Women's Work, Women's Health: Myths and Realities* (New York: Pantheon Books, 1977), p. 5.

4. Associated Press, "Two-Thirds of Mothers Due to Hold Jobs in 1990, Book Says," *The Washington Post*, October 1979.

5. Addie Wyatt, "What's Happening to Working Women in America?" *The Church and the Wage Earner*, paper no. 5, 1974, pp. 26-32.

6. Jane Roberts Chapman, *Economic Independence for Women: The Foundation for Equal Rights*, (Beverley Hills, Calif.: Sage Publication, 1976).

7. Howe, *Pink Collar Workers*, pp. 3-4.

8. Ibid., p. 4.

9. "Women in the Economy: Preferential Mistreatment. A Report to the 1977 Working Women's Conference," *Employed Women*, Chicago, 1977.

10. Howe, *Pink Collar Workers*, pp. 5-8.

11. Ibid., p. 10.

12. Ibid., p. 11.

13. Stellman, *Women's Work, Women's Health*, pp. 56-57.

14. Ibid., p. 67.

15. Valerie Kincade Oppenheimer, *The Female Labor Force in the United States: Factors Governing Its Growth and Changing Composition* (Berkeley, University of California: Institute of International Studies, Population Monograph Series no. 5, 1970).

16. Ellie Grassman, "Women Still Earn Less," *The South Middlesex News*, Framingham, Massachusetts, 3 April 1977.

17. "Women in Science: Breaking the Barrier," *The Chronicle of Higher Education*, 31 October 1977.

18. Rosebeth Moss Kanter, *Men and Women of the Corporation* (New York: Basic Books, 1977), p. 17.

19. Howe, *Pink Collar Workers*, p. 3.

20. "Women Are Government's Scapegoats in the Unemployment Crunch," *Liberation News Service*, no. 842, January 1977.

21. Nancy Seifer, "Absent from the Majority: Working Class Women in America," *The National Project on Ethnic America* (New York American Jewish Committee, Institute of Women Relations, 1973).

22. Myra MacPherson, "Blue Collar Women: The Gap Widens," *The Washington Post*, 19 June 1977.

23. Judith Papachriston, ed., "A Brief History of Wage-Earning Women: 1820-1914," *Women Together* (New York: Knopf, 1976), chapter 8.

24. Phyllis Chesler and Emily Jane Goodman, *Women, Money and Power* (New York: William Morrow and Co., 1976), p. 230.

25. Barbara M. Wertheimer, *We Were There: The Story of Working Women in America* (New York: Pantheon Books, 1977), pp. 189-208.

26. Ibid.

27. Burleigh Gardner, "Awakening of the Blue-Collar Woman," *Intellectual Digest*, New York, March 1974.

28. Alice Lake, "Divorcees: The New Poor," *McCalls* 103 (1976):12.

29. I. Pearlin and S. Jackson, "Marital Status, Life-Strains, and Depression," *American Sociological Review* 47 (1977):704.

30. James M. Kahn, "Working Women and the Male Work Day," *Christianity and Crisis* 37 (1977):2.

31. Alan Campbell, director, Office of Personnel Management, "Policy Statement and Definition of Sexual Harassment," 12 December 1979, Washington, D.C.

32. Ibid.

33. Dorothy McGhee, "Dangerous Jobs: Sterilized Women Only," *San Francisco News Service*, 22 September 1977.

34. Stellman, *Women's Work, Women's Health*, p. 35.

35. Ibid., p. 19.

36. Vilma K. Hung, "Occupational Health Problems of Pregnant Women: A Report of the Secretary of Health, Education and Welfare," no. SA-5340-75, 30 April 1975.

37. Richard Saltus, "Women's Hearts Work Better," *San Francisco Examiner*, 5 March 1980.

38. Stellman, *Women's Work, Women's Health*, pp. 89-92.

39. Ibid., p. 35.

40. Judith A. Fair, *The Chains of Protection: The Judicial Response to Women's Labor Legislation* (Westport, Conn.: Greenwood Press, 1978).

41. Mary Witt and Patricia K. Naherny, "Women Work-Up From, 878: A Report on the DOT Research Project," *Women's Educational Resources* (Madison: The University of Wisconsin, January 1975).

42. Chesler and Goodman, *Women, Money and Power*, p. 77.

43. Ibid., p. 80.

44. Ibid., p. 77.

45. Ibid.

46. Ibid., pp. 233-234.

47. "Special Issue on Day Care," *The Urban and Social Change Review*, 12:2 (Chestnut Hill, Massachusetts: Boston College Graduate School of Social Work, Winter 1979).

48. Ibid.

49. Women's Bureau, Employment Standards Administration, U.S. Department of Labor, "20 Facts on Women Workers," February 1973.

50. "Special Issue on Day Care," p. 5.

51. Ibid., p. 2.

52. Ibid., p. 3.

53. Women's Bureau, "Day Care Services: Industries Involvement," Employment Standards Commission, Bulletin no. 296, Washington, D.C., Department of Labor, 1971.

54. Grace Hermandez Cargill, "Child Care on Campus," *Young Children* (Washington, D.C.: National Association for Education of Young Children, January 1977).

55. Dale A. Masi, *Exploring Italian Social Work* (Rockville, Md.: National Institute of Mental Health, DHEW publication no. 72-9025, 1972).

56. Ibid.

57. "Women in Science," p. 7.

58. Cynthia Harrison, "Working Women Speak," *Education Training Counseling Needs* (Washington, D.C.: U.S. Department of Health, Education and Welfare, Office of Education, July 1979), pp. 26-27.

59. Kathleen Fink, "Strategies to Increase Participation of Women in Scientific and Engineering Fields," (Paper for Women's Caucus, Boston College, Massachusetts, April 1978).

60. Tillie Olsen, *Silences* (New York: Delacorte Press, Seymour Lawrence, 1978), p. 258.

Chapter 4

1. *The Holy Bible* (New York: Benziger Brothers, 1941), Gen. 2-3.

2. Aristotle, *De Generatione Animalium* (I,20), (II,3).

3. Thomas Aquinas, *The Summa Theologica of St. Thomas Aquinas* (New York: Benzigu Brothers, 1947). I-92, 1.

4. Theodore Reik, *Pagan Rites in Judaism* (New York: Farrar, 1964), p. 69.

5. Louis Ginzberg, *The Legends of the Jews* (Philadelphia Jewish Publications Society, 1909), vol. 1, p. 97.

6. Paolo Mantegazza, *The Sexual Relations of Mankind* (Baltimore, Md.: Eugenics Publishing Co., 1935), pp. 121-122.

7. Susan Lydan, "The Politics of Orgasm," in Robin Morgan, ed., *Sisterhood Is Powerful* (New York: Vintage Books, 1970), p. 220.

8. William Masters and Virginia Johnson, *Human Sexual Response* (Boston: Little Brown, 1966), p. 7.

9. Shere Hite, *The Hite Report* (New York: Dell Publishing Co., 1976), p. 257.

10. Ibid., p. 232.

11. Masters and Johnson, *Human Sexual Response.*

12. Phyllis Chesler and Emily Jane Goodman, *Women Power and Money* (New York: William Morrow & Co., 1976), p. 106.

13. Ibid., p. 122.

14. Ibid., p. 123.

15. Bella Abzug (D-N.Y.), HR 3217.

16. Barbara Jordan (D-Tex.), HR 12645.

17. (Advanced by NOW) California has enacted a law (AB 1940 of 1974) introduced by Assemblyman McAllister.

18. "Displaced Homeworkers Form Network," *Women's Agenda* 3 (1978):2.

19. Ibid., p. 3.

20. Ibid.

21. Ibid.

22. Wendy Coppedge Sanford, "Abortion," in *Our Bodies Ourselves* (New York: Simon and Schuster, 1976), p. 216.

23. Lawrence Lader, *Abortion* (Boston: Beacon Press, 1967).

24. George F. Will, The Hyde Amendment: A Value Judgment," *The Washington Post*, 6 July, 1980.

25. Sanford, "Abortion," p. 217.

26. Association for Voluntary Sterilization (AVS), *The Case for Voluntary Sterilization* (New York: AVS, August 1968), p. 9.

27. Planned Parenthood Federation of America, Inc., Laws Relating to Birth Control and Family Planning.

28. Lucinda Cisler, "Unfinished Business: Birth Control and Women's Liberation," in *Sisterhood Is Powerful*, p. 249.

29. *Consumers Union Report on Family Planning* (Mt. Vernon, N.Y.: Consumers Union, 1966), p. 26.

30. Cisler, "Unfinished Business," p. 252.

31. Ernest Havemann, *Birth Control* (New York: Time-Life Books, 1967), p. 35.

32. U.S. Department of Health, Education and Welfare, Food and Drug Administration, Advisory Committee on Obstetrics and Gynecology, *Report on Intrauterine Contraceptive Devices* (U.S. Government Printing Office, January 1968).

33. Association for Voluntary Sterilization, *Blue Cross-Blue Shield and Medicaid Insurance for Voluntary Sterilization,* rev. (New York: AVS, March 1969).

34. Cisler, "Unfinished Business," p. 256.

Chapter 5

1. Susan Brownmiller, *Against Our Will: Men, Women and Rape* (New York: Bantam Books, 1975), p. 6.

2. Gail Abarbanel, "Helping Victims of Rape," *Journal of Social Work* 21 (1976).

3. Ibid., p. 6.

4. Martin Symonds, "The Rape Victim: Psychological Patterns of Response," *American Journal of Psychoanalysis* 36 (1976):27-34.

5. Rape Crisis Center, "Rape: A Reverence for Women in D.C." Washington, D.C., 1972, pp. 2-3.

6. *American Civil Liberties Union Handbook* (New York: Discus Books, 1973).

7. Susan Ross, *The Rights of Women* (C-01 Way, Ltd Eureka, Calif.: Sunrise Books, 1973), p. 180.

8. Karen DeCrow, *Sexist Justice: How Legal Sexism Affects You* (New York: Random House, 1974), p. 210.

9. Ibid.

10. Ross, *The Rights of Women*, p. 181.

11. Ibid.

12. Ibid.

13. Ibid., p. 182.

14. DeCrow, *Sexist Justice*, p. 210.

15. Ann Burgess and Lynda Holstrom, *Rape: Victims of Crisis* (Bowie, Md.: Prentice-Hall, Robert J. Brady Co., 1974), p. 4.

16. Ibid., p. 6.

17. Ibid., p. 7.

18. Ibid., p. 38.

19. Ibid., p. 40.

20. Ibid., p. 41.

21. "Rape," p. 1.

22. DeCrow, *Sexist Justice*, p. 215.

23. Elaine Hilberman, *The Rape Victim* (New York: Basic Books, 1976), p. 62.

24. William Ryan, *Blaming the Victim* (New York: Vintage Books, 1976), p. 6.

25. Ibid., p. 11.

26. Lenore E. Walker, *The Battered Woman* (New York: Harper and Row Publishers, 1979), pp. 19-20.

27. Ibid., p. 19.

28. Ibid., p. 21.

29. Ibid., pp. 21-22.

30. Ibid., p. 22.

31. Del Martin, *Battered Wives* (San Francisco, Calif.: Glide Publications, 1976), p. 51.

32. Ibid., p. 52.

33. Ibid.

34. Walker, *Battered Woman*, p. 36.

35. Terry Davidson, *Conjugal Crime: Understanding and Changing the Wife-Beating Pattern* (New York: Hawthorn Books, 1978), p. 51.

36. Ibid.

37. Martin, *Battered Wives*, p. 73.

38. Davidson, *Conjugal Crime*, pp. 237-255.

39. Jennifer Baker Fleming, *Stopping Wife Abuse: A Guide to the Emotional, Psychological, and Legal Implications for the Abused Woman and Those Helping Her* (Garden City, N.Y.: Anchor Books/Doubleday, 1979), p. 399.

40. Robert Richard and Suzanne Stengel, *Mental Health Service for Victims, Policy Paradigm, Evaluation and Change* (Minneapolis Medical Research Foundation, Inc., Minnesota 1980), p. 6.

41. Edith Gomberg, *State of Knowledge Today* (New York: NCA Publication, 1976).

42. Edith Lynn Hornik, *The Drinking Woman* (New York: Association Press, 1977), p. 19.

43. Ibid., pp. 19-20.

44. Barbara Ehrenreich and Deirdre English, *Complaints and Disorders: The Sexual Politics of Sickness* (New York: Glass Mountain Pamphlet no. 2, the Feminist Press, 1973).

45. Mark Lendor, "A History of Women and Alcohol" (Paper, New Brunswick, N.J.: Rutgers University, Rutgers Center for Alcohol Studies, Summer 1978).

46. Enrenreich and English, *Complaints and Disorders.*

47. Hornik, *Drinking Woman*, p. 20.

48. John L. Horn, Kenneth Warberg, *Females Are Different: On the Diagnosis of Alcoholism in Women*, Proceedings of the First Annual Alcoholism Conference (Washington: U.S. DHEW, 1973), p. 349.

49. Susan Bower, Strategies for Reaching Women with Alcohol Problems (Washington: National Clearinghouse for Alcohol Information, 1979).

50. Edith Gomberg, "Women and Alcoholism," in V. Franks & V. Burtle, eds., *Women in Therapy*, (New York: Brunner/Mazel, 1974), pp. 169-170.

51. Valerie Pinkas, Sex Guilt and Focus of Control in Alcoholic Women (Ph.D. diss., New York University, 1973).

52. Gomberg, "Women and Alcoholism," p. 175.

53. E.S. Lisansky, "Alcoholism in Women, 1 Social History Data," Rutgers, N.J.: *Quarterly Journal Studies on Alcohol* 18 (1957):588.

54. D. Cahalan, *Problem Drinkers* (San Francisco: Jossey-Bass, 1970).

55. Sandie Johnson and Sally Kay Garzon, "Women and Alcoholism: Past Imperfect and Future Indefinite" (Paper presented at the Annual Research Conference of the Association for Women in Psychology, St. Louis, Mo., 3-6 February 1977), p. 1.

56. Ibid., p. 2.

57. Ibid.

58. Marc Schuckit, *Depression and Alcoholism in Women.* Reprint from Proceedings of the First Annual Alcoholism Conference of NIAAA USDHEW, ADAMHA, 1973, p. 357.

59. NIAAA Report to Congress, *Alcohol and Health*, Washington, D.C., 1979.

60. Henry Wechsler, "Epidemiology of Male/Female Drinking" (Topic paper no. 1, prepared for NIAAA Workshop on Alcoholism and Alcohol Abuse among Women, Jekyll Island, Ga., 2-5 April 1978).

61. G. Winokur, P.J. Clayton, R. Reich, *Manic Depressive Illness* (St. Louis: Mosby, 1969).

62. Marc Schuckit, *Depression and Alcoholism in Women*, p. 362.

63. Gomberg, *State of Knowledge Today*, p. 8.

64. Eileen Corrigan, "Women and Problem Drinking," in *Addictive Diseases*, pp. 215-222 (Spectrum Publications, 1974).

65. Marcia Guttentag, Susan Salasin, Wendy Legge, and Bray Helen Wilson, "Sex Differences in the Utilization of Publicly Supported Mental Health Facilities: The Puzzle of Depression" (A collaborative grant with the Mental Health Services Branch of NIMH, MH26523-02, 1977), p. 238.

66. Ibid., p. 239.

67. Ibid., p. 240.

68. Ibid., p. 246.

69. J.K. Broverman, D.M. Broverman, F.E. Clarkson, P.S. Rosenkrantz, and Susan R. Rozel, "Sex-Role Stereotypes and Clinical Judgments of Mental Health," *Journal of Consulting and Clinical Psychology* 34 (1970):1-7.

70. Johnson and Garzon, "Women and Alcoholism," p. 1.

71. Jean Kirkpatrick, Women for Sobriety (chapter 10, this book).

72. Jean Kirkpatrick, *Turnabout* (New York: Doubleday, 1978), pp. 165-178.

73. J.E. James, "Symptoms of Alcoholism in Women: A Preliminary Series of AA Members," *Quarterly Journal of Alcoholism* 36 (1975):254-1569.

74. E. Morrissey and M. Schuckit, "Physicians and Alcohol," *Newsletter* 12 (1977):1.

75. Eileen Corrigan, *Alcoholic Women in Treatment* (N.Y.: Oxford University Press, 1980).

76. Jacquelyn Hall, "State Responsibilities for the Well-Being of Women in Alcohol, Drug Abuse, and Mental Health Programs" (Presentation for the 1979 ADAMHA Annual Conference of State and Territorial Alcohol, Drug Abuse and Mental Health Authorities, Silver Springs, Maryland, 6 November 1979), p. 10.

77. Dale A. Masi, "Alcohol and the Working Woman" (Los Angeles: Motivational Media, 1978), film.

78. Dale A. Masi, "The Employed Female Alcoholic," *Labor Management Journal* 6 (May-June 1977):43.

79. Jackie Gaines, "Studies on the Black Woman Alcoholic" (Paper presented at the NCA Forum, Milwaukee, Wisconsin, April 27-May 2, 1975), pp. 8-9.

80. Ibid., p. 9.

81. Linda S. Lidell, "Psychotropic Drug Use by Women: Health, Attitudinal, Personality and Demographic Correlates" (Paper presented at the American Psychological Association Meeting, San Francisco, California, 28 August 1977), p. 1.

82. Ibid., p. 2.

83. Ibid., p. 1.

84. An Alliance of Regional Coalitions, National Research and Communications Associates, *Drugs, Alcohol and Women's Health* (Prepared under DHEW Contract no. 271-77-1280, NIDA, 1978, Washington, D.C.), p. 37.

85. Lidell, "Psychotropic Drug Use by Women," p. 1.

86. Ellen Frankfort, *Vaginal Politics* (New York: Quadrangle Books, 1972), pp. 107-108.

87. DHEW Publication no. (FDA) 79-3084, *Tranquilizers: Use, Abuse and Dependency Consumer* (U.S. Government Printing Office, 1979), pp. 31, 274-281.

88. Susan Schiefelbein, "The Female Patient Heeded? Hustled? Healed? *Saturday Review*, 29 March 1980.

89. Robert Seidenberg, "Does Misogyny Sell Mind Drugs?" (Paper presented at a Conference sponsored by Alternatives for Women, Inc., Lexington, Kentucky, 19 February 1977), p. 37.

90. Robert Seidenberg, "Advertising and Drug Acculturation" (Statement made before the Subcommittee on Monopoly, Senate Small Business Committee, 23 July 1971), p. 19.

91. *Drugs, Alcohol and Women's Health* p. 37.

92. House of Representatives, Hearing before the Select Committee on Narcotics Abuse and Control, "Women's Dependency on Prescription Drugs," 96th Congr., 1st sess. 13 September 1979, SCNAC-96-1-8, Washington, D.C., p. 28.

93. Linda Lidell, "Put Her Down on Drugs: Prescribed Drug Usage in Women" (Paper presented at the Western Psychological Association Meeting, Anaheim, California, 12 April 1973), p. 72.

94. Robert Seidenberg, "Images of Health, Illness and Women in Drug Advertising," *Journal of Drug Issues* (1974):264-266.

95. Ruth Cooperstock, "Sex Differences in the Use of Mood-Modifying Drugs: An Explanatory Model," *Journal of Health and Social Behavior* 12 (1971):238-244.

96. *Drugs, Alcohol and Women's Health*, pp. 32-36.

97. Ibid., p. 36.

98. Ibid., p. 38.

99. Ibid.

100. Ibid., p. 25.

101. Robert Seidenberg, "Drug Advertising and Perception of Mental Illness," *Mental Hygiene* 55 (1971):23.

Chapter 6

1. Priscilla Cummings, "Women in Prisons," *Richmond News Leader,* 17-21 March 1980.

2. Ibid.

3. National League of Cities and the U.S. Conference of Mayors, Nang Loving and Lynn Olson, *Proceedings, National Conference on Women and Crime* (Washington, D.C.: 26-27 February 1976), p. 5.

4. Cummings, "Women in Prison."

5. Freda Adler, *Sisters in Crime: The Rise of the New Female Criminal* (New York: McGraw-Hill, 1975), pp. 26-27.

6. National League of Cities, *Proceedings*, p. 5.

7. Cummings, "Women in Prison," March 18.

8. National League of Cities, *Proceedings*, p. 9.

9. Cummings, "Women in Prison," March 17.

10. Katherine Watterson Burkhart, *Women in Prison* (New York: Popular Library, 1976), p. 127.

11. Ibid., p. 265.

12. Cummings, "Women in Prison," March 19.

13. Ibid., March 20.

14. Brenda G. McGowan and Karen Blumenthal, *Why Punish the Children: A Study of Children of Women Prisoners* (National Council on Crime and Delinquency, 1978), p. ix.

15. Cummings, "Women in Prison," March 20.

16. Ibid.

17. Ibid., March 21.

18. Offender Aid and Restoration Annual Report, (Charlottesville, Va., OAR: 1979), p. 7.

19. Omar Hendrix, "A Study in Neglect: A Report on Women Prisoners, July 15, 1972-October 15, 1972" (New York: The Women's Prison Association), pp. 41-44.

20. Edward T. Weaver, "Public Assistance and Supplemental Security Income," *Encyclopedia of Social Work* (Washington, D.C.: NASW, 1977), p. 1121.

21. Irwin Garfinkel, ed., *Toward an Executive Income Support System* (Madison: Institute for Research on Poverty, University of Wisconsin, 1974).

22. Weaver, "Public Assistance," p. 1124.

23. Irene Cox, "Administration of Public Assistance and Supplemental Security Income," *Encyclopedia of Social Work* (Washington, D.C.: NASW, 1977), p. 1137.

24. George Haskins, "AFDC as Child Welfare," in Alwin Schan, ed., *Children and Decent People*, (New York: Basic Books, 1974), pp. 114-141.

25. An Historic Debate Revisited: Protection vs. Equality—The Dilemmas and Contradictions of Social Work and the Women's Movement, unpublished paper, p. 12.

26. Ibid., no. 6, p. 8.

27. Betty Mandell, "Welfare and Totalitarianism. Part I: Theatrical Issue," *Social Work* 16 (1971):17-26.

28. Nancy J. Brennan, "The Scarlet Letter Revisited" (Paper, School of Social Work, University of Minnesota, Minneapolis, March 1975).

29. U.S. Congress, Joint Economic Committee, Subcommittee on Fiscal Policy, *Income Security for American: Recommendation of the Public Welfare Study* (Washington: U.S. Government Printing Office, 1973), p. 15.

30. Mollie Orshansky, "The Shape of Poverty in 1966," *Social Security Bulletin* 32 (1968):4.

31. E. Waldman and B.J. McEaddy, "Where Women Work?" *Monthly Labor Review* 97 (1974): 10-11.

32. U.S. Senate, Committee on Finance, *Child Care: Data and Materials*, 93d Congr., 2d sess. (U.S. Government Printing Office, 1974), p. 48.

33. U.S. Congress, Joint Economic Committee, Subcommittee on Fiscal Policy, *Income Security for Americans: Recommendations of the Public Welfare Study*, p. 7.

34. Donald M. Fraser, "Child Support Collection," Congressional Record, E3626-E3627, 8 July 1975.

35. Nancy Marshall, "The Public Welfare System," in *Lives in Stress: A Context for Depression* (Stress and Families Project, October 1979, NIMH Grant no. 28830), pp. 380-383.

36. Comptroller General of the United States, *Social Services and Do They Help Welfare Recipients Achieve Self-support on Reduced Dependency?* (U.S. Government Printing Office, 1973).

37. Interview with two former welfare recipients.

38. Ibid., no. 19.

39. Ibid.

40. Ibid.

41. Ibid.

42. The President's Commission on Mental Health, *Women and Mental Health: Report of the Special Populations Subpanel* (U.S. Government Printing Office, 1978).

43. Ibid.

44. Ibid.

45. Jean Baker Miller, *Toward a New Psychology of Women* (Boston, Beacon Press, 1976), p. 4.

46. Ibid., p. 6.

47. Ibid., p. 8.

48. Ibid., p. 6.

49. J.B. Lazar, "The Status on Research for Women in the 70s" (Paper for the President's Commission on Mental Health, 1977).

50. L. Radloff, "Sex Differences in Depression: The Effects of Occupation and Marital Status," *Sex Roles: A Journal of Research* 1 (1975).

51. W. Gove and J. Tuder, "Adult Sex Roles and Mental Illness," *American Journal of Sociology* 78 (1973).

52. Ibid.

53. Ibid.

54. National Institute of Mental Health, Division of Biometry and Epidemiology (unpublished data).

55. Gerald Corey, *Theory and Practice of Counseling and Psychotherapy* (Belmont, Calif.: Wadsworth Publishing Co., 1977), p. 6.

56. Ibid., p. 7.

57. Ibid.

58. Ibid.

59. Ibid.

60. Ibid.

61. Ibid.

62. Ibid.

63. Ibid.

64. Ibid.

65. Alfred Adler, "Sex," in Jean Baker Miller, ed., *Psychoanalysis and Women: Contributions to New Theory and Therapy* (New York: Brunner Mazel, 1973), pp. 33-42.

66. Ibid.

67. Kay F. Shaffer, *Sex Role Issues in Mental Health* (Philippines: Manila Addison-Wesley Publishing Co., 1980), pp. 160-163.

68. Ibid.

69. Ibid.

70. Ibid.

71. Ibid.

72. Ibid.

73. Natalie Shainess, "A Psychiatrist's View: Images of Women—Past and Present Overt and Obscured," in Robin Morgan, ed., *Sisterhood Is Powerful* (New York: Vintage Books, 1970), p. 262.

74. Ibid.

75. Ibid.

76. Robin Morgan, ed., "The Oppressed Majority: The Way It Is," in *Sisterhood Is Powerful*, p. 37.

77. Phyllis Chesler, "Women as Psychiatric and Psychotherapeutic Patients," *Journal of Marriage and the Family* 33, 4.

78. Ibid., p. 150.

79. Ruth Moulton, "Psychoanalytic Reflections on Women's Liberation," *Journal of Contemporary Psychoanalysis* 8 (1972):197-223.

80. Betty Kronsky, "Feminism and Psychotherapy," *Journal of Contemporary Psychotherapy*, 3 (1971):89-98.

81. Ibid.

82. Sherry Podolsky, "Feminist Therapy" (unpublished paper for Women's Course, Boston College, Mass., April 1977), pp. 1-4.

83. Gerstin Grimstad and Susan Rennie, eds., *The New Women Survival Sourcebook* (New York: Alfred A. Knopf, 1975), p. 60.

84. Joyce Walstedt, *The Anatomy of Oppression: A Feminist Analysis of Psychotherapy* (Pittsburgh: KNOW, Inc., 1971).

85. Jeanette Silveira, *The Effect of Sexism on Thought: How Male Bias Hurts Psychology and Some Hopes for a Women's Psychology* (Pittsburgh: KNOW, Inc., 1972).

86. Sherry Podolsky, "A Functional Description of *Focus*: The Process and Rationale for Organizing *Focus*," (Boston: Focus, Inc., 1975) p. 1.

87. Podolsky, "Feminist Therapy," pp. 1-4.

88. Ibid.

89. Ibid.

90. Ibid.

91. Ibid.

92. Ibid.

93. Susan Amelia Thomas, "Theory and Practice in Feminist Therapy," *Social Work* 24 (1977):447-454.

94. Ibid., p. 452.

95. Ibid., p. 453.

96. The President's Commission on Mental Health, *Women and Mental Health*.

Chapter 7

1. *The Federal Women's Program: Putting Women in Their Place* (U.S. Government Printing Office, 1979), p. 7.

2. Ibid.

3. Ibid.

4. Ibid.

5. Ibid., p. 5.

6. Ibid., pp. 9-10.

7. Ibid., p. 8.

8. Ibid., p. 19.

9. Interview with Ms. Ellis Jones, senior equal opportunity specialist, Office of the Federal Women's Program.

10. Interview with Ms. Joannel Littrel, Federal Women's Program Manager, Department of Agriculture, Beltsville, Maryland.

11. Interview with Ms. Ellis Jones.

12. Interview with Ms. Littrell.

13. Interview with Ms. Ellis Jones.

Index

Index

About the Author

Dale A. Masi is the director of the Office of Employee Counseling Services, Department of Health and Human Services, Washington, D.C. She is also a professor at the School of Social Work and Community Planning and an adjunct professor at the College of Business and Management, University of Maryland. Dr. Masi has consulted for many organizations, including the White House, the National Institutes of Alcohol, Drug Abuse, and Mental Health, the Bechtel Corporation and the Stanford Research Institute. She was a Senior Fulbright Scholar and a postdoctoral Fellow of the American Association of University Women. In addition, Dr. Masi has published many articles and has appeared in the movie *Alcohol and the Working Woman.*